PAUL TERRY

TOP 10 OF EVERYTHING 2015

FIREFLY BOOKS

WHAT'S INSIDE?

TOP **10** OF EVERYTHING

2015

A Firefly Book

Published by Firefly Books Ltd. 2014

Copyright © 2014 Octopus Publishing Group Ltd

First printing

Publisher Cataloguing-in-Publication Data (U.S.)

A CIP record for this title is available from the Library of Congress

Library and Archives Canada Cataloguing in Publication

A CIP record for this title is available from Library and Archives Canada

Published in the United States by
Firefly Books (U.S.) Inc.
P.O. Box 1338, Ellicott Station
Buffalo, New York 14205

Published in Canada by
Firefly Books Ltd.
50 Staples Avenue, Unit 1
Richmond Hill, Ontario
L4B 0A7

Produced by SHUBROOK BROS. CREATIVE

Printed in China

SECTION ONE
MECHANICAL MARVELS

SECTION TWO
ANIMAL KINGDOM

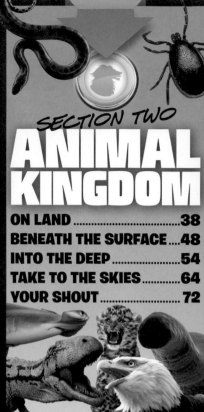

SECTION SIX
MUSIC MASH-UP

SECTION SEVEN
EPIC STRUCTURES

SECTION THREE
GAMING GALAXY

SECTION FOUR
SPORT ZONE

SECTION FIVE
FORCES OF NATURE

SECTION EIGHT
MOVIE SHOWTIME

SECTION NINE
ONLY HUMAN

SECTION TEN
INFINITE SPACE

WELCOME

Top 10 Of Everything returns with MORE pictures, facts, quizzes, and incredible lists than ever before! We don't just focus on the number one spot, we delve WAY beyond to uncover things you would never have imagined possible. T-10 examines subjects with amazing detail and eye-popping facts that will blow your mind. From terrifying dinosaurs to road-shredding cars, billion-dollar movies, and sky-scraping structures, it's all right here...

FIRST THINGS FIRST...
MEET MR. T-10

Greetings! How's it going? Ready for a seriously mad mash-up of EVERYTHING that makes our planet pretty cool? GOOD!

For the past nine months, I've been embracing the trivia nerd that lurks within me to gather up thousands of facts that I hope will fascinate, surprise, and often, make you gasp in disbelief... But that's the truly crazy thing... It's all TRUE! We certainly do live in a strange, unpredictable, exciting, and often inspiring world—something that the T-10 Team and I have worked super-hard to try and capture for you within these 320 pages...

... And talking of "strange and unpredictable," welcome to my life so far! I've been very lucky to have worked with the guys behind *The Simpsons*, LEGO, and *Star Wars*. I've also made movies (and even played a werewolf in one), worked on a video game magazine, recorded albums, and now I get to hunt down these Top 10 facts for you! I really hope you enjoy this book—it was a LOT of fun putting it together.

OK, I'm off to read a pile of comics and re-play *Journey* on the PS3...

Paul Terry

FRIENDLY CONTENT

It's really important to Team T-10 that you get to enjoy ALL the content featured in this book. Therefore, all games and movies are rated PG-13 / 12A or under.

OK, I'M READY!
HOW DO I GET THE MOST OUT OF MY T-10 BOOK?

Some info books yawn out endless lists of number ones... Others are a splurge of bizarre and whacky things that feel like, "we've got no idea where you should start reading any of this either." *Top 10 Of Everything* wants to give you an astounding and inspiring EXPERIENCE. Here's how it works...

The book is split into 10 sections. Each section focuses on a genre. Let's take Animal Kingdom as an example: it's bursting with dozens of lists like *Top 10 Biggest Human Parasites* and *Top 10 Biggest Prehistoric Carnivores*. Accompanying these lists are stacks of special features including: Xtreme Facts, Stat Attacks, Check It Outs, and many more. These are there to amaze you and expand your mind even further. At the end of each section you'll be faced with Your Shout—a series of challenges to test your new-found knowledge: picture quizzes, wordsearches, and even a Career Quiz. These questions will reveal who you may want to be in the future. Marine biologist? Explorer? Rock star? It's all up to you...

MECHANICAL MARVELS

FASTEST MANNED VEHICLES

It's the acceleration face-off to end them all! Combining all of the different modes of transport, this is how the top speeds match up...

01 ROCKET*

02 PLANE

03 JET-ENGINE CAR

04 CAR

05 MOTORCYCLE

06 TRAIN**

07 BOAT

08 HELICOPTER

09 HOVERCRAFT

10 AIRSHIP

VEHICLE NAME	COUNTRY	YEAR	TOP SPEED (KPH)	TOP SPEED (MPH)
APOLLO 10	USA*	1969	39,897	24,791
LOCKHEED SR-71 BLACKBIRD	USA	1976	3,529.6	2,193.2
THRUSTSSC	USA	1997	1,223.66	760.35
BLUEBIRD CN7	AUSTRALIA	1964	690	429
TOP 1 OIL-ACK ATTACK	USA	2010	605.7	376.36
SCMAGLEV	JAPAN	2003	581	361
SPIRIT OF AUSTRALIA	AUSTRALIA	1978	511.12	317.6
EUROCOPTER X3	FRANCE	2013	486	302
DISCOVERHOVER ONE	PORTUGAL	1995	137.4	85.38
ZEPPELIN LUFTSCHIFFTECHNIK LZ N07-100	GERMANY	2004	125	77.7

*Returning from the moon to USA
**Magnetic Levitation Train (no contact with railtrack)

XTREME FACT
APOLLO 10

Where have you been for a week's holiday? Between May 18 and 26 in 1969, Apollo 10 astronauts Thomas Stafford, John Young, and Eugene Cernan spent eight days, three minutes, and 23 seconds on a trip to the moon and back!

DANGER!
The bigger the machine, the greater the potential danger. About 700 passengers were killed in the Saint-Michel-de-Maurienne train derailment of December 12, 1917.

MOST EXPENSIVE VEHICLES OF ALL

TOP 10

Team T-10 battles to find you the craziest facts, and we think the expenses behind making these machines are definitely some of the wildest we've seen...

01 TRAIN/RAILWAY SYSTEM
02 AIRCRAFT CARRIER
03 ROCKET
04 PRIVATE BOAT
05 PLANE
06 SUBMARINE
07 TANK
08 HELICOPTER
09 AIRSHIP
10 PRODUCTION CAR

VEHICLE NAME	COUNTRY	COST ($)
SCMAGLEV	JAPAN	33.1 BILLION
USS GERALD R FORD	USA	14 BILLION
COLUMBIA SPACE SHUTTLE	USA	13 BILLION
HISTORY SUPREME	UK	4.8 BILLION
B-2 SPIRIT STEALTH BOMBER	USA	2.4 BILLION
SSN-774 VIRGINIA-CLASS	USA	2.3 BILLION
AMX-56 LECLERC	FRANCE	27.183 MILLION
AGUSTAWESTLAND AW101 VVIP	UK	21 MILLION
ZEPPELIN NT MODEL LZ N07-101	GERMANY	14.5 MILLION
BUGATTI VEYRON 16.4 SUPER SPORT	FRANCE	2.4 MILLION

COST 13 BILLION DOLLARS

XTREME FACT

SCMAGLEV

No, it's not part of a set for an apocalyptic sci-fi movie... This is Nagoya station in Aichi, Japan, where the Central Japan Railway Co are preparing construction of the new 310.7 mph (500 kph) magnetic levitation train.

CHECK IT OUT!

Columbia Space Shuttle: tragically, all seven crew members were killed when this rocket disintegrated upon re-entering Earth's atmosphere on February 1, 2003.

BIGGEST VEHICLES OF ALL

In this Top 10, size is ALL that matters. From the biggest battleship to the coolest airship, here are the 10 titans of the machine world...

	VEHICLE NAME	COUNTRY / COUNTRIES	SIZE (M)	SIZE (FT)
01 TRAIN	AAR STANDARD S-4200	CANADA	3,658	12,001
02 LAND TRANSPORTER	F60 OVERBURDEN CONVEYOR	GERMANY	502.01	1,647
03 SHIP	SEAWISE GIANT OIL TANKER	JAPAN	458.46	1,504.1
04 AIRCRAFT CARRIER	DDH 183 IZUMO	JAPAN	248	813.7
05 SUBMARINE	TYPHOON-CLASS	SOVIET UNION (NOW RUSSIA)	175	574.15
06 SPACE STATION	INTERNATIONAL SPACE STATION	USA, CANADA, RUSSIA, JAPAN, EUROPE	108.5*	356*
07 PLANE	ANTONOV AN-225 MRIYA	UKRAINE	88.4**	290**
08 AIRSHIP	BULLET 580	USA	71.63	235
09 HELICOPTER	MIL V-12	SOVIET UNION (NOW RUSSIA)	37	121.39
10 TANK	CHAR 2C / FCM 2C	FRANCE	10.27	33.7

*All measurements are vehicle lengths except: *width and **wingspan*

FASTEST MACHINES IN SPORT

The world of sport is pretty much all adrenaline-fuelled but, with these machines, things get REALLY pulse-racing...

		TOP SPEED (KPH)	(MPH)
01	TOP FUEL DRAGSTER	515	320
02	SPEEDBOAT	511	317.5
03	AIRSHOW STUNT PLANE	426	264.7
04	FORMULA ONE CAR	370	230
05	MOTOR RALLY (NASCAR, ETC)	342.4	212.8
06	SNOWMOBILE	338	210
07	MOTORCYCLE	312	194
08	JETSKI	289.7	180
09	MONSTER TRUCK	154.5	96
10	HOVERCRAFT	137.4	85.4

SPEED
230
MPH

XTREME FACT
HOVERCRAFT

Yes, the World Hovercraft Championships is an actual thing! Some 24 countries take part in the annual event. Check out www.hovercraft.org.uk/whf to see more.

XTREME FACT
DDH 183 IZUMO

This beast weighs 19,812 t and is now the world's largest aircraft carrier/warship. It's scheduled to be in operation from March 2015. This photo shows its launch ceremony, held at Japan Marine United Isogo Shipyard in Yokohama, Kanagawa, on August 6, 2013.

LENGTH 813.7 FT

CHECK IT OUT!

Typhoon-class Submarine: Tom Clancy's novel *The Hunt For Red October* features a Typhoon-class sub of the title. The story also became a Sean Connery-starring movie in 1990.

STAT ATTACK

FORMULA ONE CAR

Number of seats	One
Gears	Seven forward and one reverse
RPM	15,000
Official first race	1946
Official first championship	1950

XTREME FACT
FORMULA ONE

The first-ever proper F1 video game was *Microprose Formula One Grand Prix*, created by Geoff Crammond back in 1992. It was beloved for its detail and accuracy to the sport, including the way you could change the driver as well as the car to your preferred specification.

CHECK IT OUT!

DPV (Desert Patrol Vehicle): used to be known as an FAV (Fast Attack Vehicle). It can travel over 210 miles (338 km) on a full tank of fuel, and can carry up to 1,500 lb (680 kg) of equipment/people, making it an extremely useful vehicle.

TOP 10 FASTEST MILITARY MACHINES EVER

Gathering intelligence for potential combat strategies requires quick thinking, and even quicker hardware... But these machines have no trouble with speed!

		VEHICLE NAME	COUNTRY	SPEED (KPH)	SPEED (MPH)
01	HYPERSONIC CRUISE VEHICLE	FALCON HTV-2*	USA	20,921.47	13,000
02	PLANE	GENERAL DYNAMICS FB-111A	USA	2,655	1,650
03	UNMANNED AERIAL VEHICLE	BARRACUDA*	GERMANY/SPAIN	1,041.3	647
04	HELICOPTER	WESTLAND LYNX	UK	400.87	249.1
05	TRUCK	IFAV (INTERIM FAST ATTACK VEHICLE)	USA	156.11	97
06	SHIP	HMCS BRAS D'OR (FHE 400)	CANADA	117	73
07	LIGHT ATTACK VEHICLE	DPV (DESERT PATROL VEHICLE)	USA	96.56+	60+
08	TANK	S 2000 SCORPION	UK	82.23	51.10
09	SUBMARINE	ALFA-CLASS	RUSSIA	74	46
10	AIRCRAFT CARRIER	USS GERALD R FORD (CVN-78)**	USA	55.56+	34.52+

XTREME FACT

WESTLAND LYNX HELICOPTER

This British beast of an aircraft (originating from a design and manufacturing team based in Yeovil, Somerset, UK) really is a super-copter... It can actually fly in a loop motion and even perform a barrel-roll.

*Still being tested and developed

**The actual top speed of aircraft carriers remains classified, but some have calculated they may be able to achieve up to 97.82 mph (157.42 kph)

TOP 10 SPACE RACE NATIONS

Which nations have ruled the rocket race? Here are the first 10 true rockets that were successfully launched into space, highlighting the two sides of the construction contest...

#	Nation	Rocket Name	Date of Launch
01	USA	V-2	FEB 20, 1947
02	SOVIET UNION (NOW RUSSIA)	SPUTNIK 2	NOV 3, 1957
03	USA	USAF EXPLORER 1	JAN 31, 1958
04	USA	JUPITER IRBM AM-13	DEC 13, 1958
05	SOVIET UNION (NOW RUSSIA)	LUNA 1	JAN 2, 1959
06	SOVIET UNION (NOW RUSSIA)	R2	JULY 2, 1959
07	SOVIET UNION (NOW RUSSIA)	LUNA 2	SEPT 12, 1959
08	SOVIET UNION (NOW RUSSIA)	LUNA 3	OCT 4, 1959
09	USA	MERCURY-REDSTONE	JAN 31, 1961
10	SOVIET UNION (NOW RUSSIA)	VOSTOK 3A	APR 12, 1961

SPEED 60+ MPH

Xtreme Fact

USA MERCURY-REDSTONE

Mercury-Redstone 2 was all about monkey business–Chimpanzee Ham was inside and ready for action! He was named after the Holloman Aerospace Medical base that helped him get ready for his important space mission.

DATE JAN 31, 1961

TOP 10 FASTEST PRODUCTION CARS

Piston-heads, brace yourselves... We've compiled the cars with the craziest top speeds, ever!

#		YEAR BUILT	TOP SPEED (KPH)	(MPH)
01	BUGATTI VEYRON 16.4 SUPER SPORT	2010	431	267.8
02	SSC ULTIMATE AERO	2007	412.2	256.14
03	BUGATTI VEYRON 16.4	2005	408.5	253.8
04	KOENIGSEGG AGERA S	2012	400	248.5
05	MCLAREN F1	1992	372	231
06	PAGANI HUAYRA	2012	372	231
07	LAMBORGHINI AVENTADOR	2011	370	230
08	MCLAREN P1	2013	349	217
09	JAGUAR XJ220	1992	343	213
10	BUGATTI EB110 GT	1991	336	209

TOP 10 FASTEST PRODUCTION BIKES

When it comes to thrill rides, the roaring raw power of a motorcycle can propel you to some insane speeds...

#		YEAR(S) RELEASED	SPEED (KPH)	(MPH)
01	SUZUKI HAYABUSA GSX1300R	1999–2000	312	194
02	DUCATI DESMOSEDICI RR	2007–08	307.3	191
03	BMW S1000RR	2010–PRESENT	303	188
=	MV AGUSTA F4 R 312	2007–PRESENT	303	188
05	KAWASAKI ZX-14	2006–PRESENT	299.3	186
06	KAWASAKI ZX-12R	2000–06	299.2	185.9
07	HONDA CBR1100XX SUPER BLACKBIRD	1996–2007	290	180
08	KAWASAKI NINJA ZX-11	1990–2001	282	175
09	BIMOTA YB6 EXUP	1989–90	270	167.8
10	KAWASAKI GPZ900R NINJA	1984–96	254	158

 XTREME FACT SUZUKI HAYABUSA

Its reputation of being the fastest motorcycle has a great association with its name. Hayabusa is Japanese for "Peregrine Falcon," which is the world's fastest animal.

XTREME FACT

BUGATTI VEYRON
16.4 SUPER SPORT

Having flashy rims for your ride is one thing, but when the actual wheels cost this much, and are this complex, it gets a little crazy. At $25,000 per set, they can only be put on by a specialist team... In France... At a cost of another $70,000!

SPEED 267.8 MPH

SPEED 213 MPH

X-PLORE
SPEED KING STATUS

The Hennessey Venom GT reached 270.49 mph (435.31 kph) on February 14, 2014, so it's now the fastest production car, right? Wrong. It is being refused the World Record for a production car's speed because it only achieved it once, plus, only 29 Venom GTs are being made—and the record rule makers say 30 cars must be made to achieve "production car" status.

...& ANOTHER THING!

Ceramic brakes slow the Veyron down faster than it can accelerate—2.3 seconds to a dead stop from 62 mph (100 kph).

K091 YUD

XTREME FACT

JAGUAR XJ220

This iconic sports car is not as common as you might think. With 3,000 unique parts, just 281 were made between October 1991 and June 1992.

SPEED 194 MPH

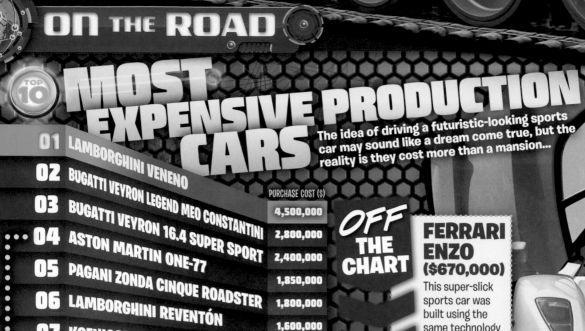

MOST EXPENSIVE PRODUCTION CARS

TOP 10

The idea of driving a futuristic-looking sports car may sound like a dream come true, but the reality is they cost more than a mansion...

#	Car	PURCHASE COST ($)
01	LAMBORGHINI VENENO	4,500,000
02	BUGATTI VEYRON LEGEND MEO CONSTANTINI	
03	BUGATTI VEYRON 16.4 SUPER SPORT	2,800,000
04	ASTON MARTIN ONE-77	2,400,000
05	PAGANI ZONDA CINQUE ROADSTER	1,850,000
06	LAMBORGHINI REVENTÓN	1,800,000
07	KOENIGSEGG AGERA R	1,600,000
08	MAYBACH LANDAULET	1,600,000
09	PAGANI HUAYRA	1,380,000
10	FERRARI LA FERRARI	1,300,000
		1,300,000

OFF THE CHART

FERRARI ENZO ($670,000)

This super-slick sports car was built using the same technology behind Formula One racing cars! Its butterfly doors hinge upward and open by the side-view mirrors.

PRICE 1.85 MILLION DOLLARS

X TREME FACT
ASTON MARTIN ONE-77

Does this have a 48-valve, V12 engine? Can it go zero to 62 mph (100 kph) in a blink-and-you'll miss-it 3.7 seconds? Uh-huh. It also takes 2,000 man-hours to build one of them! Check out its full stats at: www.astonmartin.com/cars/one-77.

TOP 10 MOST POWERFUL ENGINES

Size is all relative here, as we're focusing on the power of each vehicle to determine the best ones...

		MODEL	HORSEPOWER
01	ROCKET	Saturn V	160,000,000
02	PLANE	Boeing 777	145,000
03	HOVERCRAFT	Zubr-class LCAC	59,180
04	TRAIN	IORE	14,483
05	HELICOPTER	Mil Mi-26	11,240
06	AIRSHIP	Various	4,800
07	BOAT	Cigarette AMG Electric Drive	2,200
08	PRODUCTION CAR	SSC Ultimate Aero	1,287
09	QUADRICYCLE	Dodge Tomahawk	500
10	MOTORCYCLE	MTT Y2K Turbine Superbike	320

HORSEPOWER 500

CHECK IT OUT!

Quadricycle: although Dodge (the makers of the Tomahawk) proudly states that its top speed is 300 mph (480 kph), to date, no rider has ever dared reach it.

DID YOU KNOW?

This super-bike could cost you up to $700,000. For that amount, Team T-10 would like a full-scale working version of the Batpod, too, thank you very much!

ON THE ROAD

TOP 10 — FASTEST 0-60 MPH

Here, we're not interested in the size of your engine or the cost of the car, we just want to know which models can accelerate from zero to 60 mph the quickest...

0-60 2.2 SECONDS

#		PRODUCTION YEAR	0-60 MPH (SEC)
01	LINGENFELTER CHEVROLET CORVETTE	2002	1.97
02	SRT VIPER HENNESSEY VENOM 1000TT	2002	2.2
03	ARIEL ATOM 500 (V-8)	2012	2.3
04	BUGATTI VEYRON 16.4 SUPER SPORT	2011	2.4
=	BUGATTI VEYRON EB 16.4	2009	2.4
06	CAPARO T1	2007	2.5
=	HENNESSEY VENOM GT	2012	2.5
=	BUGATTI VEYRON 16.4 GRAND SPORT	2010	2.5
09	PAGANI ZONDA R	2010	2.6
=	ULTIMA GTR720	2006	2.6

Xtreme Fact — SRT VIPER

From 2013, this car got a name change. Formerly called the Dodge Viper, it's now known as the SRT Viper (but it's still made by Dodge).

TOP 10 — CRAZIEST CELEB RIDES

THE T-10 UNOFFICIAL

#		CELEBRITY
01	1951 CUSTOM CHEVROLET DELUXE WITH HEART-SHAPED BRAKE LIGHTS	KAT VON D
02	1958 VW BEETLE MODIFIED BEYOND ALL RECOGNITION	WILL.I.AM
03	PERSONALIZED PINK SMART CAR	KATY PERRY
04	MAYBACH EXELERO	JAY Z
05	PLATINUM MOTORSPORTS' CUSTOMIZED 2010 CAMARO	DAVID BECKHAM
06	CUSTOM 1967 FORD F-100	ROB ZOMBIE
07	FERRARI CALIFORNIA	USAIN BOLT
08	ROLLS ROYCE PHANTOM DROPHEAD	TIMBALAND
09	VINTAGE 1955 JAGUAR XK140	HARRISON FORD
10	FERRARI 458 ITALIA SPIDER	DEADMAU5

CHECK IT OUT!

Ferrari 458 Spider: here's deadmau5 (aka Canadian producer/songwriter Joel Zimmerman) and his $260,000 mean machine.

CHECK IT OUT!

Caparo T1: this was built by Caparo Vehicle Technologies, founded by two former McLaren F1 engineers in 2006.

0–60
2.5
SECONDS

TOP 10

COOLEST GADGETS IN PRODUCTION CARS

THE
T-10
UNOFFICIAL

		GADGET'S PURPOSE
01	NIGHT VISION	Just like Batman's The Tumbler, dark roads are no longer a worry
02	HEAD-UP DISPLAY	Like the video game world, speedometers can now be shown ON the windshield
03	COMMUNICATORS	Chat to friends in other cars, without using your phone
04	VOICE-ACTIVATED SYSTEMS	Choose to text, call, use satellite navigation, radio, and more, with just your voice
05	BUTTON IGNITION	No need to turn a key anymore
06	BED SEATS	Seats that transform into an inflatable bed
07	DIAGNOSTIC PACK	Linked to your smartphone, you can see what's wrong with your car
08	USB CIGARETTE LIGHTER CHARGERS	Simple but brilliant way to charge smartphones, tablets, etc
09	TAILGATE CAMERA WITH NIGHT VISION	Reverse-parking has never been so easy
10	PORTABLE BATTERY JUMP-STARTER	No need to ever worry about a flat battery with this gadget

CHECK IT OUT!

Button Ignition: it may be a common feature now, but Mercedes had developed a push-button ignition for a car back in the 1930s!

ENGINE
START
STOP

AMAZING CONCEPT CARS

TOP 10

THE T-10 UNOFFICIAL

01	DUBAI 2030 AMPHIBIOUS VEHICLE
02	ALESSIAN 2012
03	LEXUS LF-NX
04	PEUGEOT ONYX
05	MERCEDES-BENZ BIOME
06	BMW 328 HOMMAGE
07	VOLKSWAGEN NILS
08	LAMBORGHINI ESTOQUE
09	KIA TRACK'STER
10	VW AQUA (A HOVERCAR)

✗TREME FACT

PEUGEOT ONYX

Talk about an amazing collision of materials: the Onyx's bodywork combines pure copper for the doors and wings with matte black carbon graphite for the rest.

GREATEST TORQUE

TOP 10

Power is important in a car, but whereas the power normally determines the top speed, the torque affects the rate of acceleration. These 10 talk the torque...

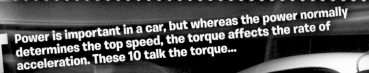

		TORQUE (LB-FT)	RELATIVE SCALE:
01	HENNESSEY VIPER VENOM 1000	1,155	100%
02	BUGATTI VEYRON SUPERSPORT	1,106	96%
03	SSC ULTIMATE AERO TT	1,094	95%
04	BRABUS 850 6.0 BITURBO	1,069	93%
05	ZENVO ST	1,055	91%
06	BRISTOL FIGHTER T	1,036	90%
07	BRABUS ROCKET	970	84%
08	BUGATTI VEYRON	922	80%
09	HENNESSEY VENOM 800	900	78%
10	MELLING HELLCAT	880	76%

OFF THE CHART

EVANTRA V8

This super-car was revealed for the first time at the Top Marques Monaco in April 2013. It's impressive: 624 lb-ft of torque, and 0–62 mph (0–100 kph) in 3.2 seconds.

TORQUE 624 LB-FT

X-PLORE

VOLKSWAGEN NILS

This compact, single-seat electric car doesn't generate any noise or carbon emissions. It's also being supported by the German Federal Ministry of Transport, Building, and Urban Development.

MOTOR-TAINMENT

TOP 10 BIGGEST CAR MOVIES

Love cars? Love movies? We suggest you take a look at these, and watch all of them immediately...

#	Title	Year of Release	Box Office ($ worldwide)
01	FAST & FURIOUS 6	2013	788,679,850
02	FAST FIVE	2011	626,137,675
03	CARS 2	2011	559,852,396
04	CARS	2006	461,983,149
05	FAST & FURIOUS	2009	363,164,265
06	GONE IN 60 SECONDS	2000	237,202,299
07	2 FAST 2 FURIOUS	2003	236,350,661
08	THE FAST AND THE FURIOUS	2001	207,283,925
09	DAYS OF THUNDER	1990	157,920,733
10	SPEED RACER	2008	93,945,766

Source: IMDB.com

XTREME FACT: SPEED RACER

This was inspired by the Japanese racing franchise *Mach GoGoGo*, which dates back to 1958. A special 40th anniversary box set of the original Manga version was released in 2008, the same year as this movie.

CHECK IT OUT!

Fast Five: costing $125 million, the fifth *Fast & Furious* movie made its money back more than six times over! Its director, Justin Lin, has helmed four of the *F&F* movies.

BOX OFFICE 626 MILLION DOLLARS

10 QUICK FIRE FACTS — FAST FIVE

01 Running time of 2 hours 10 minutes
02 Certificate PG-13/12A
03 Was released April 29, 2011
04 The budget to make it was $125 million
05 The fifth movie in the *Fast & Furious* franchise
06 Director Justin Lin helmed the third to sixth *F&Fs*
07 Made $86,198,765 on its opening weekend
08 Followed by *Fast & Furious 6* (2013)
09 Stars Vin Diesel, Paul Walker, Dwayne Johnson
10 Co-star Gal Gadot will play Wonderwoman in 2016

24

MAGNIFICATION

BIGGEST ROBOT MOVIES

TOP 10

The *Transformers* franchise was always going to feature strongly here, but you'll be surprised who has robo-smashed their way to Number One...

		ROBOT TYPE(S)	YEAR OF RELEASE	BOX OFFICE ($ WORLDWIDE)
01	IRON MAN 3	Remote-controlled Iron Man suits	2013	1,215,439,994
02	TRANSFORMERS: DARK OF THE MOON	Alien robots: Autobots & Decepticons	2011	1,123,794,079
03	STAR WARS EPISODE I: THE PHANTOM MENACE	Clone Troopers & others	1999	1,027,044,677
04	STAR WARS EPISODE III: REVENGE OF THE SITH	General Grievous and others	2005	848,754,768
05	TRANSFORMERS: REVENGE OF THE FALLEN	Alien robots: Autobots & Decepticons	2009	836,303,693
06	STAR WARS EPISODE IV: A NEW HOPE	C-3PO, R2-D2, and many more	1977	775,398,007
07	THE MATRIX RELOADED	Squid-like Sentinels	2003	742,128,461
08	TRANSFORMERS	Alien robots: Autobots & Decepticons	2007	709,709,780
09	STAR WARS EPISODE II: ATTACK OF THE CLONES	C-3PO, R2-D2, and many more	2002	649,398,328
10	IRON MAN 2	Justin Hammer's robot army	2010	623,933,331

XTREME FACT

IRONMAN 3

The power of Tony Stark... *Iron Man 3* is also the fifth most successful movie of all time! With *The Avengers* being the third most lucrative movie ever ($1,518,594,910), Marvel Studios (and *Iron Man*) are doing rather well...

TOP 10
BIGGEST SELLING RACING VIDEO GAMES

Whoa... Talk about a two-car race! Over the past 23 years, the world of video game racing has been dominated by a couple of franchises that couldn't be more different...

#	Game	Platform	Year of Release	Unit Sales (millions)
01	MARIO KART WII	Wii	2008	34.28
02	GRAN TURISMO 3: A-SPEC	PS2	2001	14.98
03	GRAN TURISMO 4	PS2	2004	11.66
04	GRAN TURISMO	PLAYSTATION	1997	10.95
05	GRAN TURISMO 5	PS3	2010	10.85
06	MARIO KART 64	N64	1996	9.87
07	GRAN TURISMO 2	PLAYSTATION	1999	9.49
08	MARIO KART 7	3DS	2011	9.14
09	SUPER MARIO KART	SNES	1992	8.76
10	NEED FOR SPEED: UNDERGROUND	PS2	2003	7.20

Source: VGChartz

UNIT SALES **9.14 MILLION**

STAT ATTACK
MARIO KART Wii

Developer .... Nintendo
Director .... Yasuyuki Oyagi
First unveiled .... E3 2007, Los Angeles (USA)
Multiplayer .... Ability to play with worldwide gamers online

XTREME FACT
MARIO KART 7

This much-loved racer is also the third biggest 3DS game of all time. And the seven? You can play as seven different Mario-verse characters. 2014's *Mario Kart 8* could take its crown though...

AMAZING CARS FOR HIRE

#	Car	Famous as...
01	K.I.T.T. (TRANS AM)	Knight Rider's sleek, intellectual sidekick
02	ECTO 1 (1959 CADILLAC AMBULANCE)	The Ghostbusters' trusty transport
03	A-TEAM VAN (GMC G20)	The crack commando unit's black and red van
04	FORD GRAN TORINO	Car of the TV detectives Starsky and Hutch
05	BULLITT (1968 FORD MUSTANG)	From one of the most famous car chases ever
06	LOVE BUG (1962 VW BEETLE)	The Disney car with the big personality
07	1981 DeLOREAN DMC-12	The time traveler from Back To The Future
08	BUMBLEBEE (2010 CHEVROLET CAMARO)	The very yellow Transformer
09	1978 LOTUS ESPRIT	James Bond's iconic underwater car
10	GENERAL LEE (1969 DODGE CHARGER)	The Dukes of Hazzard's turbo-charged wagon

Note: All cars are replicas

Xtreme FACT
K.I.T.T.

Artificially intelligent K.I.T.T. (Knight Industries Two Thousand) from the 1980s TV series *Knight Rider* got a Super Pursuit Mode in season four. It transformed and exceeded 300 mph (483 kph)!

FORD GRAN TORINO

CHECK IT OUT!

General Lee: the Dodge Charger (from '79-'85 TV series *The Dukes Of Hazzard*) had its doors welded shut for super-quick, jump-in access.

BEEN & SEEN

Seen the movie? Tick it off the list and then seek out the other ones!

- [ ] **IRON MAN 3**
- [ ] **BACK TO THE FUTURE**
- [ ] **TRANSFORMERS:** REVENGE OF THE FALLEN
- [ ] **PACIFIC RIM**
- [ ] **TRANSFORMERS:** DARK OF THE MOON
- [ ] **THE DARK KNIGHT RISES**
- [ ] **STAR TREK**
- [ ] **STAR WARS EPISODE III:** REVENGE OF THE SITH
- [ ] **STAR TREK** INTO DARKNESS
- [ ] **STAR WARS EPISODE II:** ATTACK OF THE CLONES

WATER
JETLEV JETPACK

XTREME FACT
ENERGON
TRANSFORMERS' FUEL

Energon is a fuel/energy source that powers the Transformers. In their mythology, it can be found in solid, gas, and liquid states, and is stored in Energon cubes.

TOP 10 MOST AWESOME POWER SOURCES

THE T-10 UNOFFICIAL

		MACHINE	ORIGIN
01	EYE OF HARMONY (EXPLODING STAR)	TARDIS/DOCTOR'S LIFEFORCE	*Doctor Who*
02	FLUX CAPACITOR	DeLOREAN DMC-12	*Back To The Future* movie trilogy
03	DILITHIUM CRYSTALS' PLASMA	USS ENTERPRISE	*Star Trek* TV series and movies
04	ARC REACTOR	TONY STARK'S CHEST PIECE	*Iron Man* comics and movies
05	ENERGON	FUEL FOR TRANSFORMERS	*Transformers* animated TV series and movies
06	NUCLEAR REACTOR	GYPSY DANGER	*Pacific Rim* movie
07	THE SUN	THE GOLDEN CONDOR	*The Mysterious Cities Of Gold* animated TV series
08	DIATIUM POWER CELL	LIGHTSABER	Jedi's weapon of choice in the *Star Wars* universe
09	WATER	JETLEV JETPACK	Real-life water-powered jetpack
10	GAS	GRAPPLING GUN	Batman's utility belt

CHECK IT OUT!

Diatium Power Cell: in September 2013, Harvard and MIT University physics teams accidentally caused photons to interact so strongly, that they formed a beam very similar to a *Star Wars* lightsaber!

XTREME FACT

THE DARK KNIGHT

Nathan Crowley, production designer of The Batpod, wanted to approach it as a functional machine, not as a motorcycle. Weighing over 700 lb (317.5 kg), the escape pod (from the critically damaged Tumbler) has two engines: one in each wheel.

BOX OFFICE 1.004 BILLION DOLLARS

BIGGEST "VEHICLE IS A STAR" MOVIES

No "robots in disguise" presented as vehicles here, just movies where actual cool cars, planes, boats, and bikes have significant "role" and screen time...

#	Movie	VEHICLE(S) FEATURED	YEAR OF RELEASE	BOX OFFICE ($ WORLDWIDE)
01	TITANIC	British passenger liner *RMS Titanic*	1997	2,186,772,302
02	SKYFALL	Aston Martin DB5 and many more	2012	1,108,561,013
03	THE DARK KNIGHT RISES	The Bat, The Batpod, prototype military Tumblers	2012	1,084,439,099
04	PIRATES OF THE CARIBBEAN: DEAD MAN'S CHEST	Pirate galleons	2006	1,066,179,725
05	PIRATES OF THE CARIBBEAN: ON STRANGER TIDES	Pirate galleons	2011	1,043,713,802
06	THE DARK KNIGHT	The Tumbler, The Batpod, The Joker's trucks	2008	1,004,558,444
07	PIRATES OF THE CARIBBEAN: AT WORLD'S END	Pirate galleons	2007	963,420,425
08	FAST & FURIOUS 6	Hundreds, including 1969 Dodge Charger Daytona	2013	788,679,850
09	PIRATES OF THE CARIBBEAN: THE CURSE OF THE BLACK PEARL	Pirate galleons	2003	654,264,015
10	FAST FIVE	Over 20 cars, including Dodge Charger	2011	626,137,675

Source: IMDB.com

OFF THE CHART

CASINO ROYALE

This Aston Martin DBS V12 was a star of Daniel Craig's 2006 debut Bond outing. The movie took $599,045,960 worldwide.

29

TOP 10 SMALLEST DRONES

As technology progresses, things get faster, and much smaller. In the world of UVAs (Unmanned Aerial Vehicles), or drones, things are getting seriously sci-fi...

			DEVELOPED BY	WINGSPAN (CM)	WINGSPAN (IN)
01	ROBOBEE		Harvard School of Engineering and Applied Sciences, USA	3	1.18
02	DELFLY MICRO		DelFly, Netherlands	10	3.94
03	NANO HUMMINGBIRD		AeroVironment, Inc, USA	16	6.30
04	DELFLY II		DelFly, Netherlands	30	11.81
05	WASP		AeroVironment, Inc, USA	33	13
06	MOSQUITO		Israel Aerospace Industries, Israel	35	13.78
07	WASP III		AeroVironment, Inc, USA	72.3	28.47
08	SCOUT		Aeryon Labs, Canada	80	31.50
=	ZALA 421-08		ZALA Aero, Russia	80	31.50
10	BIRD-EYE 100		Israel Aerospace Industries, Israel	85	33.47

WINGSPAN 3.94 IN

XTREME FACT

DELFLY MICRO

This weighs just 0.11 oz (3 g)! It's the result of Delft University of Technology's brilliant refinement process: DelFly I had a wingspan of 19.7 in (50 cm), then DelFly II was 11 in (28 cm).

WINGSPAN 51.2 IN

OFF THE CHART

RQ-11 RAVEN

Just missing out on a position in the Top 10 is the RQ-11 Raven. Developed by the US's AeroVironment, Inc, and first used in 1999, it has a wingspan of 51.2 in (130 cm). Here, we see it being used by Allied forces to search for hidden weapons in Afghanistan, in 2009.

CHECK IT OUT!

DelFly II: here is super-smart Dutch engineer Guido de Croon. He's demonstrating the DelFly II's ability to fly like a hummingbird at the Engineering-École des Mines in Nantes, France, on April 7, 2011.

MOST INTELLIGENT MACHINES

THE T-10 UNOFFICIAL

		TYPE	FAMOUS FOR
01	KIROBO	Robot companion for Japanese Space Station workers	Launched into space (2013)
02	PLEO	Robot baby dinosaur that has the capacity to learn	Being a leap forward in cyber-pet technology
03	CURIOSITY	Mars Science Laboratory robot	Exploring Mars since its Aug 6, 2012, touchdown
04	JOHNNY FIVE	Military robot that becomes self-aware	*Short Circuit* movies (1986 and 1988)
05	ATLAS	Military robot	Rescuing people from battlefields
06	EVE	Extraterrestrial Vegetation Evaluator 'bot	*WALL·E* (2008)
07	COMPRESSORHEAD	Heavy metal robot band	YouTube cover of Motörhead's "Ace Of Spades"
08	WATSON	IBM supercomputer	Defeating two *Jeopardy!* champions (2011)
09	RUBOT II	Puzzle-solving robot	Solving a Rubik's cube in 21 seconds
10	THE GENERAL	Speed-learning supercomputer	*The Prisoner* TV series (1967-68)

XTREME FACT

PLEO

PLEO is a baby dinosaur robot that acts and learns like a real animal using RFID responsive learning technology. It reacts to touch, light, and sound.

CHECK IT OUT!

PLEO: the first generation machine (pictured) from 2007 came before the PLEO rb, launched in 2011. It costs $469 and comes with accessories to help it learn, including a training leaf. See www.pleoworld.com.

XTREME FACT

KIROBO

This 13.4 in (34 cm)-tall, 2.2 lb (1 kg) robo-hero was launched into space on August 4, 2013, and arrived at the International Space Station on August 10. It speaks Japanese, has voice and face recognition, and can help with zero-gravity experiments!

GADGETS & ROBOTS

XTREME FACT
JAEGERS

These building-sized movie machines are operated by two human pilots that are connected to each other by a neural bridge. One of the visual effects geniuses behind the Jaegers was Shane Mahan who helped create the *Iron Man* suits.

TOP 10
GREATEST SCI-FI HUMAN + MACHINE COMBOS & CYBORGS

THE T-10 UNOFFICIAL

#		FROM	YEAR(S)
01	IRON MAN	*Iron Man & The Avengers* (comics & movies)	1963–PRESENT
02	JAEGERS	*Pacific Rim* (movie)	2013
03	CAMERON	*Terminator: The Sarah Connor Chronicles* (TV series)	2008–09
04	DARTH VADER	*Star Wars* (movies, video games & comics)	1977–PRESENT
05	NUMBER SIX	*Battlestar Galactica* (TV series)	2004–09
06	THE BORG	*Star Trek: The Next Generation* (TV series & franchise)	1989–PRESENT
07	INSPECTOR GADGET	*Inspector Gadget* (cartoon series & movies)	1983–2003
08	MARCUS WRIGHT	*Terminator Salvation* (movie)	2009
09	SURROGATES	*Surrogates* (comic & movie)	2009
10	DEADPOOL	Marvel Comics and *X-Men Origins: Wolverine* (movie)	1991–PRESENT

CHECK IT OUT!

Marcus Wright: played by Australian actor Sam Worthington, he is the fourth version of a Terminator model, after the T-800 (Arnold Schwarzenegger), T-1000 (Robert Patrick), and T-X (Kristanna Loken).

32

MOST EXPENSIVE RC VEHICLES

If you're ever thinking about upgrading any of your remote-controlled toys, maybe steer well clear of these... Unless you know a billionaire!

B-52

	RC VEHICLE	MADE BY	BUILT (COUNTRY)	PRICE TAG ($)
01	ADASTRA	FULL-SIZE BOAT*	JOHN SHUTTLEWORTH	UK	23.4 MILLION
02	LAMBORGHINI AVENTADOR LP 700-4	CAR	ROBERT WILHELM GÜLPEN	GERMANY	4.7 MILLION
03	YAMAHA RMAX	HELICOPTER	YAMAHA	JAPAN	1 MILLION
04	RTR 1/10 GRAVE DIGGER	MONSTER TRUCK	TRAXXAS	USA	80,000
05	B-52	MILITARY PLANE	GORDON NICHOLS	UK	12,000**
06	CATERPILLAR 345 EXCAVATOR	EXCAVATOR	WEDICO	USA	6,950
07	CATERPILLAR 966G II WHEEL LOADER	DIGGER TRUCK	WEDICO	USA	5,850
08	RMS TITANIC 50" LIMITED	CRUISE LINER	TITANIC UNIVERSE	UK	2,800
09	A340-300 AIRBUS	COMMERCIAL JET	HOBBY WING	CHINA	1,950
10	BLACK PETERBILT TRUCK	TRUCK CAB	WEDICO	USA	1,500

*Can be remote-controlled by an iPad.
**Cost of the engines alone

MOST POWERFUL COMPUTERS

As your PS4 or Xbox One has incredible graphics and sound capabilities, it may feel like the peak of computer technology. However, this lot make them look like a pencil and paper...

	LOCATION	YEAR	COST ($)	CALCULATIONS PER SECOND (QUADRILLIONS)
01	TIANHE-2	CHINA	2013	390 MILLION	33.86
02	TITAN	USA	2012	97 MILLION	17.59
03	SEQUOIA	USA	2013	250 MILLION	16.32
04	K COMPUTER	JAPAN	2011	1 BILLION	10.51
05	MIRA	USA	2013	50 MILLION	8.59
06	STAMPEDE	USA	2013	27.5 MILLION	5.17
07	JUQUEEN	GERMANY	2013	(CLASSIFIED)	5.01
08	VULCAN	USA	2013	(CLASSIFIED)	4.29
09	SUPERMUC	GERMANY	2012	86 MILLION	2.90
10	TIANHE-1A	CHINA	2010	88 MILLION	2.57

XTREME FACT

SEQUOIA

This supercomputer takes up 3,014 sq ft (280 sq m), and was created for the National Nuclear Security Administration of USA to simulate scenarios involving nuclear weapons.

YOUR SHOUT

This part of the book is all about challenging your knowledge on the wonderful world of machines!

YOUR PICK OF THE... MACHINES

Now that you've gone through all of the lists, tell us your ultimate top 10 machines...

01

02

03

04

05

06

07

08

09

10

ROUND 1: MULTIPLE CHOICE

01 Which of these wave-makers is on our Fastest Machines In Sport list?

A CATAMARAN
B SUBMARINE
C HOVERCRAFT

02 The Lingenfelter Chevrolet Corvette is the fastest car ever to go from 0 to 60 mph, but how quickly can it achieve this speed?

A 1.97 SEC
B 1.99 SEC
C 2.61 SEC

03 Which of the following is the smallest UAV (Unmanned Aerial Vehicle) with a 3 in (1.18 cm) wingspan?

A DELFLY MICRO
B ROBOBEE
C WASP III

ROUND 2: QUESTION TIME

01 The three top spots on the Fastest Manned Vehicles list belong to Apollo 10, Lockheed SR-71 Blackbird, and the ThrustSSC, but in which country were they all produced?

ANSWER:

ROUND 3:
PICTURE PUZZLES

Can you name this vehicle in the Top 10 Most Powerful Engines list?

01

ANSWER:

Do you know which machine this sci-fi power source belongs to?

02

ANSWER:

Can you tell us the fastest manned vehicle ever, seen here below?

03

ANSWER:

ROUND 4:
WORDSEARCH

Study the jumbled letters on the left and then see how many of these machines you can spot that are hidden:

```
A D M S D O N H J S A N
U W N P R W B X M D H D
W A H E L I C O P T E R
S B D E N M K D V J S O
U C S D S G L L K E C N
B H L B T D O T E T V E
M I Z O X E X F B S J J
A T R A I N K F M K O F
R A X T D S R C R I L O
I N O W M G S C O C X J
N K K W K O A F A R C A
E X W I O K N S J E I F
```

HELICOPTER

DRONE

SPEEDBOAT

SUBMARINE

TRAIN

ROCKET

JETSKI

TANK

FIND THE ANSWERS ON PAGE 312

02 Which New York-loving rapper owns a Maybach Exelero, as featured in our Top 10 Unofficial Craziest Celeb Rides?

03 Kirobo *(right)* is one of the most intelligent robots ever built, but where was it sent to to help out humans in 2013?

ANSWER:

MACHINES
CAREER
QUIZ

Which of these activities would you most like to do?

◼ A PARAGLIDING
◼ B GO KARTING
◼ C ROCK CLIMBING

Which of these would you rather go to school in?

◼ A A JET PACK
◼ B A BUGATTI VEYRON
◼ C A TANK

Which of these movies do you like the most?

◼ A PLANES
◼ B FAST & FURIOUS 6
◼ C IRON MAN 3

If your plane crash-landed on a desert island, would you...

◼ A REBUILD THE PLANE AND SEE IF IT CAN GET YOU HOME
◼ B USE THE PARTS TO MAKE A BUGGY TO HELP YOU EXPLORE
◼ C USE THE PLANE'S RADIO TO TRY AND GET HELP

Which of the following video games do you play the most?

◼ A FLIGHT SIMULATOR X
◼ B GRAN TURISMO 3: A-SPEC
◼ C CIVILIZATION REVOLUTION

Which place is most suited to you for a fun day out?

◼ A AN AIRSHOW
◼ B A CAR SHOW
◼ C A TRANSPORT MUSEUM

Which of the following statements best fits you?

◼ A I GET A THRILL FROM HEIGHTS
◼ B I LOVE GOING FAST
◼ C I LIKE TO INVENT AND BUILD STUFF

Find out which machine-related job is best suited to you on page 312

ANIMAL KINGDOM

TOP 10
FASTEST ON LAND

Be it on four legs or two, here are the animals that can race across the plains the quickest...

		SPEED (KPH)	SPEED (MPH)
01	CHEETAH	113	70.2
02	PRONGHORN ANTELOPE	98	60.9
03	SPRINGBOK	97	60.3
04	AMERICAN QUARTER HORSE	86	53.4
05	LION	80	49.7
06	OSTRICH	72	44.7
=	AFRICAN WILD DOGS	72	44.7
=	ELK	72	44.7
09	EASTERN GREY KANGAROO	70	43.5
10	COYOTE	69	42.9

XTREME FACT
LION

Lions do something very similar to domesticated pet cats... When they greet each other, lions rub their heads against one another to show the bond they have as well as to leave a scent.

CHECK IT OUT!

American Quarter Horse: its unusual name comes from a surprisingly simple truth. American colonists in the 17th century developed this breed to be the fastest in races up to one-quarter of a mile.

OFF THE CHART
RED KANGAROO

Australia's Red Kangaroo can also run at 42.9 mph (69 kph). With males growing to 9.2 ft (2.8 m) long, it's the biggest of all the 'roos.

SPEED
49.7
MPH

TOP 10 CRYPTOZOOLOGICAL LAND BEASTS

#	Name	HOW IT IS DESCRIBED IN SIGHTINGS
01	ARICA	Velociraptor-type creature
02	SASQUATCH	Huge hairy biped
03	QILIN	Dragon-esque, unicorn-like, flame-covered tiger
04	OLITIAU	Very large bat-like reptile
05	FLATWOODS MONSTER	Possible alien, 12 ft tall, red-faced
06	GAROU	Werewolf-type monster
07	ENFIELD HORROR	Grey, three legs, slimy skin, red eyes, and claws
08	YA-TE-VEO	Man-eating tentacled tree
09	BLACK SHUCK	Massive red-eyed wolf-apparition
10	CHUPACABRA	Small, spiny, demonic-looking quadruped, "Goat sucker"

XTREME FACT — QILIN

Here is a bronze statue of the mythical Qilin guarding the Hall of Benevolence and Longevity, based at the Summer Palace in Beijing, China. Although often shown with flames over its body, the Qilin is believed to be a positive omen.

CHECK IT OUT!

Jaguar: these big cats are also excellent swimmers, and those jaws are so powerful, they can break a turtle's shell!

WEIGHT 308.6 LB

TOP 10 LARGEST BIG CATS

Believe it or not, the kitty on your street is a direct descendant of the huge feline predators that strike fear into their wild backyards...

#	Name	WEIGHT (KG)	(LB)
		420	925.9
01	TIGER	270	595.2
02	LION	140	308.6
03	JAGUAR	120	264.5
04	COUGAR	73	160.9
05	SNOW LEOPARD	64	141.1
06	LEOPARD	55	121.2
07	CHEETAH	35	77.2
08	LYNX	25	55.1
09	CLOUDED LEOPARD	20	44.1
10	CARACAL		

XTREME FACT — LYNX

Although it died out in the UK 750 years ago, biologists are looking to reintroduce the lynx into the west coast of Scotland.

39

TOP 10
BIGGEST PREHISTORIC CARNIVORES

Millions of years ago, the lords of the landscape were MUCH bigger. Here are the 10 meat-eating dinosaurs that towered over all others...

		LENGTH (M)	LENGTH (FT)
01	SPINOSAURUS	18	59
02	CARCHARODONTOSAURUS	13.2	43.3
=	GIGANOTOSAURUS	13.2	43.3
04	CHILANTAISAURUS	13	42.7
05	TYRANNOSAURUS REX	12.3	40.4
06	TYRANNOTITAN	12.2	40
07	TORVOSAURUS	12	39.4
=	ALLOSAURUS	12	39.4
09	ACROCANTHOSAURUS	11.5	37.7
10	DELTADROMEUS	11	36.1

Source: David Martill, Palaeobiologist

LENGTH 39.4 FT

CHECK IT OUT!

Allosaurus: fossil remains of old "Al" are rarely found outside of American soil. Al was also the main dino in Arthur "creator of Sherlock Holmes" Conan Doyle's 1912 novel, *The Lost World*.

XTREME FACT
CARCHARODONTOSAURUS

Shark fans may recognize the first part of this dinosaur's name—it actually comes from the shark family *Carcharodon* (Greek for "sharp, jagged teeth"). The most well-known of this family is the Great White Shark, *Carcharodon carcharias*. Carcharodontosaurus' teeth were massive, too, and measured up to 7.9 in (20 cm) long!

DANGER!

Wanna experience dinosaurs up close? Check out the amazing full-sized puppetry of *Walking With Dinosaurs The Arena Spectacular*: www.dinosaurlive.com

XTREME FACT

THE CHITAURI SPACE EEL

Although the Chitauri race have appeared in Marvel comic books, this skyscraper-smashing space eel-type monster was created by the writers of 2012 movie *The Avengers*, Joss Whedon (the director, too) and Zak Penn.

TOP 10 MOST SUCCESSFUL MASSIVE MONSTER ATTACK MOVIES

We know that Transformers are big mechanical creatures, BUT, this list is only concerned with movies about oversized nonmetallic monstrosities attacking towns/cities...

		MOVIE	YEAR	BOX OFFICE ($ WORLDWIDE)
		The Avengers	2012	1,511,757,910
01	THE CHITAURI SPACE EEL	The Lord Of The Rings: The Return Of The King	2003	1,119,929,521
02	NAZGÛL	The Lost World: Jurassic Park	1997	618,638,999
03	TYRANNOSAURUS REX	War Of The Worlds	2005	591,745,540
04	TRIPOD ALIENS	King Kong	2005	550,517,357
05	KONG	Pacific Rim	2013	406,744,226
06	THE KAIJUS	Godzilla	1998	379,014,294
07	GODZILLA	Ghostbusters	1984	291,632,124
08	STAY PUFT	The Incredible Hulk	2008	263,427,551
09	ABOMINATION	Super 8	2011	259,936,677
10	ALIEN			

Source: IMDB.com

CHECK IT OUT!

Godzilla: since Ishirō Honda's 1954 film, there have been 31 Godzilla-starring movies made!

MASS 551 LB

XTREME FACT
VARANIDAE/ KOMODO DRAGON

Growing to a terrifying 10 ft (3 m) in length, this huge lizard is not to be messed with. Although it mainly eats deer, the Varanidae has also attacked humans who share its Indonesian home.

CHECK IT OUT!

Boidae: just in the Boidae family alone, there are 43 different species of snakes.

TOP 10
BIGGEST REPTILE FAMILIES

The 10 biggest reptiles are mostly species of crocodiles and alligators, so we've ranked them by "family," which gives us a much broader range of these cold-blooded creatures...

REPTILE NAME	MAXIMUM RECORDED MASS (KG)	(LB)	RELATIVE SCALE:
Saltwater Crocodile	2,000	4,410	100%
Black Caiman	1,310	2,888	66%
Gharial	977	2,154	49%
Leatherback Sea Turtle	932	2,055	47%
Galápagos Tortoise	400	882	20%
Green Anaconda	250	551	13%
Komodo Dragon	166	366	8%
Reticulated Python	158	348	8%
Gaboon Viper	20	44	1%
King Cobra	12.7	28	1%

01 CROCODYLIDAE
02 ALLIGATORIDAE
03 GAVIALIDAE
04 DERMOCHELYDAE
05 TESTUDINIDAE
06 BOIDAE
07 VARANIDAE
08 PYTHONIDAE
09 VIPERIDAE
10 ELAPIDAE

XTREME FACT
GAVIALIDAE/ GHARIAL

With its very long and narrow snout, India's Gharial mainly hunts fish and is actually also known as the fish-eating crocodile. As well as growing huge in mass, it can also reach 20.5 ft (6.25 m) in length.

LONGEST PREHISTORIC NECKS

Long bodies is an obvious list to do, so we thought it would be more fun to compare which dinosaurs had the longest necks...

		TOTAL LENGTH		NECK LENGTH	
		(M)	(FT)	(M)	(FT)
01	MAMENCHISAURUS SINOCANADORUM	35	114.8	18	59
02	SUPERSAURUS VIVIANAE	34	111.6	14	45.9
03	SAUROPOSEIDON PROTELES	45	147.6	11.5	37.7
04	ARGENTINOSAURUS HUINCULENSI	35	114.8	9.5	31.2
05	MAMMENCHISAURUS HOCHUANENSIS	22	72.2	9.3	30.5
06	DIPLODOCUS HALLORUM	33	108.3	8	26.2
07	MAMENCHISAURUS YOUNGI	16	52.5	6.5	21.3
08	ELASMOSAURUS	14	46	6	19.7
=	THALASSOMEDON	12	39.4	6	19.7
10	ARAMBOURGIANIA	11	36.1	3	9.8

Source: David Martill, Palaeobiologist

CHECK IT OUT!

Brachiosaurus: the first seven in the T-10 list are all an order of dinos called sauropods, and Brachiosaurus is one of the most well-known. Something less well-known is that the asteroid belt "9954 Brachiosaurus" was named after it!

MOST BRUTAL WEAPONRY

THE T-10 UNOFFICIAL

		WEAPONRY
01	SALTWATER CROCODILE	"Death roll" spinning action
02	BABIRUSA	Hooked tusks
03	ASHE'S SPITTING COBRA	Spits poison through hollow fangs
04	ELK	Massive spiky antlers
05	LION	Huge claws and teeth
06	HUNTSMAN SPIDER	Big fangs
07	SCORPION	Whiplash stinger on its tail
08	ANACONDA	Colossal body crushes prey
09	ARMY ANT	Scythe-looking hooked jaws
10	HIPPOPOTAMUS	Jagged teeth, powerful jaws, large mass

XTREME FACT
SCORPION

Although there are more than 1,750 different species of scorpion all over the world, only 25 of them have the ability to kill a human with their venomous stinger.

DANGER!

If you're not a fan of scorpions, best be careful if you ever find yourself in Mexico, as 1,000 people are killed there every year from scorpion stings!

43

DID YOU KNOW?

We really do love our four-legged friends' tales... 48 movies about dogs have taken more than $1 million at the box office!

BOX OFFICE
117
MILLION DOLLARS

TOP 10 BIGGEST BOX OFFICE DOG MOVIES

Here, "it's all gone to the dogs" doesn't mean anything other than awesome! What we like to call our T-10 "Best In Show" list, these are the biggest pooch-powered box office hits...

		YEAR OF RELEASE	BOX OFFICE ($ WORLDWIDE)
01	101 DALMATIANS (LIVE-ACTION)	1996	320,689,294
02	BOLT	2008	309,979,994
03	SCOOBY-DOO	2002	275,650,703
04	MARLEY & ME	2008	242,717,113
05	101 DALMATIANS	1961	215,880,014
06	CATS & DOGS	2001	200,687,492
07	BEVERLY HILLS CHIHUAHUA	2008	149,281,606
08	BEETHOVEN	1992	147,214,049
09	HOTEL FOR DOGS	2009	117,000,198
10	LADY AND THE TRAMP	1955	93,602,326

Source: IMDB.com

XTREME FACT
HOTEL FOR DOGS

Based on the 1971 children's novel of the same name by Lois Duncan, nearly 70 dogs starred in this film. Something even better is that many were rescued from dog pounds and then adopted by the movie's crew members. Aww...

M. S.

TOP 10 COOLEST PET MOVIES

THE T-10 UNOFFICIAL

		YEAR
01	BABE	1995
02	BOLT	2008
03	HOW TO TRAIN YOUR DRAGON	2010
04	K-9	1989
05	THE CAT RETURNS	2002
06	FRANKENWEENIE	2012
07	101 DALMATIANS	1961
08	TURNER & HOOCH	1989
09	LADY & THE TRAMP	1955
10	BEETHOVEN	1992

CHECK IT OUT!

Frankenweenie: this superb 2012 stop-motion animation took $81,491,068 worldwide. It was actually inspired by *Frankenweenie* creator Tim Burton's live action short film of the same name, which he made in 1984. Both are based on Mary Shelley's 1818 novel, *Frankenstein.*

DID YOU KNOW?

HOW TO TRAIN YOUR DRAGON: LIVE SPECTACULAR

Inspired by the 2010 animated movie, this arena show is on a three-year world tour right now! There are 23 animatronic dragons (some with a 46-foot wingspan) like Toothless *(left)* in the show. Check out www.dreamworksdragonslive.com

TOP 10 DEADLIEST SPIDERS

THE T-10 UNOFFICIAL

01 BRAZILIAN WANDERING
02 FUNNEL-WEB
03 SIX-EYED SAND
04 HOBO
05 BROWN RECLUSE
06 REDBACK
07 BLACK WIDOW
08 BROWN WIDOW
09 WOLF
10 CHILEAN RECLUSE

X-TREME FACT
BLACK WIDOW

This spider's name has nothing to do with its appearance. It's called the Black Widow because of its extremely dark behavior... The female EATS her husband after their mating is over!

X-PLORE SPIDER VENOM

The reason why Team T-10 couldn't present to you the definitive 10 deadliest spiders

is because it's almost impossible to rank the toxicity of all spiders. Some of their venom can kill small animals, but not humans. For example, as little as 0.006 mg of the Brazilian Wandering Spider's venom can kill a mouse, whereas the Brown Recluse's bite can necrotize human flesh.

CHECK IT OUT!

Funnel-web Spider: with 40 species of Funnel-webs out there, that's more than enough to be wary of. These spiders live in Australia and Tasmania, and thrive in forest environments, but they are just as happy in suburbia too... Argh!

MAGNIFICATION

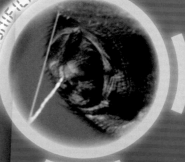

Silverback Mountain Gorilla: it can live about 35 years and is critically endangered.

880 REMAINING

XTREME FACT

SUMATRAN RHINOCEROS

As well as being the only Asian rhinoceros with two horns, the Sumatran Rhino is the smallest of them all. In the last 16 years, only two females in captivity have actually had young. Cruel poaching threatens to completely wipe out this rhinoceros.

ENDANGERED LAND MAMMALS

TOP 10

Of all the threatened species of land mammals, the World Wildlife Fund (WWF) is focusing on these, as protecting their habitat does not guarantee their survival...

		ESTIMATED NUMBER REMAINING
01	WONDIWOI TREE KANGAROO	POSSIBLY EXTINCT
02	NORTHERN WHITE RHINOCEROS	4
03	AMUR LEOPARD	7–12 (CHINA), 20–25 (RUSSIA)
04	JAVAN RHINOCEROS	LESS THAN 50
05	SUMATRAN RHINOCEROS	LESS THAN 200
06	CROSS RIVER GORILLA	250–300
07	MOUNTAIN GORILLA	880
08	GIANT PANDA	1,600
09	GREATER ONE-HORNED RHINOCEROS	2,900
10	TIGER	3,200

XTREME FACT

AMUR LEOPARD

The Amur Leopard and Tiger Alliance (ALTA) has been set up by 15 international and Russian conservation groups to help stop the rare animals from becoming extinct. To find out all about ALTA, visit www.altaconservation.org.

27–37 REMAINING

BIGGEST HUMAN PARASITES

TOP 10

If you're eating something right now, we suggest you STOP or read this list a bit later! These gross creatures enjoy making a home inside the intestines of humans...

		LENGTH	
		(M)	(FT)
01	PORK TAPEWORM	50	164.04
02	BEEF TAPEWORM	12	39.37
03	RAW FISH TAPEWORM	9.14	30
=	WHALE TAPEWORM	9.14	30
05	ROUNDWORM	1	3.28
06	RAT TAPEWORM	0.6	1.97
07	BERTIELLA TAPEWORM	0.13	0.43
08	FASCIOLA GIGANTICA FLATWORM	0.10	0.33
=	CYCLOPHYLLIDEA TAPEWORM	0.10*	0.33
10	FASCIOLOPSIS BUSKI FLUKE	0.075	0.25

*Larval stage

LENGTH 3.28 FT

XTREME FACT ROUNDWORM

As repulsive and as sci-fi as it sounds, the roundworm is currently using a QUARTER of the world's population as hosts...

OFF THE CHART

HOOKWORM

It's only 0.51 in (13 mm) long, but the hookworm is the second most common human parasite.

DANGER!

In 2013, a British woman volunteering in Madagascar nearly died from Pork Tapeworms making their way into her brain! It took two years for her to fully recover.

LENGTH 164 FT

XTREME FACT PORK TAPEWORM

Here's an extreme close-up of a Pork Tapeworm, showing its effective (but disgusting) double row of hooks by its mouth parts. The parasite can produce 50,000 eggs and stay in the small intestine for YEARS...

XTREME FACT

SEA LAMPREY

Extreme angler and explorer Jeremy Wade, from TV series *River Monsters*, encountered tales of this ancient, suction-cup-faced, blood-sucking fish actually attacking humans in the May 2013 episode called *Vampires Of The Deep*.

STAT ATTACK

TICK

Type	Arachnid
Legs	Eight
Diet	Blood
Eating habit	Parasitic, burrowing into flesh
Eggs	Up to 18,000
Lifespan	Up to two years

TOP 10

DEADLIEST BURROWERS IN NATURE

THE T-10 UNOFFICIAL

		TYPE	BURROWING/PARASITIC STYLE
01	MOSQUITO	INSECT	None more deadly: this blood sucker's proboscis is like a needle and the insect spreads fatal diseases
02	TONGUE-EATING LOUSE	CRUSTACEAN	Enters a fish's gills, attaches to its tongue, rots its tongue away, and then becomes its new tongue
03	SEA LAMPREY	FISH	Eel-like, with a mouth of razor-sharp, circular teeth, they latch on to its host and suck its blood
04	GREEN-BANDED BROODSAC	FLATWORM	Invades host's eyes, makes them look like caterpillars, birds eat them, it then lays eggs in bird's rectum
05	CANDIRU	FISH	Tiny but deadly catfish that eats its way inside larger fish and feeds on their insides
06	TICK	ARACHNID	They latch on to flesh and drink blood, sometimes digging under the skin of the host
07	PIRANHA	FISH	In a feeding frenzy, sharp-teethed piranha gnaw their way inside their victim at a lightning rate
08	BOTFLY	INSECT	The maggots chew their way inside the host, using the hole they have created to breathe
09	SACCULINA	BARNACLE	Females creep inside a crab via its joints and use the crab's insides to reproduce/spread
10	GUINEA WORM	ROUNDWORM	Infected water carries larvae into the host, then a worm measuring 3 ft (1 m) emerges

49

LARGEST LAND BURROWERS

There are many more mammals that dig shelters and homes than you'd think, including some pretty BIG ones...

		LENGTH	
		(CM)	(IN)
01	POLAR BEAR	339	133.5
02	AARDVARK	220	86.6
03	NORTH AMERICAN RIVER OTTER	157	61.8
04	GIANT ARMADILLO	150	59.1
05	EUROPEAN OTTER	140	55.1
=	RED FOX	140	55.1
07	COMMON WOMBAT	130	51.2
08	MONGOOSE	120	47.2
09	NORTHERN HAIRY-NOSED WOMBAT	100	39.4
10	COYPU	95	37.4

XTREME FACT
MONGOOSE

There are 33 different kinds of mongoose. Some are extremely solitary, whereas others prefer to live as a group. Rikki-Tikki-Tavi is the name of a mongoose from Rudyard Kipling's 1894 book, *The Jungle Book*.

LENGTH 47.2 IN

SMALLEST LAND BURROWERS

We've looked at the biggest, so now it's time for the littlest mammals that love to dig...

		LENGTH	
		(CM)	(IN)
01	NAKED MOLE-RAT	10	3.9
02	TOWNSEND'S MOLE	21	8.3
03	COLLARED PIKA	23	9.1
04	LONG-EARED JERBOA	24	9.4
05	TOWNSEND'S CHIPMUNK	27.9	11
06	NORTH AMERICAN WATER VOLE	33	13
07	BANNER-TAILED KANGAROO RAT	35.6	14.1
08	DESERT TORTOISE	36	14.2
09	EUROPEAN HAMSTER	40	15.8
=	GREAT GERBIL	40	15.8

XTREME FACT
NAKED MOLE-RAT

Look closely at this Mole-rat and you'll see special sensory hairs near its snout, and it also has them by its tail to help it judge spaces. It lives in East Africa, deep underground.

LENGTH 3.9 IN

BEEN & SEEN

If you've ever seen any of these for real, tick them off!

- [ ] WORM
- [ ] MOLE
- [ ] BADGER
- [ ] TORTOISE
- [ ] HAMSTER
- [ ] RABBIT
- [ ] FERRET
- [ ] VOLE
- [ ] GERBIL
- [ ] OTTER

XTREME FACT

EUROPEAN OTTER

Although the European Otter's daily diet is usually a fishy one, during winter, it also feeds on frogs, insects, and sometimes small birds or beavers.

CHECK IT OUT!

Red Fox: the largest of the foxes, the Red Fox's den is usually 8.2 ft (2.5 m) deep. A successful scavenger, it has survived mankind developing buildings next to its natural habitat.

LENGTH 55.1 IN

DANGER!

It may be cute but, like any wild animal, the Red Fox carries diseases that can be damaging to humans, such as rabies and tapeworms. So absolutely no stroking!

BURROWING TOOLS OF THE TRADE

TOP 10

THE T-10 UNOFFICIAL

		BURROWING "TOOLS"
01	MOLE	Wide, spade-like claws and paws
02	GEODUCK	Muscular clam's siphon can dig deep and get a strong hold
03	RABBIT	Strong claws and paws for rapid digging
04	TERMITE	Massive mandibles (jaws) for digging and moving materials
05	HERMIT CRAB	Slender, curly body can be inserted into new shell homes
06	ANECIC EARTHWORM	Thin, slimy body that it flexes to burrow vertically
07	POLAR BEAR	Huge claws to dig its den for giving birth
08	GROUNDHOG	Powerful and stocky build for excellent burrowing
09	SEA URCHIN	Flexible oval shape for digging into sand
10	GIANT BURROWING FROG	Spade-like legs make for excellent digging

STAT ATTACK

HERMIT CRAB

Average lifespan .... 1-10 years
Size .... 0.8-4 in (2-10 cm)
In existence from ... Late Cretaceous
Environment .... Varying depths of saltwater
Number of species .... over 500

CHECK IT OUT!

Termite: soldier termites are like the Terminators of the colony. They have thicker, tougher plating, and bigger jaws to defend against ants. Their jaws are often so huge that they cannot eat without being fed by their buddies!

XTREME FACT
MOLE

The mole is an air-breathing mammal, so how does it not suffocate while burrowing underground? Well, it has super blood. A special protein allows it to reuse the air it inhaled earlier, above ground. That means hunting worms deep down is not a problem.

XTREME FACT

CLOVERFIELD

The Blu-ray of *Cloverfield* has an Investigation Mode that reveals the main creature as being 350 ft (106.7 m) high, 1,200 ft (365.7 m) long, and weighing 12,800,128 lb (5,806.4 t). It was also covered in 2,000 parasites that were as large as dogs and attacked humans. Bites from the parasites caused death from a lethal toxin.

BOX OFFICE 170.7 MILLION DOLLARS

TOP 10 BIGGEST SUBTERRANEAN BEAST MOVIES

Some creatures of the cinematic realm strike terror into our very core, and some like to lurk in underground lairs...

	MOVIE(S)	YEAR OF RELEASE	BOX OFFICE ($ WORLDWIDE)
01 THE MUMMY	10 *Mummy* movies	1932–2008	1,250,075,319*
02 GODZILLA	31 *Godzilla* movies	1954–PRESENT	396,476,272**
03 BURROWING ALIEN	*Super 8*	2011	260,095,986
04 CREATURE & ITS PARASITES	*Cloverfield*	2008	170,764,026
05 UNDERGROUND HIBERNATING DRAGONS	*Reign Of Fire*	2002	82,150,183
06 GRABOIDS	*Tremors*	1990	48,572,000
07 GIANT SPIDERS	*Eight Legged Freaks*	2002	45,867,333
08 GIANT ALLIGATOR IN THE SEWERS	*Alligator*	1980	6,459,000
09 GIANT ANTS	*Them!*	1954	2,727,971
10 THE PHANTOM	*The Phantom Of The Opera*	1925	2,000,000

*Based on box office takings of *The Mummy* trilogy (1999-2008), as box office data between 1932 and 1967 is unknown
**Based on box office data available for some of the *Godzilla* movies

CHECK IT OUT!

The Phantom: actor Lon Chaney (1883-1930), above, starred as the horrifying title character who lived in the catacombs of Paris. Chaney created all his make-up effects himself, by hand.

TOP 10 FASTEST IN THE SEA

New oceanic intelligence is in! Of all the fish, whales, dolphins, and other marine life, these are the 10 quickest...

		SPEED	
		(KPH)	(MPH)
01	BLACK MARLIN	128.75	80
02	SAILFISH	110	68.3
03	MAKO SHARK	95	59
04	WAHOO	78	48.5
05	BLUEFIN TUNA	70	43.5
06	GREAT BLUE SHARK	69	42.9
07	BONEFISH	64	39.8
=	SWORDFISH	64	39.8
09	GREAT WHITE SHARK	56.3	35
10	KILLER WHALE	56	34.8

XTREME FACT
MAKO SHARK

The fastest shark on the planet, the Mako Shark is a formidable predator. For example, in May 2013, scientists discovered a 200 lb (90.7 kg) sea lion inside the stomach of a massive 12.1 ft (3.7 m)-long, 1,322.8 lb (600 kg) Mako. Fast AND hungry!

TOP 10 BIGGEST SHARKS

Team T-10 loves these amazing creatures, so here are the 10 biggest that are roaming the oceans today...

		LENGTH	
		(M)	(FT)
01	WHALE SHARK	12.7	41.7
02	BASKING SHARK	12.3	40.4
03	GREAT WHITE SHARK	8	26.2
04	TIGER SHARK	7.4	24.3
=	PACIFIC SLEEPER SHARK	7.4	24.3
06	GREENLAND SHARK	6.4	21
07	GREAT HAMMERHEAD SHARK	6.1	20
08	THRESHER SHARK	6	19.7
09	BLUNTNOSE SIXGILL SHARK	4.8	15.7
10	BIGEYE THRESHER SHARK	4.6	15.1

RELATIVE SCALE: 100% 97% 63% 58% 58% 50% 48% 47% 38% 36%

LENGTH 41.7 FT

XTREME FACT
WHALE SHARK

A true carry-over from the prehistoric era, current scientific knowledge puts the Whale Shark as a species that originated 60 million years ago. Living for 70 years, this gentle giant only eats tiny organisms called plankton.

SPEED 59 MPH

MAGNIFICATION

X-PLORE
BONEFISH

The Bonefish is a near-threatened species that can grow up to 3.3 ft (1 m) in length and weigh 19 lb (8.6 kg). Its declining number is due to the fact that it's a popular game

SPEED 39.8 MPH

fish: these are fish that are seen as a challenge for anglers to try to hook, land, and photograph.

CHECK IT OUT!

Great Hammerhead Shark: the largest of the nine different species of Hammerhead, like many sharks, it is endangered, due to the terrible act of capturing and finning it for shark fin soup. Check out this shark documentary to learn more: www.sharkwater.com.

LENGTH 20 FT

&...ANOTHER THING!

The width of the cephalofoil (the hammer shape) is 23-27% of the body length.

HEAVIEST IN THE OCEAN

There are plenty of huge fish in Earth's seas, but it's the air-breathing marine mammals that tip the scales into astonishing figures...

TOP 10

		WEIGHT (T)	WEIGHT (LB)
01	BLUE WHALE		
02	RIGHT WHALE		
03	FIN WHALE	120	264,554
04	BOWHEAD WHALE	80	176,369
05	SPERM WHALE	75	165,346
06	GRAY WHALE	60	132,277
07	HUMPBACK WHALE	50	110,231
=	BRYDE'S WHALE	40	88,184
		30	66,138
09	SEI WHALE	30	66,138
10	GIANT BEAKED WHALE	25	55,115
		12	26,455

XTREME FACT
RIGHT WHALE

There are actually three species of Right Whale: North Atlantic, North Pacific, and the Southern, each weighing up to 176,369 lb (80 t).

OFF THE CHART
KILLER WHALE
WEIGHT: 9,920 LB (4.5 T)

The award-winning 2013 documentary *Blackfish* shines a light on the dark truths behind Killer Whales kept in captivity by SeaWorld. Check it out: www.blackfishmovie.com.

WEIGHT 132,277 LB

XTREME FACT
BOWHEAD WHALE

This is a kind of "baleen whale," which describes the baleen bristles (made of the same substance as hair) that the whales have in their jaws. The bristles filter out food sources from mouthfuls of water.

WEIGHT
176,369
LB

CHECK IT OUT!

Colossal Squid: this amazing photo was taken on February 22, 2007 in New Zealand waters. It captured the moment that, for the first time ever, a live adult male Colossal Squid was successfully brought aboard a boat.

LENGTH
46
FT

LARGEST OCTOPI & SQUID

TOP 10

For many years, these highly intelligent creatures, which grow to gigantic sizes, were considered the stuff of legends. However, now we know the truth...

		TYPE	LENGTH (M)	(FT)
		SQUID	14	46
01	COLOSSAL SQUID	SQUID	13	42.7
02	GIANT SQUID	SQUID	8	26.2
03	BIGFIN SQUID	OCTOPUS	6.1	20
04	GIANT PACIFIC OCTOPUS	SQUID	5.5	18
05	ASPEROTEUTHIS ACANTHODERMA	SQUID	4+	13.1+
06	ROBUST CLUBHOOK SQUID	GLASS SQUID	4+	13.1+
=	COCKATOO SQUID	OCTOPUS	4	13.1
08	SEVEN-ARM OCTOPUS	GLASS SQUID	2.7	8.9
09	MEGALOCRANCHIA FISHERI	SQUID	2.3	7.5
10	DANA OCTOPUS SQUID			

XTREME FACT

GIANT SQUID

This very special specimen of a Giant Squid is kept preserved at the Natural History Museum in London, UK. Measuring 28.3 ft (8.62 m) in length, this squid is brought out and displayed when conditions are correct.

BIGGEST CORAL REEFS

Incredible as it may sound, coral reefs are made up and created by living, breathing marine organisms called... Corals!

		AREA		LENGTH	
	LOCATION	(KM²)	(MI²)	(KM)	(MI)
01 GREAT BARRIER REEF	Coral Sea, Australia	344,400	132,974	2,600+	1615.6+
02 RED SEA CORAL REEF	Red Sea	LESS THAN 50	19.3	1,900	1180.6
03 NEW CALEDONIA BARRIER REEF	Pacific Ocean	15,000	5,792	1,500	932.1
04 MESOAMERICAN BARRIER REEF	Atlantic Ocean	1,400	541	943	586
05 FLORIDA REEF	Atlantic Ocean	1,153	445.2	322	200.1
06 ANDROS BARRIER REEF	Bahamas	6,000	2,316.6	200	124.3
07 ZHONGSHA ISLANDS	South China Sea	6,448	2,490	81	50.3
08 SAYA DE MALHA BANKS	Indian Ocean	40,000	15,444	515	320
09 GREAT CHAGOS BANK	The Maldives	12,000	4,633	162.5	100
10 REED TABLEMOUNT	South China Sea	8,866	3,423	100	62.1

XTREME FACT

THE GREAT BARRIER REEF

Not only is this amazing sight (above) actually made entirely of living organisms across 2,900 reefs, it is so massive that it can be seen from space.

LITERARY LEGENDS OF THE SEA

THE T-10 UNOFFICIAL

	NOVEL/STORY/POEM	AUTHOR	YEAR FIRST PUBLISHED
01 CTHULHU	The Call Of Cthulhu	H. P. Lovecraft	1928
02 MOBY-DICK	Moby-Dick; Or, The Whale	Herman Melville	1851
03 THE KRAKEN	The Kraken	Alfred Tennyson	1830
04 ALIENS FROM THE OCEANS	The Kraken Wakes	John Wyndham	1953
05 THE DEEP ONES	The Shadow Over Innsmouth	H. P. Lovecraft	1936
06 GREAT WHITE SHARK	Jaws	Peter Benchley	1974
07 THE WATCHER IN THE WATER	The Fellowship Of The Ring	J. R. R. Tolkien	1954
08 SEVEN GIANT SQUID	20,000 Leagues Under The Sea	Jules Verne	1870
09 SHOGGOTH	At The Mountains Of Madness	H. P. Lovecraft	1936
10 MANY GIANT SQUID	The Sea Raiders	H. G. Wells	1896

XTREME FACT

THE KRAKEN

There have been many tales and illustrations (like this one from 1650) depicting a Kraken, a massive squid or octopus, attacking a ship. Some reports date back as far as 1250!

CHECK IT OUT!

Elasmosaurus: this kind of plesiosaur had an unusually thin and extremely long neck, much more so than its fellow oceanic reptiles. Scientists estimate it weighed 4,409.2 lb (2,000 kg).

LENGTH 46 FT

TOP 10 BIGGEST PREHISTORIC OCEAN BEASTS

You may think the seas are full of weird and wonderful creatures nowadays, but millions of years ago the REAL monsters lurked beneath the surface...

		TYPE	LENGTH (M)	(FT)
01	MAUISAURUS	Reptile	20.1	66
02	MEGALODON	Fish	20	65.6
03	LIOPLEURODON	Reptile	18	59
04	LEEDSICHTHYS	Fish	16	52.5
05	MOSASAURUS	Reptile	15.2	49.9
	HAINOSAURUS	Reptile	15.2	49.9
07	ELASMOSAURUS	Reptile	14	46
08	PLIOSAURUS	Reptile	12.2	40
	MEGALNEUSAURUS	Reptile	12.2	40
	PLOTOSAURUS	Reptile	12.2	40

OFF THE CHART

PROGNATHODON

A kind of marine reptile from the mosasaur family, Prognathodon just misses out on a spot on our Top 10 by being around 30 ft (9.1 m) in length.

XTREME FACT

MEGALODON

This set of prehistoric jaws are from the much-loved Megalodon, an ancient shark that was a terrifying 59 ft (18 m) long! To put that into perspective, the Great White Shark is "just" 26.2 ft (8 m)!

Source: *David Martill & Luke Hauser, Palaeobiologists*

TOP 10

MOST ENDANGERED AQUATIC CREATURES

The World Wildlife Fund (WWF) is working hard to try to save these amazing oceanic animals, whose population numbers are critically low...

		EST. NUMBER REMAINING
01	YANGTZE RIVER DOLPHIN	
02	CHINESE PADDLEFISH	POSSIBLY EXTINCT
03	IRRAWADDY DOLPHIN	POSSIBLY EXTINCT
04	VAQUITA	78–111
05	NORTH ATLANTIC RIGHT WHALE	200
06	KEMP'S RIDLEY TURTLE	300–500
07	INDUS RIVER DOLPHIN	1,000
08	FINLESS PORPOISE	1,100
09	GANGES RIVER DOLPHIN	1,200–1,400
10	HECTOR'S DOLPHIN	1,200–1,800
		7,400

Source: WWF

ESTIMATED **1,200** REMAINING

ESTIMATED **1,000** REMAINING

CHECK IT OUT!

Kemp's Ridley Turtle: the Deepwater Horizon oil spill that began in the Gulf of Mexico on April 20, 2010, damaged the population of this turtle so badly that efforts were made to collect 70,000 eggs from beach nests before the hatchlings swam into the oil.

XTREME FACT

FINLESS PORPOISE

This is the only porpoise that doesn't have a pronounced dorsal fin, but does have very large pectoral fins. It lives in Asian waters, including Bangladesh, India, China, Korea, and Japan.

DEADLIEST RIVER MONSTERS

THE T-10 UNOFFICIAL

TOP 10

01	GIANT FRESHWATER STINGRAY
02	WELS CATFISH
03	GIANT WOLF FISH
04	PACU
05	GOLIATH TIGERFISH
06	ELECTRIC EEL
07	ARAPAIMA
08	NEW ZEALAND LONGFIN EEL
09	SHORT-TAILED RIVER STINGRAY
10	CANDIRU

XTREME FACT
ELECTRIC EEL

This isn't actually a kind of eel at all, it's a type of knifefish, which describes the way its body tapers toward the tail. It can reach an impressive length of 8.2 ft (2.5 m).

DANGER!

Electric Eels can produce 600 volts of electricity, more than enough to kill a human! They can also live for 15 years. If you're ever in the Amazon, beware...

CRAZIEST SEA CREATURES

THE T-10 UNOFFICIAL

TOP 10

01	COLOSSAL SQUID
02	GOBLIN SHARK
03	DEEPSTARIA ENIGMATICA (A KIND OF JELLYFISH)
04	SLOANE'S VIPERFISH
05	POLYCHAETE WORM
06	VAMPIRE SQUID
07	FRILLED SHARK
08	BLOBFISH
09	EASTERN PACIFIC BLACK GHOSTSHARK
10	PREDATORY TUNICATE

XTREME FACT
SLOANE'S VIPERFISH

This may look like the stuff of nightmares, but don't worry. Not only does it only grow to around 13.8 in (35 cm) in length, it also resides at deep, DEEP depths of up to 8,202 ft (2,500 m), so it is well out of our way. Sloane's Viperfish also holds the record for the fish with the biggest teeth in relation to its head size. We can see why!

BIGGEST CRUSTACEANS

TOP 10

With their thick shells and grabbing claws, all of these super-tough creatures are some of the strangest on our planet...

		SIZE (CM)	SIZE (IN)
01	JAPANESE SPIDER CRAB	380	149.8
02	ALASKAN KING CRAB		
03	AMERICAN LOBSTER	152.4	60
04	COCONUT CRAB	110	43.3
05	COLOSSENDEIS COLOSSEA SEA SPIDER	100	39.37
=	TASMANIAN GIANT CRAB	91	35.83
07	GIANT ISOPOD	91	35.83
08	ATLANTIC HORSESHOE CRAB	76	29.9
09	PENNELLA BALAENOPTERAE (PARASITIC BARNACLE)	60	23.6
10	SUPERGIANT AMPHIPOD	32	12.6
		28	11

SIZE
149.8
IN

XTREME FACT

JAPANESE SPIDER CRABS

These are absolute monsters. Like an aquatic alien, these crabs can weigh up to 42 lb (19 kg). Despite their scary appearance and very long pincers, fishermen who encounter them report that they are pretty placid creatures.

SIZE
43.3
IN

CHECK IT OUT!

American Lobster: here is the heavyweight champion of the crustacean world! The American Lobster just tips the scales against the Japanese Spider Crab (42 lb/19 kg), weighing in at a hefty 44.3 lb (20.1 kg). This very large lobster has a "crusher" claw and one for detailed "tearing" action.

CRYPTOZOOLOGICAL SEA & LAKE MONSTERS

TOP 10

THE T-10 UNOFFICIAL

#	Name	HOW IT IS DESCRIBED IN SIGHTINGS
01	LOCH NESS MONSTER	Plesiosaur-type creature
02	AKKOROKAMUI	394 ft (120 m)-long squid-like creature
03	DOBHAR-CHÚ	Otter and dog-like fish
04	WENDIGO	Giant, skeletal, human-eating monster
05	BROSNO DRAGON	Lake monster
06	OGAPOGO	Sea serpent
07	BUNYIP	Water spirit/beast, a mix of features: flippers, tusks, and a horse's tail
08	CHAMP	Lake monster
09	NĀGA	Serpentine lake creature
10	BEAST OF BUSCO	Massive 500 lb (227 kg) snapping turtle

XTREME FACT — WENDIGO

This is a particularly frightening legend from the Algonquians (native Americans who live by the Atlantic coastline). The Wendigo is said to possess humans, turning them into something demonic and cannibalistic.

CHECK IT OUT!

Loch Ness Monster: Sightings of this legendary cryptid date back to the sixth century, and it's one of the most famous lake monsters in the world. To see more, check out www.nessie.co.uk.

XTREME FACT — NĀGA

This is the famous Nāga statue at Wat Khaek near Nong Khai in Thailand. This theme park features colossal Buddhist and Hindu sculptures. Nāga means "great snake," and the cryptid is often described as a human form that becomes a snake from the waist down.

TOP 10 FASTEST IN THE AIR

New info is in about the breakneck speeds our feathered friends can achieve! Here are the quickest dive-bomb and flight speeds...

		MAXIMUM KNOWN SPEED		RELATIVE SCALE:
		(KPH)	(MPH)	
01	PEREGRINE FALCON	389	241.7	100%
02	GOLDEN EAGLE	320	198.8	82%
03	GYRFALCON	209	129.9	54%
04	SWIFT	171	106.3	44%
05	EURASIAN HOBBY	161	100	41%
06	FRIGATEBIRD	153	95.1	39%
07	SPUR-WINGED GOOSE	142	88.2	37%
08	RED-BREASTED MERGANSER	130	80.8	33%
09	CANVASBACK	116	72.1	30%
10	EIDER	113	70.2	29%

XTREME FACT — FRIGATEBIRD

This massive bird is built for a life of gliding above the open ocean, and that's exactly what it does. Rarely on land, the Frigatebird catches its food while flying over the seas.

TOP 10 WIDEST EAGLE WINGSPANS

Dinosaur fans: did you know that birds of prey are known as "raptors," which means "seize"? You do now! Eagles are among the most iconic, so here are the 10 largest...

		LARGEST WINGSPAN	
		(M)	(FT)
01	WEDGE-TAILED EAGLE	2.84	9.3
02	HIMALAYAN GOLDEN EAGLE	2.81	9.22
03	MARTIAL EAGLE	2.6	8.53
04	WHITE-TAILED SEA EAGLE	2.53	8.30
05	STELLAR'S SEA EAGLE	2.5	8.20
06	BALD EAGLE	2.3	7.55
=	VERREAUX'S EAGLE	2.3	7.55
08	HARPY EAGLE	2.24	7.35
09	PHILIPPINE EAGLE	2.20	7.22
10	CROWNED EAGLE	1.9	6.23

CHECK IT OUT!

White-tailed Sea Eagle: closely related to the Bald Eagle, this bird of prey weighs a meaty 15.2 lb (6.9 kg). Although it hunts fish and small mammals, it's also an effective scavenger.

XTREME FACT — BALD EAGLE

This striking bird is the national animal of the USA, hence the American Bald Eagle's appearance on the official seal of the country.

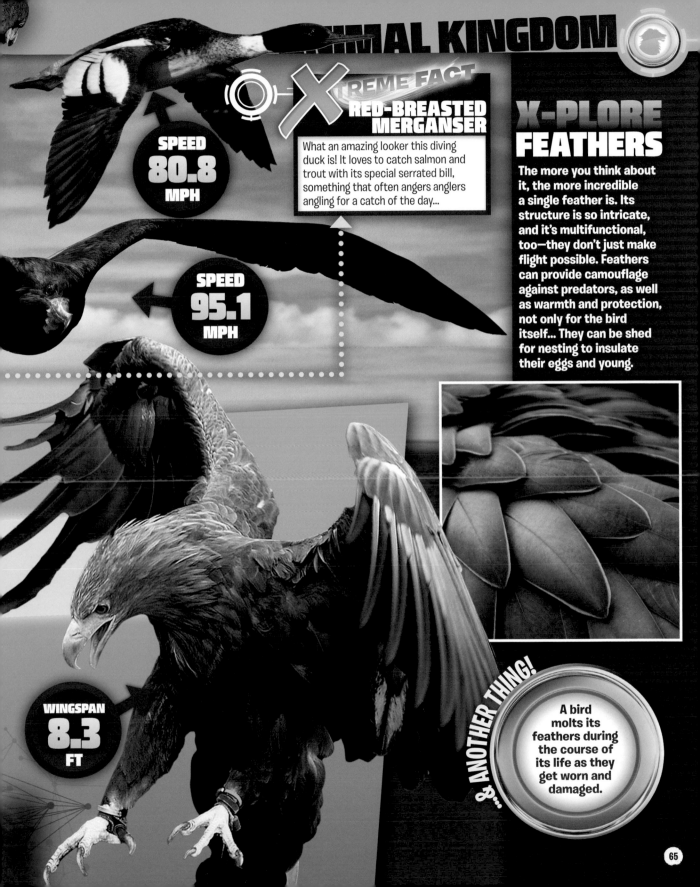

X-TREME FACT
RED-BREASTED MERGANSER

What an amazing looker this diving duck is! It loves to catch salmon and trout with its special serrated bill, something that often angers anglers angling for a catch of the day...

SPEED 80.8 MPH

SPEED 95.1 MPH

WINGSPAN 8.3 FT

X-PLORE FEATHERS

The more you think about it, the more incredible a single feather is. Its structure is so intricate, and it's multifunctional, too—they don't just make flight possible. Feathers can provide camouflage against predators, as well as warmth and protection, not only for the bird itself... They can be shed for nesting to insulate their eggs and young.

&...ANOTHER THING!

A bird molts its feathers during the course of its life as they get worn and damaged.

SMALLEST BIRDS IN THE SKY

Sometimes looks can be deceiving. A bird that seems quite long may weigh a lot less than its smaller relations. Therefore, we've ranked the smallest birds by their length, not their weight...

		SMALLEST SIZE (LENGTH)	
		(CM)	(IN)
01	BEE HUMMINGBIRD	5	1.97
02	BANANAQUIT	7.5	2.95
03	WEEBILL	8	3.15
=	STRIATED PARDALOTE	8	3.15
05	GOLDCREST	8.5	3.35
06	BROWN GERYGONE	9	3.54
=	LESSER GOLDFINCH	9	3.54
08	CRIMSON CHAT	10	3.94
=	GOLDEN-HEADED CISTICOLA	10	3.94
10	TROPICAL PARULA	11	4.33

CHECK IT OUT!

Golden-headed Cisticola: this species of warbler is a bit cheeky to say the least, because it has a special nest-perfecting technique. It takes spiders' webs to weave its nest together. What a creative architect!

LENGTH
3.94
IN

FASTEST INSECT WINGS

That whiny, annoying sound you hear when a mosquito flies close to your ear? That is its wings beating at an insane rate per second...

		BEATS PER SECOND
01	MIDGE	1,046
02	GNAT	950
03	MOSQUITO	600
=	BUMBLEBEE	600
05	FRUIT FLY	300
06	WASP	247
07	HOUSEFLY	190
08	BLOWFLY	150
09	HOVERFLY	120
10	HORNET	100

XTREME FACT
BUMBLEBEE

Although there are around 250 different species of bumblebee, in many places they are dangerously endangered due to our use of pesticides. Search online for the Bumblebee Specialist Group to get more information on the pollinators.

600
BEATS PER SECOND

XTREME FACT
GOLDCREST

The Goldcrest actually wins the number one spot in the UK as its smallest bird. This little chirper loves to grab insects hiding between pine needles.

LENGTH
3.35
IN

TOP 10 FLYING INSECTS THAT BUG US THE MOST

THE T-10 UNOFFICIAL

01	LOCUST
02	MOSQUITO
03	GNAT
04	WASP
05	HORNET
06	FLYING ANT
07	STAG BEETLE
08	HOUSEFLY
09	MIDGE
10	BLACK FLY

CHECK IT OUT!

Locust: in cases where a locust cloud covers hundreds of square miles, literally BILLIONS of locusts can make up the devastating swarm.

MAGNIFICATION

XTREME FACT

ATLAS MOTH

This massive moth's name comes from the god of Greek mythology, Atlas, who was so big that he held up the Earth on his back.

LENGTH
10.3
IN

TOP 10 BIGGEST FLYING INSECTS

Insects get a LOT bigger than your common housefly... Check out the sizes of these flying freaks!

ACTUAL SIZE

		SIZE (LENGTH)		RELATIVE SCALE:
		(MM)	(IN)	
01	CHAN'S MEGASTICK	567	22.3	100%
02	BORNEO STICK INSECT	546	21.5	96%
03	WHITE WITCH MOTH	310*	12.2	55%
04	QUEEN ALEXANDRA'S BIRDWING	310*	12.2	55%
05	GIANT AFRICAN STICK INSECT	265	11.6	47%
06	ATLAS MOTH	262*	10.3	46%
07	MEGALOPREPUS CAERULATUS DAMSELFLY	190*	7.5	34%
08	HERCULES BEETLE	175	6.9	31%
09	TITAN BEETLE	167	6.6	29%
10	GIANT WATER BUG	120.7	4.75	21%

*Wingspan, the rest are lengths

CHECK IT OUT!

Giant Water Bug: it may be a bug, but this critter attacks and feeds on amphibians, fish, and even snakes!

WORST INSECT SWARMS

TOP 10

THE T-10 UNOFFICIAL

		LOCATION	DATE/SEASON
01	MOSQUITO	North Slope, Alaska (USA)	Summer 2013
02	LOCUST	Negev Desert (Israel)	May 2013
03	YELLOW JACKET WASP	California (USA)	September 1989
04	AFRICANIZED BEE	Pantego, Texas (USA)	July 2013
05	FIRE ANT	Mississippi (USA)	September 1999
06	TERMITE	New Orleans, Louisiana (USA)	May 2013
07	MORMON CRICKET	Elko, Nevada (USA)	July 2009
08	BEDBUG	New York (USA)	August 2010
09	GYPSY MOTH	Milwaukee, Wisconsin (USA)	Summer 2004
10	FLYING ANT	Across the UK	August 2013

XTREME FACT

BEDBUG

Like ticks, these are nasty little vampiric bugs that only feed on blood. In 2009, New York City had 10,000 cases of bedbugs reported: a third more than in 2008.

WEIRDEST FLYERS

TOP 10

THE T-10 UNOFFICIAL

01	DRACO LIZARD
02	DEVIL RAY
03	PYGMY GLIDING POSSUM
04	FLYING SQUIRREL
05	FLYING FISH
06	FLYING GECKO
07	SUGAR GLIDER
08	FLYING FROG
09	PHILIPPINE FLYING LEMUR
10	FLYING SNAKE

CHECK IT OUT!

Flying Frog: due to the extra-wide webbing between its toes, this frog can glide over great distances. More than 3,000 different species of can achieve this clever kind of froggy flight.

CRYPTOZOOLOGICAL FLYING FREAKS

TOP 10

THE T-10 UNOFFICIAL

		HOW IT IS DESCRIBED IN SIGHTINGS
01	MOTHMAN	Winged, bird-like man with red eyes
02	THUNDERBIRD	Like a pterosaur
03	DEVIL BIRD	Bird that lets out a hellish, human-like cry
04	ROPEN	Giant bat-like creature
05	WAKWAK	Human-abducting vampiric creature
06	OWLMAN	Very similar to the Mothman, except seen in Cornwall (UK)
07	OLITIAU	Gigantic bat-like demon
08	IMPUNDULU	Human-sized bird that summons lightning
09	POPOBAWA	Shape-shifting evil spirit
10	EKEK	Bird-like humans with a craving for blood

XTREME FACT

THUNDERBIRD

Described by Native Americans as a colossal, supernatural bird, it's often shown on top of totem poles. Modern sightings describe it as similar to a pterosaur.

DID YOU KNOW?

Cryptozoology (from the Greek *kryptos*, which means "hidden") is the study of creatures that may exist due to reported sightings, but no scientific evidence has been found so far.

HEAVIEST BIRDS

TOP 10

Birds that can weigh as much as professional wrestlers?! You'd better believe it...

		WEIGHT (KG)	(LB)
01	OSTRICH	156.8	346
02	DOUBLE-WATTLED CASSOWARY	85	187
03	EMU	60	132
04	GOLD-NECK CASSOWARY	58	128
05	EMPEROR PENGUIN	45.4	100
06	GREATER RHEA	40	88
07	DARWIN'S RHEA	28.6	63
08	LITTLE CASSOWARY	26	57
09	KING PENGUIN	16	35
10	DALMATIAN PELICAN	15	33

WEIGHT 33 LB

CHECK IT OUT!

Dalmation Pelican: surely this is the mouthiest of all birds! Its wingspan can reach over 11.5 ft (3.5 m)!

BIGGEST PREHISTORIC FLYERS

TOP 10

Giant winged reptiles once ruled our skies millions of years ago. Here are the 10 biggest that have been unearthed so far...

		WINGSPAN (M)	WINGSPAN (FT)
01	HATZEGOPTERYX		
02	ARAMBOURGIANIA		
03	QUETZALCOATLUS	13	42.7
04	PTERANODON	11	36.1
05	COLOBORHYNCHUS	9	29.5
=	MOGANOPTERUS	8	26.2
07	TUPUXUARA	7	23
=	ORNITHOCHEIRUS	7	23
09	CEARADACTYLUS	6	19.7
10	THALASSODROMEUS	6	19.7
		5.5	18
		4.5	14.8

Source: David Martill, Palaeobiologist

WINGSPAN 29.5 FT

XTREME FACT

QUETZALCOATLUS

This prehistoric flying reptile was given a name suited to its size. Quetzalcóatl was a feathered, snake-like mythical god in ancient Aztec times. He was also the god of intelligence and self-reflection.

DANGER!

In *Jurassic Park III* (2001), pterosaurs feature in one of the movie's most terrifying sequences as the bumbling human characters find themselves inside the biggest "bird cage" they've ever seen...

& ...ANOTHER THING!

Life-sized Quetzalcoatlus models stood on London, England's South Bank in June 2010.

5458433
5645445641-1545
514351-4564
213453434-4545433-4545435
5345435-4534354
42-45425
639363-535398
4533653-565
1253854-15862

YOUR SHOUT

This section of the book is dedicated to testing your knowledge of awesome animals...

YOUR PICK OF THE... ANIMALS

You've seen the lists... You've read the facts... Now, tell us your ultimate top 10 animals, EVER!

01

02

03

04

05

06

07

08

09

10

ROUND 1: MULTIPLE CHOICE

01 What is the second fastest animal on land, clocked at 60.9 mph (98 kph)?

A **PRONGHORN ANTELOPE**
B **LION**
C **COYOTE**

02 The largest land burrower is the polar bear, but on average, what length do they grow to?

A **112 IN (284.5 CM)**
B **133.5 IN (339 CM)**
C **149 IN (378.5 CM)**

03 The Giant Water Bug is the tenth largest insect on the planet, but what does it feed on?

A **AMPHIBIANS, FISH, & SNAKES**
B **MICE, RABBITS, & MOLE RATS**
C **LOBSTERS, CRABS, & MUSSELS**

ROUND 2: QUESTION TIME

01 The Coral Sea in Australia is home to the longest coral reef in the world. It is a massive 1,615.6 mi (2,600 km) in length and is so huge that it can be seen from space. Can you tell us its great name?

ANSWER:

ROUND 3:
PICTURE PUZZLES

Which arachnid does this deadly venomous weapon belong to?

01

Can you name this tiny mammal that tops our list of Smallest Land Burrowers?

02

Do you know the web-footed creature that can glide through the air?

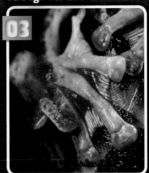

03

ANSWER:

ANSWER:

ANSWER:

ROUND 4:
WORDSEARCH

Take a look at this jumble of letters on the left and see how many of these animals you can find:

```
D A R T Z E Y Q U E A S
F R I N R X N A O T I P
Z I B R W A D H I F S R
N W U S X O K I E F A I
Y C S A C W L H W N N G
L R I W C B Q F C Y A B
F A A R D V A R K X C B
W O T Q V Z F W A H O O
O C X W U E I S V W N K
L Y N X G M I A V B D X
B A F N M U E W B O A G
S D N D C I V C W A D H
```

BLOWFLY

SPRINGBOK

WOLF

AARDVARK

EMU

WAHOO

ANACONDA

LYNX

FIND THE ANSWERS ON PAGE 312

02 The animal on the right is number three on our Top 10 Largest Cats' list, behind the tiger and the lion. Do you know what it is?

03 Which bird, placed sixth in our Top 10 Widest Eagle Wingspan list, is also the national bird of the USA?

ANSWER:

ANIMAL CAREER QUIZ

In which of these places would you most like to live?
- A BY THE SEA
- B THE COUNTRYSIDE
- C ON A PRAIRIE

Which would you rather have as a pet?
- A A FISH
- B A DOG
- C A LIZARD

Which of these movies do you like the most?
- A FINDING NEMO
- B DOCTOR DOLITTLE
- C JURASSIC PARK

If you were faced with an enraged lion, which of these actions would you take?
- A THROW WATER AT IT FROM YOUR FLASK AND RUN
- B STICK AROUND AND TRY TO WORK OUT WHY HE'S ANGRY
- C STAY CALM AND BACK AWAY QUIETLY AND SLOWLY

Which of the following aquatic activities would you prefer to do?
- A SCUBA DIVE BY CORAL
- B SWIM WITH DOLPHINS
- C CAGE DIVE WITH SHARKS

Which place is most suited to you for a fun day out?
- A AN AQUARIUM
- B A PETTING FARM
- C THE ZOO

Which of the following statements best fits you?
- A I ENJOY SWIMMING A LOT
- B I'M ALWAYS READING BOOKS
- C I LOVE OFF-ROAD BMXING

Find out which animal-related job is best suited to you on page 312

73

GAMING
GALAXY

TOP 10
BIGGEST SELLING CONSOLE GAMES OF ALL TIME

Of all the games in the whole world, it's quite a shock to see that ALL of the 10 bestsellers ever are from Nintendo-created consoles...

#	Title	GENRE	RELEASED	CONSOLE/PLATFORM	SALES (MILLIONS)
01	WII SPORTS	Sports	2006	Wii	81.82
02	SUPER MARIO BROS.	Platform	1985	NES (Nintendo Entertainment System)	40.24
03	MARIO KART WII	Racing	2008	Wii	34.31
04	WII SPORTS RESORT	Sports	2009	Wii	32.22
05	POKÉMON RED/BLUE/GREEN	RPG	1996	Game Boy	31.37
06	TETRIS	Puzzle	1989	Game Boy	30.26
07	NEW SUPER MARIO BROS.	Platform	2006	DS	29.37
08	WII PLAY	Party	2006	Wii	28.78
09	DUCK HUNT	Shooter	1984	NES (Nintendo Entertainment System)	28.31
10	NEW SUPER MARIO BROS. WII	Platform	2009	Wii	27.22

Source: VGChartz

CHECK IT OUT!

Wii Sports Resort: Nintendo added 12 new activities, plus the Wii MotionPlus accessory with this release. You can find out all about the game at www.wiisportsresort.com.

SALES
29.37
MILLION

XTREME FACT
NEW SUPER MARIO BROS.

A new power-up in the game saw Super Mario grow to an incredible size for a short time. Due to its phenomenal success, the sequel *New Super Mario Bros. Wii* was released in 2009 with an added twist: four players could play at the same time.

X-PLORE
PS4 & XBOX ONE

The war of the "next generation" consoles rages on! Sony's PS4 was released on November 15, 2013, with Microsoft's Xbox One on November 22, 2013. Although they both have differing specifications, graphics and sound-wise they are on similar pars. But how did they fair during their first sales period? PS4 sold 2.1 million units after it's first few weeks on sale, with Xbox One selling 2 million, so the rival companies remain pretty neck-and-neck.

TOP 10 BIGGEST GAMING PUBLISHERS

To find out the most successful and important gaming publishers on the planet, we looked at the top 100 best-selling games and tallied up who published them...

		NO. OF GAMES IN TOP 100 SELLERS
01	NINTENDO	
02	SONY COMPUTER ENTERTAINMENT	50
=	ACTIVISION	11
04	TAKE-TWO INTERACTIVE	11
05	MICROSOFT GAME STUDIOS	8
=	ELECTRONIC ARTS	6
07	UBISOFT	6
08	BETHESDA SOFTWORKS	3
=	RED ORB	1
=	SQUARESOFT	1

CHECK IT OUT!

Nintendo: it began as a different company, but has always been a maker of games. Founded in 1889 by Fusajiro Yamauchi, Nintendo first made "Hanafuda" playing cards. The company then began developing video game systems in 1975.

GOLD COINS

BIGGEST SELLING WII U GAMES

Nintendo's awesome Wii U has only been out for a couple of years, so the games haven't reached multimillion sales just yet, but here are the 10 bestsellers...

		GENRE	RELEASED	SALES (MILLIONS)
01	NINTENDO LAND	Action	2012	2.45
02	NEW SUPER MARIO BROS. U	Action	2012	2.14
03	LEGO CITY UNDERCOVER	Action	2013	0.51
04	PIKMIN 3	Strategy	2013	0.49
05	THE LEGEND OF ZELDA: THE WIND WAKER	Action	2013	0.40
06	SONIC ALL-STARS RACING TRANSFORMED	Action	2012	0.26
=	NEW SUPER LUIGI U	Platform	2013	0.26
08	JUST DANCE 4	Party	2012	0.21
09	SCRIBBLENAUTS: UNLIMITED	Action	2012	0.18
10	SKYLANDERS GIANTS	Action	2012	0.15

Source: VGChartz

XTREME FACT

LEGO CITY UNDERCOVER

This comical adventure game was the first LEGO game to be published by Nintendo. It features the vocal talents of British comedy stars including Adam Buxton and Peter Serafinowicz. Check out www.legocityu.nintendo.com.

10 QUICK FIRE FACTS

LEGO CITY UNDERGROUND

01	Published by Nintendo
02	Developed by TT Fusion, makers of 16 LEGO games
03	Has a rating of 10+
04	Only released on the Wii U, in 2013
05	Sold 100,000 units in the USA in its first month
06	Features over 100 vehicles to use
07	The Wii U GamePad is used to scan for clues
08	Chase McCain Minifigure came with the Limited Edition
09	Has a prequel, *LEGO City Undercover: The Chase Begins*
10	Official website is www.legocityu.nintendo.com

SALES
510
THOUSAND

CHECK IT OUT!

Super Mario Galaxy: for the first Super Mario adventure to be set in space, Nintendo absolutely nailed it. In 2008, this game received the Adventure Game of the Year award from the Academy of Interactive Arts & Sciences.

BIGGEST SELLING WII GAMES

TOP 10

Nintendo's revolutionary game system is still selling truckloads more games than its rival consoles, with the sports genre stronger than ever...

		GENRE	RELEASED	SALES (MILLIONS)
01	WII SPORTS	Sports	2006	81.42
02	MARIO KART WII	Racing	2008	33.84
03	WII SPORTS RESORT	Sports	2009	31.83
04	WII PLAY	Party	2006	28.74
05	NEW SUPER MARIO BROS. WII	Platform	2009	26.83
06	WII FIT	Sports	2007	22.65
07	WII FIT PLUS	Sports	2009	21.30
08	SUPER SMASH BROS. BRAWL	Combat	2008	11.80
09	SUPER MARIO GALAXY	Platform	2007	10.86
10	JUST DANCE 3	Party	2011	9.73

Source: VGChartz

XTREME FACT

SUPER SMASH BROS. BRAWL

This title saw numerous gaming legends thrown together in a fighting game environment. Donkey Kong, Link *(above)*, Kirby, and brothers Mario and Luigi were just some of the 12 playable, battling characters.

CHECK IT OUT!

Sports Champions: exclusively a PS3 game, this was developed by San Diego Studio and Zindagi Games. It put a brand new spin on the genre in 2010 by featuring a mix of modern and ancient sports disciplines.

UNIT SALES
3.80 MILLION

TOP 10 BIGGEST SELLING PS3 GAMES

Got a PS3? Know a friend who's got one that you enjoy playing? Check out these shocking results... All but ONE of the top sellers are racing or soccer games!

		GENRE	RELEASED	UNIT SALES (MILLIONS)
01	GRAN TURISMO 5	Racing	2010	10.85
02	FIFA SOCCER 13	Sports	2012	7.09
03	FIFA SOCCER 12	Sports	2012	6.47
04	LITTLEBIGPLANET	Platform	2008	5.39
05	FIFA SOCCER 14	Sports	2013	5.25
06	FIFA SOCCER 11	Sports	2010	5.00
07	GRAN TURISMO 5 PROLOGUE	Racing	2007	4.15
08	MOTORSTORM	Racing	2006	3.80
09	SPORTS CHAMPIONS	Sports	2010	3.61
10	FIFA SOCCER 10	Sports	2009	3.55

Source: VGChartz

XTREME FACT MOTORSTORM

The 2006 *MotorStorm* marked the first of a series of off-road racing games that now features five, all released for the Sony platforms of PS3, PS2, PSP, and PS Vita. Total sales for the franchise are $6.78 million. See www.motorstorm.com.

TOP 10 BIGGEST SELLING PS VITA GAMES

Another young platform is the fantastic handheld PlayStation Vita. Released December 17, 2011, it's building up a large catalogue of games...

#	Title	GENRE	RELEASED	UNIT SALES (MILLIONS)
01	LITTLEBIGPLANET PS VITA	Platform	2012	0.66
02	NEED FOR SPEED: MOST WANTED	Racing	2012	0.57
03	FIFA SOCCER	Sports	2012	0.48
04	HOT SHOTS GOLF: WORLD INVITATIONAL	Sports	2011	0.43
05	RAYMAN ORIGINS	Platform	2012	0.41
06	GRAVITY RUSH	Action	2012	0.39
07	RAGNAROK ODYSSEY	RPG	2012	0.32
08	FIFA SOCCER 13	Sports	2012	0.31
09	MADDEN NFL 13	Sports	2012	0.27
10	NEXT HATSUNE MIKU: PROJECT DIVA	Simulation	2012	0.23

Source: VGChartz

SALES 410 THOUSAND

XTREME FACT

RAYMAN ORIGINS

Up to four players can drop in and drop out while playing *Rayman Origins*. Published by gaming giants Ubisoft, it was a multiple platform release across PS3, PS Vita, Nintendo 3DS, Nintendo Wii, Xbox 360, PC, and Mac.

CHECK IT OUT!

Gravity Rush: this wowed gaming fans by taking a different approach to its graphics. These are "cel-shaded," a technique used in 2D cartoon animation, giving it a cool comic-book look and feel.

BEEN & SEEN

When you've played any of these games, tick them off!

- [ ] LEGO MARVEL SUPER HEROES
- [ ] NI NO KUNI: WRATH OF THE WHITE WITCH
- [ ] GRAN TURISMO 5
- [ ] FIFA SOCCER 14
- [ ] GUITAR HERO: WORLD TOUR
- [ ] SONIC UNLEASHED
- [ ] EYEPET ADVENTURES
- [ ] TOP SPIN 4
- [ ] TONY HAWK: RIDE
- [ ] BUZZ! THE ULTIMATE MUSIC QUIZ

SALES
20.91
MILLION

KINECT ADVENTURES!

This was launched with the Kinect system, and changed gaming in a huge way. Xbox 360 owners can now move their whole body and have the Kinect camera system translate their motions into controlling the on-screen characters.

TOP 10

BIGGEST SELLING XBOX 360 GAMES

Look at the distance in sales between the number one and two bestsellers, but the Kinect system is still going VERY strong for Xbox 360 fans...

#	Title	Genre	Released	Sales (millions)
01	KINECT ADVENTURES!	Party	2010	20.91
02	KINECT SPORTS	Sports	2010	5.78
03	FORZA MOTORSPORT 3	Racing	2009	5.39
04	FIFA SOCCER 13	Sports	2012	5.02
05	GUITAR HERO III: LEGENDS OF ROCK	Party	2007	4.43
06	FORZA MOTORSPORT 4	Racing	2011	4.14
07	FIFA SOCCER 12	Sports	2011	4.10
08	FORZA MOTORSPORT 2	Racing	2007	4.01
09	LEGO INDIANA JONES: THE ORIGINAL ADVENTURES	Adventure	2008	3.66
10	FIFA SOCCER 11	Sports	2010	3.48

Source: VGChartz

CHECK IT OUT!

Forza Motorsport 2: look how many of Turn 10 Studios' Forza franchise dominate the Top 10 chart! The Limited Collector's Edition of *Forza Motorsport 2* features the exclusive cars Subaru Impreza S204, Saleen S281E, and Challenge Stradale.

BIGGEST SELLING 3DS GAMES

TOP 10

How cool are the 3D effects of the Nintendo 3DS?! Team T-10 absolutely loves this console. We're obsessed with *Animal Crossing*, and here are the other bestsellers...

		GENRE	RELEASED	UNIT SALES (MILLIONS)
01	POKÉMON X/Y	RPG	2013	10.14
02	SUPER MARIO 3D LAND	Platform	2011	9.24
03	MARIO KART 7	Racing	2011	9.20
04	NEW SUPER MARIO BROS. 2	Platform	2012	7.23
05	ANIMAL CROSSING: NEW LEAF	Action	2012	6.25
06	LUIGI'S MANSION: DARK MOON	Adventure	2013	3.41
07	NINTENDOGS + CATS	Simulation	2011	3.29
08	THE LEGEND OF ZELDA: OCARINA OF TIME	Action	2011	3.28
09	PAPER MARIO: STICKER STAR	RPG	2012	1.88
10	FRIEND COLLECTION: NEW LIFE	Simulation	2013	1.64

Source: VGChartz

10 QUICK FIRE FACTS

POKÉMON X/Y

01	Developers Game Freak have made many *Pokémon* games
02	Sold 4 million units on its launch weekend
03	Its released soundtrack is 3.5 hours long
04	First title in the sixth generation of *Pokémon* games
05	Directed by Junichi Masuda
06	Released exclusively on the Nintendo 3DS
07	Is the fastest-selling 3DS game ever
08	*The Cocoon Of Destruction And Diancie* (2014) is its movie
09	Added 70 new species of Pokémon
10	Official website is: www.pokemon.com

XTREME FACT
PAPER MARIO: STICKER STAR

This Mario adventure was a departure from the usual platform style. It incorporated more of a role-playing element, with the characters in a flat, 2D style against a three-dimensional environment.

CHECK IT OUT!

Pokémon X/Y: this brought no less than 70 new Pokémon and 28 new Mega Evolutions to our attention. Not only does it top our 3DS chart, it also holds the accolade of being the fastest-selling 3DS game of all time...

TOP 10 MOST AMAZING GAMING WORLDS

THE T-10 UNOFFICIAL

		RELEASED
01	JOURNEY	2012
02	ICO	2006
03	THE LEGEND OF ZELDA: OCARINA OF TIME	1998
04	LIMBO	2010
05	TRANSFORMERS: FALL OF CYBERTRON	2012
06	NI NO KUNI: WRATH OF THE WHITE WITCH	2013
07	MYST	1994
08	ANIMAL CROSSING: NEW LEAF	2012
09	SKYLANDERS: GIANTS	2012
10	SUPER MARIO WORLD	1990

CHECK IT OUT!

Transformers: Fall Of Cybertron: loved seeing Grimlock in *Transformers: Age Of Extinction*? You get to play as him in this *War Of Cybertron* follow-up. Developers High Moon Studios gave fans an epic experience on the Ark.

XTREME FACT

NI NO KUNI: WRATH OF THE WHITE WITCH

Legendary Japanese filmmakers Studio Ghibli (animated movies include *Spirited Away*, *Howl's Moving Castle*, and *Arrietty*) worked with Level-5 for five years before the game's 2013 release.

XTREME FACT
MARIO KART WII

This, the sixth main *Mario Kart* game, added a new periphery into the mix: the Wii Wheel. The Wii controller is holstered into the wheel and gives players driving-wheel reactions.

SALES
34.31
MILLION

TOP 10 MOST SUCCESSFUL GENRE LEADERS

Which gaming genres do you love the most? Want to see which are the most popular, as well as the bestsellers in each? No problem...

		TITLE	CONSOLE/PLATFORM	RELEASED	UNIT SALES (MILLIONS)
01	SPORTS	Wii Sports	Wii	2006	81.82
02	PLATFORM	Super Mario Bros.	NES	1985	40.24
03	RACING	Mario Kart Wii	Wii	2008	34.31
04	RPG	Pokémon Red/Green/Blue Version	Game Boy	1996	31.37
05	PUZZLE	Tetris	Game Boy	1989	30.26
06	SHOOTER	Duck Hunt	NES	1984	28.31
07	SIMULATION	Nintendogs	DS	2005	24.57
08	FIGHTING	Super Smash Bros. Brawl	Wii	2008	12.04
09	ADVENTURE	Myst	PC	1994	8.03
10	ACTION	The Legend Of Zelda: Ocarina Of Time	N64	1998	7.60

SALES 2.78 MILLION

SALES 3.39 MILLION

CHECK IT OUT!

Just Dance 2014: This was a launch title for the PS4 and Xbox One, and is the fifth in the *Just Dance* series.

TOP 10 BIGGEST SELLING CONSOLE GAMES OF 2013

It was a truly EPIC year for gaming, and these 10 were the biggest smash-hits across all of the consoles...

#	Title	GENRE	PLATFORM	SALES (MILLIONS)
01	POKÉMON X/Y	RPG	3DS	9.37
02	FIFA SOCCER 14	Sports	PS3	5.20
03	FIFA SOCCER 14	Sports	Xbox 360	3.60
04	LUIGI'S MANSION: DARK MOON	Platform	3DS	3.39
05	MINECRAFT	Adventure	Xbox 360	2.95
06	JUST DANCE 2014	Party	Wii	2.78
07	MADDEN NFL 25	Sports	Xbox 360	1.81
08	GRAN TURISMO 6	Racing	PS3	1.80
09	THE LEGEND OF ZELDA: A LINK BETWEEN WORLDS	Action	3DS	1.80
10	NBA 2K14	Sports	Xbox 360	1.73

Source: VGChartz

XTREME FACT
LUIGI'S MANSION: DARK MOON

Released in North America on March 24, 2013, this hugely enjoyable 2013 Luigi adventure sold 863,000 units within six months! It ended up being a massive worldwide hit as well.

SMASHER CHARACTERS

TOP 10

THE T-10 UNOFFICIAL

#	Character	GAMES FEATURED IN	YEAR OF RELEASE
01	GEORGE, LIZZIE, RALPH	Various *Rampage* titles	1986-2007
02	GODZILLA	Various *Godzilla* titles	1983-PRESENT
03	CRUSHER	*Skylanders: Giants*	2012
04	JAEGER & KAIJU	*Pacific Rim: The Video Game*	2013
05	SUPER MARIO	Various	1981-PRESENT
06	E. HONDA	*Street Fighter II*	1992-PRESENT
07	THE INCREDIBLE HULK	*The Incredible Hulk: Ultimate Destruction*	2005
08	SONIC THE HEDGEHOG	Various *Sonic The Hedgehog* titles	1991-PRESENT
09	VARIOUS ROBOTIC SUITS & PILOTS	Various *Mobile Suit Gundam* titles	1993-PRESENT
10	VARIOUS	*Spore*	2008

CHECK IT OUT!

Sonic The Hedgehog: the speedy, spiky dude, created by Yuji Naka and Naoto Ōshima, has starred in over 70 games since 1991!

10 QUICK FIRE FACTS

SONIC THE HEDGEHOG

#	Fact
01	Miles "Tails" Prower is his best friend
02	His original name was Mr. Needle Mouse
03	Has starred in comic books since 1992
04	Was featured in 2013 movie *Wreck-it Ralph*
05	He cannot swim
06	He was originally designed with big fangs
07	According to the comic, his speed is the result of a lab accident
08	His hobbies include DJing and break-dancing
09	One game suggests he can run at 3,840 mph (6,180 kph)
10	He can run just as fast backwards as he can forwards

XTREME FACT

THE INCREDIBLE HULK

The Hulk was born from the creative minds of Stan Lee and Jack Kirby back in 1962. The Marvel Comics' star has featured in eight video games since his 1984 debut in *Questprobe*.

TOTAL PLATFORMS

TOP 10 BIGGEST SELLING GAMING CONSOLES

If you were to guess which consoles were the most popular, would you get it right? Check out the ultimate 10 bestsellers since gaming began...

#	Console	MADE BY	RELEASED	WORLDWIDE SALES (MILLIONS)
01	PLAYSTATION 2	Sony	2000	157.68
02	NINTENDO DS	Nintendo	2004	154.80
03	GAME BOY/GAME BOY COLOR	Nintendo	1989/1998	118.69
04	PLAYSTATION	Sony	1994	104.25
05	WII	Nintendo	2006	100.95
06	PLAYSTATION 3	Sony	2006	82.45
07	GAME BOY ADVANCE	Nintendo	2001	81.51
08	XBOX 360	Microsoft	2005	81.11
09	PLAYSTATION PORTABLE	Sony	2004	80.72
10	NINTENDO ENTERTAINMENT SYSTEM (NES)	Nintendo	1983	61.91

SALES 154.8 MILLION

XTREME FACT: XBOX 360

If you own one, or your friends have one, you may have heard of the phrase "Red Ring Of Death." This became the term for the 360 suffering a severe hardware failure, causing the front circle to light up red.

SALES 81.11 MILLION

CHECK IT OUT!

Nintendo DS: forget the ongoing "feud" between gaming fans of which is best, PS3 or Xbox 360? This little handheld has nearly sold the same amount of units as BOTH those home consoles combined!

TOP 10 COOLEST-LOOKING PLATFORMS

THE T-10 UNOFFICIAL

		MADE BY
01	PLAYSTATION 4	Sony
02	3DS	Nintendo
03	PS VITA	Sony
04	GAME BOY	Nintendo
05	PLAYSTATION 3	Sony
06	GAMECUBE	Nintendo
07	XBOX ONE	Microsoft
08	SNES	Nintendo
09	XBOX 360	Microsoft
10	WII	Nintendo

XTREME FACT GAMECUBE

Since its launch in 2001, it was beloved by gamers until being discontinued in 2007, making way for the Wii. The GameCube also pioneered a form of online gaming before it became the norm of today.

TOP 10 BIGGEST SELLING HOME CONSOLES

Since last year, Sony's PS3 has taken over global sales of Microsoft's Xbox 360, but they are still way behind Sony's earlier, all-conquering systems...

		MADE BY	RELEASED	UNIT SALES (MILLIONS)
01	PLAYSTATION 2	Sony	2000	157.68
02	PLAYSTATION	Sony	1994	104.25
03	WII	Nintendo	2006	100.95
04	PLAYSTATION 3	Sony	2006	82.45
05	XBOX 360	Microsoft	2005	81.11
06	NINTENDO ENTERTAINMENT SYSTEM (NES)	Nintendo	1983	61.91
07	SUPER NINTENDO ENTERTAINMENT SYSTEM (SNES)	Nintendo	1990	49.10
08	NINTENDO 64 (N64)	Nintendo	1996	32.93
09	GENESIS/MEGA DRIVE	Sega	1988	29.54
10	ATARI 2600	Atari	1977	27.64

CHECK IT OUT!

Playstation 3: the original version of the PS3 *(pictured)* was launched in November 2006, and its slimmer, quieter, and cheaper successor was released in September 2009.

PLATFORMS WITH THE MOST GAMES

Those arguments of "my console's the most popular because it has the most games" are OVER: here are the revealing stats…

#	Platform	MADE BY	RELEASED	TOTAL GAMES MADE
01	PC (MICROSOFT WINDOWS)	Microsoft	1985	7,853
02	NINTENDO DS	Nintendo	2004	3,968
03	PLAYSTATION	Sony	2000	3,548
04	XBOX 360	Microsoft	2005	3,487
05	PLAYSTATION 3	Sony	2006	2,987
06	WII	Nintendo	2006	2,753
07	PLAYSTATION	Sony	1994	2,679
08	PSP	Sony	2004	1,757
09	GAME BOY ADVANCE	Nintendo	2001	1,639
10	GAME BOY/GAME BOY COLOR	Nintendo	1989/1998	1,607

CHECK IT OUT!

Wii: October 20, 2013 was a significant day in the Wii's history… Nintendo decided to discontinue the console, paving way for its follow-up machine, the Wii U.

CONTROLLERS WITH THE MOST BUTTONS

With control pads, it's definitely a case of "more, more, MORE"! Check out how the amount of separate buttons has evolved over the years to give us even greater combos…

#	Controller	RELEASED	BUTTONS
01	PLAYSTATION 4 DUALSHOCK 4	2013	17
=	PLAYSTATION 3 DUALSHOCK 3 SIXAXIS	2007	17
=	PLAYSTATION 2 DUALSHOCK 2	2000	17
=	PLAYSTATION DUAL ANALOG	1997	17
05	GAMECUBE WAVEBIRD	2002	14
=	XBOX 360	2005	14
=	WII U GAMEPAD	2012	13
07	XBOX ONE	2013	13
=	DREAMCAST CONTROLLER & VMU	1998	12
09	NINTENDO (N64)	1996	11
10			

CHECK IT OUT!

GameCube WaveBird: this GameCube controller was wireless, BUT Nintendo had already invented infrared wireless controllers decades earlier in 1989 for its NES console.

XTREME FACT

PLAYSTATION 4 DUALSHOCK 4

Of its many new features, the addition of a headphone socket on this controller means gamers can plug in and experience sounds privately.

XTREME FACT

PLAYSTATION VITA

Not just a handheld console in its own right, the PS Vita can also be synced to a PS4 to play games from it, remotely! You can even use it as a second screen for the PS4. Sony has truly made a little 'n' large gaming hardware combo.

PlayStation

SALES
7.39
MILLION

BEEN & SEEN

If you've used any of these pieces of technology, tick them off!

- [ ] **NINTENDO 3DS**
- [ ] **PS VITA**
- [ ] **GAME & WATCH**
- [ ] **IPHONE 5**
- [ ] **PSP**
- [ ] **GAME BOY**
- [ ] **SONY ERICSSON XPERIA PLAY**
- [ ] **ATARI LYNX**
- [ ] **NINTENDO DS**
- [ ] **GAME BOY ADVANCE**

TOP 10 BIGGEST SELLING HANDHELD PLATFORMS

Gaming-on-the-go is as popular as ever, especially with smartphones bringing more amazing handheld gaming into the mix. Console-wise, these are the champions...

		MADE BY	RELEASED	UNIT SALES (MILLIONS)
01	NINTENDO DS	Nintendo	2004	154.80
02	GAME BOY/GAME BOY COLOR	Nintendo	1989/1998	118.69
03	GAME BOY ADVANCE	Nintendo	2001	81.51
04	PLAYSTATION PORTABLE	Sony	2004	80.72
05	NINTENDO 3DS	Nintendo	2011	42.69
06	GAME GEAR	Sega	1990	10.62
07	PLAYSTATION VITA	Sony	2011	7.39
08	N-GAGE	Nokia	2003	3
09	NEO GEO POCKET/POCKET COLOR	SNK	1998/1999	2
10	TURBOEXPRESS	NEC	1990	1.5

CHECK IT OUT!

Game Boy Advance: the follow-up to the Game Boy Color, this awesome Nintendo handheld was manufactured for seven years, between 2001 and 2008.

GAME BOY ADVANCE

TOP 10 MOST POPULAR FACEBOOK GAMES

Wow, we thought all of those "Saga" games were popular on Facebook, but we had no idea just how popular...

#	Game	Developer	Players (Millions)	Relative Scale:
01	CANDY CRUSH SAGA	King	140	100%
02	PET RESCUE SAGA	King	45	32%
03	FARM HEROES SAGA	King	35	25%
04	CRIMINAL CASE	Pretty Simple	30	21%
05	DRAGON CITY	Social Point	29	21%
06	FARMVILLE 2	Zynga	27	19%
07	DIAMOND DASH	Wooga	23	16%
08	PAPA PEAR SAGA	King	19	14%
09	BUBBLE WITCH SAGA	King	18	13%
10	WORDS WITH FRIENDS	Zynga	12	9%

310.

25

CHECK IT OUT!

Diamond Dash: the fever for this game is still high, especially as it is available across Windows, iPhone, iPad, and iPod Touch platforms. It is Germany-based developer Wooga's fifth game, and was released in 2011.

XTREME FACT
FARM HEROES SAGA

Developer King really is becoming the absolute KING of the mobile and Facebook gaming scene. Founded in 2003, it has released more than 150 games!

TOP 10
BIGGEST GAMING WEBSITES

There are SO many websites dedicated to news, reviews, scoops, and guides for gaming. These 10 are the most popular on the planet...

EST. UNIQUE VISITORS PER MONTH (MILLIONS)

01	IGN	
02	GAMESPOT	17.5
03	GAMEFAQS	15.9
04	GAMETRAILERS	11.5
05	KOTAKU	6.45
06	CHEATCC	4.1
07	GAMESRADAR	3.5
08	1UP	3
09	GAMESPY	2.9
10	JOYSTIQ	2.85
		2.6

CHECK IT OUT!

Gamesradar: this site covers all of the platforms (including handheld and mobile), with reviews, video guides, news features, and sneaky cheats. See www.gamesradar.com.

TOP 10
BEST MOBILE GAMES

THE T-10 UNOFFICIAL

RELEASED

01	PLANTS VS. ZOMBIES 2	2013
02	MASS EFFECT: INFILTRATOR	2012
03	JAWS	2010
04	HORN	2012
05	DEVIL MAY CRY 4 REFRAIN	2011
06	GHOST TRICK: PHANTOM DETECTIVE	2010
07	TEMPLE RUN 2	2013
08	FRUIT NINJA	2010
09	CAN YOU ESCAPE	2013
10	INFINITY BLADE	

XTREME FACT
PLANTS VS. ZOMBIES 2

PopCap's sequel to the massive *Plants Vs. Zombies* scooped no less than 30 Game Of The Year awards. Expanding from backyards, the battle between vegetation and the undead now goes all over the world, including an Ancient Egypt zone.

OUTSIDE THE BOX

TOP 10 BIGGEST VIDEO GAME MOVIE ADAPTATIONS

This year, we've combined theatrically released live-action AND animated movies based on video games! These racked up the "highest scores" with audiences around the world...

#	Movie	Released	Based on Game/Franchise	Box Office ($ Millions)
01	PRINCE OF PERSIA: THE SANDS OF TIME	2010	Prince Of Persia	336,365,676
02	LARA CROFT: TOMB RAIDER	2001	Tomb Raider	274,703,340
03	POKÉMON: THE FIRST MOVIE	1998	Pokémon	163,644,662
04	LARA CROFT TOMB RAIDER: THE CRADLE OF LIFE	2003	Tomb Raider	156,505,388
05	POKÉMON: THE MOVIE 2000	1999	Pokémon	133,949,270
06	MORTAL KOMBAT	1995	Mortal Kombat	122,195,920
07	STREET FIGHTER	1994	Street Fighter	99,423,521
08	FINAL FANTASY: THE SPIRITS WITHIN	2001	Final Fantasy	85,131,830
09	POKÉMON 3: THE MOVIE	2000	Pokémon	68,411,275
10	MORTAL KOMBAT: ANNIHILATION	1997	Mortal Kombat	51,376,861

Source: IMDB.com

BOX OFFICE **85.1** MILLION DOLLARS

CHECK IT OUT!

Pokémon: The First Movie: the *Pokémon* franchise arrived in 1996, and it didn't take long for its first animated movie. It was released in 1998 and directed by Kunihiko Yuyama, the main director of the TV series.

BOX OFFICE **163.6** MILLION DOLLARS

XTREME FACT

FINAL FANTASY: THE SPIRITS WITHIN

It may have made over $85 million, but the problem is that the movie cost $137 million to make! This is because in 2001, its photorealistic CGI (computer-generated imagery) was cutting-edge and extremely expensive to produce.

COOLEST CASTING OF GAMING CHARACTERS IN MOVIES

TOP 10

THE T-10 UNOFFICIAL

01 ANNA TORV (VOICE)

02 ANGELINA JOLIE

03 AARON PAUL

04 JAKE GYLLENHAAL

05 JASON STATHAM

06 KRISTIN KREUK

07 KYLIE MINOGUE

08 BOB HOSKINS

09 SCOTT WOLF

10 SAFFRON BURROWS

CHARACTER PLAYED	MOVIE ADAPTATION(S) OF GAME	YEAR(S)
Nariko	*Heavenly Sword*	2014
Lara Croft	*Tomb Raider* movies	2001–03
Tobey Marshall	*Need For Speed*	2014
Prince Dastan	*Prince Of Persia: The Sands Of Time*	2010
Farmer	*In The Name Of The King: A Dungeon Siege Tale*	2007
Chun-Li	*Street Fighter: The Legend Of Chun-Li*	2009
Lieut Cammy	*Street Fighter*	1994
Super Mario	*Super Mario Bros.*	1993
Billy Lee	*Double Dragon*	1994
"Angel" Deveraux	*Wing Commander*	1999

XTREME FACT

ANGELINA JOLIE: LARA CROFT

The 39-year-old American actress Angelina Jolie played tomb-raiding video game character Lara Croft twice on the big screen. The total box office takings for her action-packed outings is $431,208,728.

...& ANOTHER THING!

Writer Marti Noxon (*Buffy The Vampire Slayer*) is working on a new Lara Croft movie.

XTREME FACT

AARON PAUL: TOBY MARSHALL

Critically acclaimed actor Aaron Paul starred as *Need For Speed*'s main character Tobey Marshall: a wrongfully imprisoned street racer who avenges his friend's death. Released March 14, 2014, it had a relatively low budget (considering it's action/racing) of $66 million.

TOP 10

FIRST-EVER ANIMATED MOVIES BASED ON VIDEO GAMES

01 SUPER MARIO BROS. THE GREAT MISSION TO RESCUE PRINCESS PEACH!

02 FATAL FURY: THE MOTION PICTURE

03 STREET FIGHTER II: THE ANIMATED MOVIE

04 POKÉMON: THE FIRST MOVIE

05 POKÉMON: THE MOVIE 2000

06 POKÉMON 3: THE MOVIE

07 POKÉMON 4EVER

08 POKÉMON HEROES: LATIOS AND LATIAS

09 POKÉMON: JIRACHI WISH MAKER

10 POKÉMON: DESTINY DEOXYS

Before the trend of live-action adaptations kicked in, Japan was producing popular animated movies based on video game franchises...

BASED ON GAME FRANCHISE	RELEASED
Super Mario Bros.	JUL 20, 1986
Fatal Fury	JUL 16, 1994
Street Fighter II	AUG 8, 1994
Pokémon	JUL 18, 1998
Pokémon	JUL 17, 1999
Pokémon	JUL 8, 2000
Pokémon	JUL 7, 2001
Pokémon	JUL 13, 2002
Pokémon	JUL 19, 2003
Pokémon	JUL 17, 2004

XTREME FACT
POKÉMON

The origins of the *Pokémon* phenomenon date back to the humble Game Boy. In 1996, two interlinkable games were released, and the rest is history. To date, there are 16 movies, more than 800 TV episodes, toys, merchandise, and 43 video games!

CHECK IT OUT!

Super Mario Bros. Those powered-up Italian brothers made their first appearance in the video game world in 1983's *Mario Bros.* but it wasn't long before the *Super Mario Bros.* brand was born with 1985's NES game. The franchise has sold over 262 million units.

COOLEST COLLECTORS' EDITION EXTRAS

TOP 10

THE T-10 UNOFFICIAL

		BUNDLED WITH...
01	DRIPPY PLUSH TOY, WIZARD'S BOOK	Ni No Kuni: Wrath Of The White Witch Wizard's Edition
02	CARRY CASE, PREMIUM TURNTABLE CONTROLLER	DJ Hero: Renegade Edition
03	FIGURINES OF LINK AND PHANTOM ZELDA	The Legend Of Zelda: Spirit Tracks Ltd Edition
04	HISTORY OF MARIO BOOK, SOUNDTRACK	Super Mario All-Stars: 25th Anniversary Edition
05	SLASH GUITAR FACEPLATE	Guitar Hero III: Special Edition
06	GOLD RING, DOCUMENTARY, LENTICULAR PACKAGING	Sonic Generations
07	PEWTER CREATURE, OFFICIAL STRATEGY GUIDE	Myst III: Exile
08	MICKEY FIGURINE, DVD	Epic Mickey
09	ART BOOK, SOUNDTRACK	Rayman Origins
10	MAGNETIC FOLD-OUT CASE, SOUNDTRACK	Prince Of Persia: Limited Edition

LONGEST-RUNNING CONVENTIONS

TOP 10

Loads of conventions have hundreds of thousands of attendees, but here we're interested in the ones that have been dedicated to video gaming the longest...

		LOCATION	YEAR BEGAN	TOTAL YEARS
01	COASTCON	Mississippi (USA)	1977	37
02	PLAY: THE GAMES FESTIVAL	Modena (Italy)	1982	32
03	I-CON	New York (USA)	1982	32
04	MIDSOUTHCON	Tennessee (USA)	1982	32
05	BASHCON	Ohio (USA)	1985	32
06	GENERICON	New York (USA)	1985	29
07	DRAGON CON	Georgia (USA)	1987	27
08	U-CON	Michigan (USA)	1988	26
09	DEMICON	Iowa (USA)	1990	24
10	THE GATHERING	Hamar (Norway)	1992	22

CHECK IT OUT!

PLAY: The Games Festival: this long-running Italian-based games festival has been held in several different cities, including Verona, Rome, and Modena. It's not just video gaming on offer, as PLAY also features board games, collectible card games, role-playing games, and many others...

TOP 10 LONGEST-RUNNING TV SHOWS BASED ON VIDEO GAMES

These stars of the small screen have also conquered the OTHER small screen in our lives... Television!

01	POKÉMON
02	DIGIMON
03	KIRBY: RIGHT BACK AT YA!
04	SATURDAY SUPERCADE
05	SONIC X
06	MEGA MAN STARFORCE
07	MONSTER RANCHER
08	THE SUPER MARIO BROS. SUPER SHOW!
09	ADVENTURES OF SONIC THE HEDGEHOG
10	BOMBERMAN JETTERS

BASED ON GAME FRANCHISE	YEARS ON AIR	TOTAL EPS	RELATIVE SCALE:
Pokémon	18 (1997–PRESENT)	800+	100%
Digimon	12 (1999–2011)	332	42%
Kirby	2 (2001–03)	100	13%
Various	2 (1983–85)	97	12%
Sonic The Hedgehog	2 (2003–05)	78	10%
Mega Man	2 (2006–08)	76	10%
Monster Rancher	2 (1999–2001)	73	9%
Super Mario Bros.	1 (1989)	65	8%
Sonic The Hedgehog	3 (1993–96)	67	8%
Bomberman	1 (2002–03)	52	7%

TOP 10 BEST VIDEO GAME SOUNDTRACKS

THE T-10 UNOFFICIAL

01	JOURNEY
02	SUPER MARIO BROS.
03	ACTRAISER
04	MACHINARIUM
05	THE LEGEND OF ZELDA: OCARINA OF TIME
06	XENON 2: MEGABLAST
07	SHADOW OF THE COLOSSUS
08	SHADOW OF THE BEAST
09	UMJAMMER LAMMY
10	TETRIS

COMPOSER	RELEASED
Austin Wintory	2012
Koji Kondo	1985
Yuzo Koshiro	1990
Tomáš Dvořák	2009
Koji Kondo	1998/2011
Bomb The Bass & David Whittaker	1989
Kow Otani	2005
David Whittaker	1989
Masaya Matsuura	1999
Hirokazu Tanaka/Russian folk song "Korobeiniki"	1989

XTREME FACT
SHADOW OF THE BEAST

Heard how good Psygnosis' *Shadow Of The Beast* (1989) was? Heavy Spectrum Entertainment Labs are developing a brand new version exclusively for the PS4. The project was announced at Germany's 2013 Gamescom.

TOP 10 BIGGEST MOVIES ABOUT VIDEO GAMING

We've looked at movie adaptations of video game franchises, but what of the movies ABOUT gaming? Here come the 10 box office champions...

		RELEASED	BOX OFFICE ($ MILLIONS)
01	WRECK-IT RALPH	2012	471,222,889
02	TRON LEGACY	2010	400,062,763
03	SPY KIDS 3D: GAME OVER	2003	197,011,982
04	WARGAMES	1983	79,567,667
05	SCOTT PILGRIM VS. THE WORLD	2010	47,664,559
06	TRON	1982	33,000,000
07	THE LAST STARFIGHTER	1984	28,733,290
08	STAY ALIVE	2006	27,105,095
09	THE WIZARD	1989	14,278,900
10	CLOAK & DAGGER	1984	9,719,952

Source: IMDB.com

BOX OFFICE **400** MILLION DOLLARS

XTREME FACT

TRON LEGACY

Released in 2010 as a direct sequel to *Tron* (1982), *Tron Legacy* had a budget of $170 million—10 times more than *Tron's*. French songwriting duo Daft Punk provided all of the original music for the movie (24 tracks) and even had a cameo appearance as DJs.

CHECK IT OUT!

Spy Kids 3D - Game Over: the third instalment in the *Spy Kids* series starred Selena Gomez and Sylvester Stallone (playing four different roles). The movie went on to make over five times its budget of $38 milion.

10 QUICK FIRE FACTS

TRON LEGACY

01	Directed by Joseph "*Oblivion*" Kosinski
02	Written by *Lost's* Eddy Kitsis and Adam Horowitz
03	Stars Jeff Bridges, Garrett Hedlund, Olivia Wilde
04	Released on December 17, 2010
05	Took $44,026,211 on its opening weekend
06	Rated PG-13/12A
07	Running time of 2 hours 5 mins
08	Cost $170 million to make
09	Was shown in 3,451 cinemas
10	Nominated for an Academy Award: Sound Editing

YOUR SHOUT

It's time to download your knowledge on the world of gaming into these pages... Don't crash!

YOUR PICK OF THE... GAMING

You've played some of the games, you've read all the facts, now tell us your top 10 gaming things...

01
02
03
04
05
06
07
08
09
10

ROUND 1: MULTIPLE CHOICE

01 What genre is the biggest-selling console game of all time?

A **PLATFORM**
B **SPORT**
C **RACING**

02 The biggest-selling games console is the PlayStation 2, but how many units has it sold?

A **157.68 MILLION**
B **84.36 MILLION**
C **12.8 MILLION**

03 The longest-running games convention, Coastcon, has been running for 37 years. Do you know where it takes place each year?

A **MISSISSIPPI, USA**
B **MODENA, ITALY**
C **HAMAR, NORWAY**

ROUND 2: QUESTION TIME

01 The top three PS Vista games are *LittleBigPlanet PS Vita*, *FIFA Soccer*, and *Need For Speed: Most Wanted*. Can you give us the year in which they were all released?

ANSWER:

ROUND 3:
PICTURE PUZZLES

Can you name the gaming character seen in this extreme close-up?

We've cropped this picture of a cool console. Can you name it from what you can see?

Can you tell us the biggest selling Xbox 360 game that this emblem belongs to?

01

02

03

ANSWER:

ANSWER:

ANSWER:

ROUND 4:
WORDSEARCH

Scan your eye to the left... See that grid of letters? How many of these games developers can you find within it?

```
E D A N I N T E N D O X
F G V A B M E H Q U F B
S D F O E V D R A M V E
C G M T I O P V C W N R
S F I M I O M W T V N M
A I C R N U M U I E V E
B U R S V A B X V C K F
X B O X S E X I I T I O
Z A S Q U A R E S O F T
X D O X N W B W I O I P
S C F E G M I X O E F U
A D T C V T S O N Y U T
```

NINTENDO
SONY
ACTIVISION
XBOX
SQUARESOFT
MICROSOFT
EA
UBISOFT

FIND THE ANSWERS ON PAGE 312

02 Can you name the gaming console that this controller (with an awesome 17 buttons) belongs to?

03 *Pet Rescue Saga* is the second most popular game on Facebook. Can you name the number one, which has 140 million players?

ANSWER:

GAMING
CAREER
QUIZ

What is your preferred gaming genre?

- ◼ A ACTION
- ◼ B ADVENTURE
- ◼ C FIGHTING

Which would you rather get as a present?

- ◼ A HUGE PILES OF LEGO
- ◼ B A KEYBOARD
- ◼ C A DIGITAL JOURNAL

Which of these movie characters do you like the most?

- ◼ A TONY STARK
- ◼ B SOUNDWAVE
- ◼ C CLARK KENT

Which subject do you most enjoy?

- ◼ A ART & DESIGN
- ◼ B MUSIC
- ◼ C ENGLISH

Which of the following activities would you prefer to do?

- ◼ A DESIGNING CHARACTERS
- ◼ B LISTENING TO MUSIC
- ◼ C READING GAMING MAGS

Which of these is most suited to you for a fun day out?

- ◼ A A THEME PARK
- ◼ B A POP CONCERT
- ◼ C GOSSIPING AT A FRIEND'S HOUSE

Which of the following statements best fits you?

- ◼ A I HAVE A GREAT IMAGINATION
- ◼ B MY MP3 PLAYER IS ALWAYS ON
- ◼ C I'M ALWAYS ASKING QUESTIONS

Find out which gaming-related job is best suited to you on page 312

QUICKEST "FAST TWITCH" SPORTSMEN (DIFFERENT EVENTS)

We've done an exhaustive amount of calculations to bring you the speediest sportsmen on the planet who all specialize in short distance, "fast twitch" events…

#	Name	COUNTRY	ATHLETIC EVENT	DISTANCE	YEAR	TIME	AVERAGE SPEED (KPH)	(MPH)
01	USAIN BOLT	Jamaica	Track	100 M	2009	0:09.58	37.58	23.35
02	USAIN BOLT	Jamaica	Track	200 M	2009	0:19.19	37.52	23.31
03	MICHAEL JOHNSON	USA	Track	400 M	1999	0:43.18	33.35	20.72
04	DAVID RUSHIDA	Kenya	Track	800 M	2012	1:40.91	28.54	17.73
05	CÉSAR CIELO	Brazil	Swimming: Freestyle	50 M	2009	0:20.91	8.61	5.35
06	RAFAEL MUÑOZ	Spain	Swimming: Butterfly	50 M	2009	0:22.43	8.02	4.98
07	CÉSAR CIELO	Brazil	Swimming: Freestyle	100 M	2009	0:46.91	7.67	4.77
08	LIAM TANCOCK	UK	Swimming: Backstroke	50 M	2009	0:24.04	7.49	4.65
09	MICHAEL PHELPS	USA	Swimming: Butterfly	100 M	2009	0:49.82	7.23	4.49
10	PAUL BIEDERMANN	Germany	Swimming: Butterfly	200 M	2009	1:42.00	7.06	4.39

SPEED 5.35 MPH

CHECK IT OUT!

César Cielo: the Brazilian is certainly built for powerhouse sprint swimming—he's 6.4 ft (1.95 m) and 194 lb (88 kg). He's also the most successful Brazilian swimmer, ever. In 2010, *Sport Life* magazine also named Cielo the Best Athlete of the Decade.

XTREME FACT USAIN BOLT

Here he is—the fastest human being on the planet! Jamaican Usain St. Leo "Lightning" Bolt's 100 m record of 9.58 sec is the fastest speed a person has ever achieved across land, unassisted by machinery.

TOP 10

QUICKEST "FAST TWITCH" PARALYMPIC MEN (DIFFERENT EVENTS)

This can never really be a definitive Top 10, because there are many different classes (depending on the physical difference) in Paralympic sports. However, here are the fastest within each overall event...

#	Name	Country	Athletic Event	Distance	Class	Year	Time	Average Speed (KPH)	(MPH)
01	ALAN FONTELES CARDOSO OLIVEIRA	Brazil	Track	200 M	T43	2013	0:20:66	34.85	21.65
02	JASON SMYTH	Ireland	Track	100 M	T13	2012	0:10.46	34.42	21.39
03	LIXIN ZHANG	China	Track	400 M	T54	2008	0:45.07	31.95	19.85
04	MARCEL HUG	Switzerland	Track	800 M	T54	2010	1:31.12	31.61	19.64
05	ANDRÉ BRASIL	Brazil	Swimming: Freestyle	50 M	S10	2009	0:22.44	8.02	4.98
06	ANDRÉ BRASIL	Brazil	Swimming: Freestyle	100 M	S10	2009	0:48.70	7.39	4.59
07	ANDRÉ BRASIL	Brazil	Swimming: Butterfly	50 M	S10	2009	0:25.51	7.06	4.39
08	SEAN RUSSO	Australia	Swimming: Backstroke	50 M	S13	2013	0:27.30	6.59	4.1
09	ANDRÉ BRASIL	Brazil	Swimming: Butterfly	100 M	S10	2009	0:54.76	6.57	4.08
10	PHILIPPE GAGNON	Canada	Swimming: Freestyle	200 M	S10	2002	1:52.83	6.38	3.96

BRASIL 0221

SPEED 19.85 MPH

XTREME FACT
LIXIN ZHANG

Here is China's Lixin Zhang in action in the T54 Men's 1,500 m at the Paralympic Games, September 3, 2012, in London, England. He also won four gold medals at the 2008 Beijing Paralympics.

CHECK IT OUT!

Alan Fonteles Carduso Oliveira: he began running on wooden prostheses at 13, and by the age of 20, had won gold in the Men's 200 m T44 final at the London 2012 Paralympic Games.

EXPLOSIONS OF POWER

TOP 10 QUICKEST "FAST TWITCH" SPORTSWOMEN (DIFFERENT EVENTS)

Combining the major short distance "fast twitch" running and swimming events, here are the speediest sportswomen EVER and their events...

		COUNTRY	ATHLETIC EVENT	DISTANCE	YEAR	TIME	AVERAGE SPEED (KPH)	(MPH)
01	FLORENCE GRIFFITH JOYNER	USA	Track	100 M	1988	0:10.49	34.32	21.32
02	FLORENCE GRIFFITH JOYNER	USA	Track	200 M	1988	0:21.34	33.74	20.97
03	MARITA KOCH	Germany	Track	400 M	1985	0:47.60	30.25	18.8
04	JARMILA KRATOCHVÍLOVÁ	Czech Republic	Track	800 M	1983	1:53.28	25.42	15.8
05	BRITTA STEFFEN	Germany	Swimming: Freestyle	50 M	2009	0:23.73	7.59	4.72
06	THERESE ALSHAMMAR	Sweden	Swimming: Butterfly	50 M	2009	0:25.07	7.18	4.46
07	BRITTA STEFFEN	Germany	Swimming: Freestyle	100 M	2009	0:52.07	6.91	4.3
08	JING ZHAO	China	Swimming: Backstroke	50 M	2009	0:27.06	6.65	4.13
09	DANA VOLLMER	USA	Swimming: Butterfly	100 M	2012	0:55.98	6.43	4
10	FEDERICA PELLEGRINI	Italy	Swimming: Freestyle	200 M	2009	1:52.98	6.37	3.96

XTREME FACT
BRITTA STEFFEN

31-year-old German swimmer Britta Steffen holds the world record in the 50 m AND the 100 m freestyle! She also has an official website at www.britta-steffen.com.

XTREME FACT
FLORENCE GRIFFITH JOYNER

Better known as Flo-Jo, Florence Griffith Joyner's amazing 1988 records for running have never been broken by another female. She tragically died in her sleep from a seizure in 1998.

CHECK IT OUT!

Therese Alshammar: the Swedish swimming titan holds an insane amount of medals: 43 for European Championships, 25 World Championship medals, and three from Olympic events.

SPEED
4.72
MPH

TOP 10

QUICKEST "FAST TWITCH" PARALYMPIC WOMEN (DIFFERENT EVENTS)

Not a definitive Top 10, as comparing the different classes (depending on physical difference), skills, and speeds is an unfair comparison. This data shows the fastest times and speeds within each event overall...

	COUNTRY	ATHLETIC EVENT	DISTANCE	CLASS	YEAR	TIME	AVERAGE SPEED (KPH)	(MPH)
01 GUOHUA ZHOU	China	Track	100 M	T43	2012	0:11.91	30.23	18.8
02 OMARA DURAND	Cuba	Track	200 M	T13	2011	0:24.24	29.7	18.45
03 CHANTAL PETITCLERC	Canada	Track	400 M	T54	2004	0:51.91	27.74	17.24
04 TATYANA McFADDEN	USA	Track	800 M	T54	2013	1:44.44	27.58	17.13
05 OXANA SAVCHENKO	Russia	Swimming: Freestyle	50 M	S10	2009	0:26.54	6.78	4.21
06 SOPHIE PASCOE	New Zealand	Swimming: Butterfly	50 M	S10	2013	0:29.08	6.19	3.85
07 OXANA SAVCHENKO	Russia	Swimming: Freestyle	100 M	S10	2009	0:58.60	6.14	3.82
08 SOPHIE PASCOE	New Zealand	Swimming: Backstroke	50 M	S10	2013	0:30.49	5.9	3.67
09 VALÉRIE GRAND'MAISON	Canada	Swimming: Freestyle	200 M	S10	2008	2:08.53	5.6	3.48
10 JOANNA MENDAK	Poland	Swimming: Butterfly	100 M	S10	2009	1:05.10	5.53	3.44

SPEED 18.45 MPH

XTREME FACT

OMARA DURAND

Visually impaired Cuban runner Omara Durand won two gold medals for T13 events at the London 2012 Paralympic Games, in the 100 m and 400 m events.

CHECK IT OUT!

Chantal Petitclerc: she has 21 Olympic medals, including 14 golds! This Canadian wheelchair racer's first Paralympic Games was at Barcelona in 1992.

STAT ATTACK

FOOTBALL (FIELD GOAL)

Origin	1883
Original point value	5
Modern 3-points value from:	1909
Crossbar height	9.8 ft (3 m)
Goalposts' width	18.5 ft (5.64 m)
Football Associations	NFL, NCAA

DISTANCE
518.37 FT

TOP 10 SPORTS THAT PROPEL A BALL THE FARTHEST

Of all the ball sports in all the world, these are records of the different spheres being sent the farthest, most impressive distances...

	NAME	COUNTRY	YEAR	DISTANCE (M)	(FT)
01 LONG DRIVE GOLF	Mike Dobbyn	USA	2007	503.83	1,653
02 PGA GOLF	Mike Austin	USA	1974	471	1,545.3
03 BASEBALL (HOME RUN)	Mickey Mantle	USA	1960	193.24	634
04 CRICKET (HIT/SIX)	Shahid Khan Afridi	Pakistan	2013	158	518.37
05 BASEBALL (THROW)	Glen Gorbous	Canada	1957	135.89	445.83
06 CRICKET (THROW)	Roald Bradstock	USA	2010	132.6	435.04
07 FOOTBALL (THROW)	Various players	USA	N/A	90.53	297
08 RUGBY	Gerry Brand	South Africa	1932	77.7	254.92
09 FOOTBALL (FIELD GOAL)	Ching Do Kim	Hawaii	1944	71.32	234
10 SOCCER (THROW-IN)	Danny Brooks	UK	2010	49.78	163.32

CHECK IT OUT!

Cricket: this sport is popular in the UK, and this could be because it was invented there in the 16th century! The earliest written mention of it was spelt "creckett" in 1598.

TOP 10
SPORTS WITH THE HEAVIEST THROWN OBJECTS

		WEIGHT (KG)	(LB)
01	CABER TOSS		
02	WEIGHT THROW	79	174.17
03	KEG TOSS	25	56
04	SHOT PUT	13.5	29.7
=	HAMMER THROW	7.26	16
=	SHEAF TOSS	7.26	16
07	DISCUS	7.26	16
08	JAVELIN	2	4.4
=	PÉTANQUE (BOULES)	0.8	1.76
10	CLUB THROW*	0.8	1.76
		0.4	0.88

*For this sport, it has to be a minimum weight

There are more sports where you have to launch an object into the air than you'd think. With some very hefty items, get those muscles flexing with these...

CHECK IT OUT!

Hammer Throw: here's German Markus Esser getting prepared for hammer time in the 2013 final of the 14th IAAF World Athletics Championships.

WEIGHT
16
LB

WEIGHT
16
LB

Xtreme FACT
SHOT PUT

The origin of the shot put is thought to be from the middle ages when soldiers would throw (or put) cannonballs as a hobby. It first appeared in the Olympics in its current form in 1896.

XTREME FACT
JARED BRENNAN

Darwin-born Australian Football star Jared Brennan retired from the sport at the end of the 2013 season. His 173-game career saw him play for both the Brisbane Lions and Gold Coast Suns.

OFF THE CHART
LD WILLIAMS

Check out American LD Williams' (playing here for the French team JL Bourg-en-Bresse) leaping skills! This was taken as he scored and triumphed at the 2012 Dunk Challenge on December 30, 2012, at the Palais Omnisport de Paris-Bercy in Paris, France.

TOP 10 HIGHEST JUMPERS IN SPORT

Leaping to extreme heights with just the power of your body takes a lot of training, and these athletes are the absolute masters of jumping...

HEIGHT 40.2 IN

#	Name	Country	Sport	Height Jumped (CM)	Height Jumped (IN)
01	YAN ZHI CHENG	China	Acrobatics	246	97
02	JAVIER SOTOMAYOR	Cuba	High jump	245	96.5
03	TONY JAA	Thailand	Martial arts	200	78.7
04	KADOUR ZIANI	France	Basketball	142.2	56
05	HANUMAN	India	Parkour	137.2	54
06	LEONEL MARSHALL	Cuba	Volleyball	127	50
07	GERALD SENSABAUGH	USA	American football	117	46
08	JARED BRENNAN	Australia	Australian football	102	40.2
09	MAC BENNETT	USA	Ice hockey	86	34
10	CRISTIANO RONALDO	Portugal	Soccer	78	30.7

X TREME FACT

BLACK CAVIAR

Before she retired from racing on April 17, 2013, Black Caviar made nearly $8 million in earnings, so let's hope she got only the best quality sugar cubes and carrots! A professional racehorse with her own website? Oh, yes! See www.blackcaviar.net.au.

X-PLORE

THE LEGACY OF RED RUM

A true racehorse legend, Red Rum died on October 18, 1995, aged 30. A national treasure for the UK, Red Rum is its best-known racehorse. His most famous race was the 1973 Grand National, in which Red Rum triumphed, after being 30 lengths behind!

TOP 10 MOST SUCCESSFUL RACEHORSES

When we're talking about explosions of power in sport, we cannot forget our fine four-legged friends! Here are the greatest thoroughbred horses who never lost a race...

		COUNTRY	LIFETIME	UNDEFEATED WINS
01	KINCSEM	Hungary	1874–1887	54
02	BLACK CAVIAR	Australia	2006–PRESENT	25
03	PEPPERS PRIDE	USA	2003–PRESENT	19
04	ECLIPSE	UK	1764–1789	18
=	KARAYEL	Turkey	1970–PRESENT	18
06	ORMONDE	UK	1883–1904	16
=	PRESTIGE	France	1903–1924	16
=	RIBOT	UK	1952–1972	16
09	COLIN	USA	1905–1932	15
=	MACON	Argentina	1922–UNKNOWN	15

& ...ANOTHER THING!

In honour of Red Rum's epic career, he is buried near the winning post at Aintree race course in the UK.

TOP 10

SPORTS WITH THE FASTEST SWINGS

Do you enjoy sports where you swing a bat or racket, or bowl with your arm? Then check out these incredible speeds that these human limbs have achieved...

01	BADMINTON
02	RACQUETBALL
03	SQUASH
04	TENNIS
05	GOLF
06	LACROSSE
07	BASEBALL
08	CRICKET (BOWL)
09	TABLE TENNIS
10	SOFTBALL

NAME	COUNTRY	YEAR	HEAD SPEED (KPH)	(MPH)
Tan Boon Heong	Malaysia	2010	421	261.6
Egan Inoue	USA	1990s	307.39	191
Cameron Pilley	Australia	2011	281.64	175
Samuel Groth	Australia	2012	263	163.4
Joe Miller	UK	2010	241.4	150
Paul Rabil	USA	2010	178.64	111
Justin Upton	USA	2012	171.4	106.5
Shoaib Akhtar	Pakistan	2003	161.3	100.2
Lark Brandt	New Zealand	2003	112.5	70
Zara Mee	Australia	2006	111	69

XTREME FACT

SQUASH

A school invented a sport? Yes! In 1830, in Harrow (Northwest London), UK, squash was conceived. It quickly spread to many other schools, and its international popularity began in the late 19th century. Amazing!

SPEED
106.5
MPH

SPEED
175
MPH

CHECK IT OUT!

Baseball: here's the fastest baseball bat swinger in the world, Atlanta Braves' Justin Upton. He's hit 135 home runs in his career so far.

BIGGEST HITTERS

(BOXING/COMBAT SPORT STARS)

THE T-10 UNOFFICIAL

		COUNTRY	SPORT
01	BEC HYATT	Australia	Mixed martial arts
02	LENNOX LEWIS	UK	Boxing
03	LUCIA RIJKER	The Netherlands	Kickboxing, Boxing
04	MANNY PACQUIÁO	Philippines	Boxing
05	JAKE LAMOTTA	USA	Boxing
06	BUAKAW BANCHAMEK	Thailand	Muay Thai
07	YOKO TAKAHASHI	Japan	Mixed martial arts
08	ROCKY MARCIANO	USA	Boxing
09	TONY LOPEZ	USA	Mixed martial arts
10	SAÚL ÁLVAREZ	Mexico	Boxing

10 QUICK FIRE FACTS

MANNY PACQUIÁO

01	His was born in the Philippines on December 17, 1978
02	Manny's idol is Bruce Lee
03	His boxing record is won 55 (KO 38), lost 5 (KO 3), drawn 2
04	His nickname is Pac-Man
05	Has boxed a total of 383 rounds
06	He has held eight major world boxing titles
07	He was the first Filipino athlete to appear on a postage stamp
08	Has been in movies and had a recording career
09	He has a Jack Russell terrier who shares his nickname
10	Has competed in eight different weight classes

XTREME FACT
MANNY PACQUIÁO

Phillippines' Pacquiáo *(right)* is beating Shane Mosley and retaining the WBO welterweight title in Las Vegas, Nevada, on May 7, 2011. Pacquiáo is also a politician, and has a movie about his life, *Manny* (2014), narrated by Liam Neeson.

XTREME FACT
YUKON QUEST

It started in 1984 and, ever since, the 1,000-mile International Sled Dog Race takes place annually, between Whitehorse, Yukon, and Fairbanks, Alaska. See www.yukonquest.com.

DISTANCE 1,000 MI

DISTANCE 140.6 MI

TOP 10

LONGEST "SLOW TWITCH" SPORTS EVER

"Slow twitch" muscles are essential for long-distance sports, because they can work hard for ages without hurting. Here are the craziest endurance sporting challenges ever...

		TYPE/EVENTS INCLUDED	TOTAL DISTANCE COVERED (KM)	(MI)
01	TOUR DE FRANCE^	Cycling	5,745*†	3,569.8*†
02	GREAT DIVIDE MOUNTAIN BIKE ROUTE	Mountain biking	4,418*	2,745*
03	ULTRAMARATHON	Running and walking	1,609+*	1,000+*
04	YUKON QUEST	Dog sled race	1,609	1,000*
05	MONGOL DERBY	Horse riding	1,000**	621.37**
06	IRONMAN TRIATHALON	Swimming (2.3 mi), cycling (112 mi), marathon (26.2 mi)	226.31	140.6
07	POWERMAN ZOFINGEN DUATHALON	Hill run (6.2 mi), hill cycle (93.2 mi), hill run (18.6 mi)	190	118.06
08	QUADRATHALON	Swimming (2.48 mi), kayaking (12.4 mi), cycling (62.1 mi), running (13 mi)	145	90.1
09	CANADIAN SKI MARATHON	Skiing	160	99.42
10	RACE WALKING	Fast walking	80.5	50

† Longest ever Tour de France, staged in 1926
* Multi-day event
** Multiple horses used

CHECK IT OUT!

Ironman Triathalon: its roots began in Hawaii and, nowadays, Ironman challenges are set up all over the world. However, its origins mean that the Ironman World Championship has been held annually in Hawaii since 1978. The 2013 winners were Frederik Van Lierde (Belgium) with a time of 8 hr 12 min 29 sec and Mirinda Carfrae (Australia), 8 hr 52 min 14 sec.

X-PLORE
ULTRAMARATHON

Here's Oswaldo Lopez (USA) looking utterly focused as he powers his way through the running section of what is called the most gruelling footrace in the world, the AdventurCORPS Badwater 135 Ultramarathon race. The challenge is hosted in California's Death Valley National Park.

TOP 10
CRAZIEST MARATHON COSTUMES

THE T-10 UNOFFICIAL

We researched some of the wackiest get-ups that runners have donned for charity, and came up with these 10 winners...

01 THE HULK

02 RHINOCEROS

03 DARTH VADER

04 TOWER

05 KNIGHT & DRAGON

06 MAN ON A TOILET

07 OVER 1,500 SANTAS

08 SMURF

09 SONIC THE HEDGEHOG

10 SUMO WRESTLER

FASTEST AROUND-THE-WORLD TRIPS

For the ultimate test of mental and physical endurance, it has to be an around-the-world challenge. Here are the record holders based on their different methods...

DIRECTION	RECORD HOLDER(S)	YEAR(S)	TIME
Westbound	Tom Horne, Bud Ball, John McGrath, Ross Oetjen, Eric Parker	2013	1D, 17H, 7M
Westbound	David J. Springbett	1980	1D, 20H, 6M
Westbound	Michael Quandt	2004	1D, 16H, 31M
Westbound	Steve Fossett	2002	13.5D
Westbound	Bertrand Piccard, Brian Jones	1999	19D, 21H, 55M
Eastbound	Loïck Peyron (skipper of a crew of 13)	2012	45D, 13H, 42M, 53S
Eastbound	Francis Joyon	2008	57D, 13H, 34M, 6S
Eastbound	François Gabart	2013	78D, 2H, 16M
Eastbound	Mike Hall	2012	91D, 18H
Westbound	Jean-Luc Van Den Heede	2003-04	122D, 14H, 3M, 49S

MOST IMPORTANT MUSCLES USED IN LONG-DISTANCE RUNNING

THE T-10 UNOFFICIAL

	ROLE
01 **RECTUS FEMORIS**	Part of quadriceps: moves and flexes knees and hip joints
02 **VASTUS MEDIALIS**	Part of quadriceps: moves and flexes knees and hip joints
03 **VASTUS LATERALIS**	Part of quadriceps: moves and flexes knees and hip joints
04 **VASTUS INTERMEDIUS**	Part of quadriceps: moves and flexes knees and hip joints
05 **HAMSTRINGS**	Hip extension and knee-flexing
06 **GLUTEUS MAXIMUS**	Keeps body upright and helps hip extension
07 **ILIOPSOAS**	Hip-flexing
08 **CALF**	Flexes ankles and knees
09 **ABDOMINALS**	Core strength, holds the body, aids balance
10 **EXTERNAL & INTERNAL INTERCOSTALS**	Aids forced inhalation & exhalation to oxygenate the blood

CHECK IT OUT!

Abdominals: the abdominal wall's three layers are the external obliques, internal obliques, and transverse abdominus. As the tissues overlap, this "core" area is strong and helps maintain posture.

GREATEST TOUR DE FRANCE CHAMPIONS

It's one of the most famous cycling tournaments on the planet. These are the pedal powerhouses who have won it more times than anyone else...

		COUNTRY	YEARS CHAMPION	TOTAL
01	JACQUES ANQUETIL	France	1957, 1961, 1962, 1963, 1964	5
=	EDDY MERCKX	Belgium	1969, 1970, 1971, 1972, 1974	5
=	BERNARD HINAULT	France	1978, 1979, 1981, 1982, 1985	5
=	MIGUEL INDURAIN	Spain	1991, 1992, 1993, 1994, 1995	5
05	PHILIPPE THYS	Belgium	1913, 1914, 1920	3
=	LOUISON BOBET	France	1953, 1954, 1955	3
=	GREG LeMOND	USA	1986, 1989, 1990	3
08	LUCIEN PETIT-BRETON	France	1907, 1908	2
=	FIRMIN LAMBOT	Belgium	1919, 1922	2
=	OTTAVIO BOTTECCHIA	Italy	1924, 1925	2

XTREME FACT
MIGUEL INDURAIN

Spanish cycling legend Miguel Indurain retired in 1997, but he has certainly made his mark. Among his wins, he wore the Tour de France race leader yellow jersey for a period of 60 days.

X-PLORE
LANCE ARMSTRONG CONTROVERSY

One of the strangest and saddest twists in the world of professional sport is the tale of American Lance Armstrong. He is the reason why the Tour de France Championship record for 1999-2005 has been wiped. Armstrong won for that seven-year period and became a global hero for beating cancer between 1996-97. He also created the Lance Armstrong (now Livestrong) Foundation to provide support to cancer patients. Shockingly, after denying using performance-enhancing drugs all his career, Armstrong admitted using them in January 2013, making all of his amazing wins null and void.

OFF THE CHART

CHRIS FROOME

This is the 2013 Tour de France champion, Chris Froome. In the previous year's race, Froome rode as cycling legend Sir Bradley Wiggins' domestique, which is a kind of assistant.

TOP 10

OLDEST PROJECTILE SPORTS

Ye olden folk were enjoying being competitive with a ball, spear, or arrow way before TV coverage came along...

		YEARS AGO IT BEGAN
01	ARCHERY	
02	SHOOTING	5,000+
=	JAVELIN	4,000+
=	HOCKEY	4,000+
=	HANDBALL	4,000+
06	HURLING	4,000+
=	HARPASTUM (EARLY RUGBY)	2,500+
=	CUJU (EARLY SOCCER)	2,500+
=	POLO	2,500+
10	MESOAMERICAN BALLGAME (EARLY RACQUETBALL)	3,000+

XTREME FACT

HANDBALL

Showing how modern handball should be played, here's Icelandic Guðjón Valur Sigurðsson about to score a goal for his team THW Kiel against Rhein-Neckar Löwen on Nov 6, 2013. One of the best handballers on the planet, Sigurðsson scored 66 goals at the 2007 World Championships.

AGE 4,000+ YEARS

BEGAN 5,000+ YEARS AGO

CHECK IT OUT!

Archery: this engraving depicts archers in the Battle of Zama, which took place 202 BC. Publius Cornelius Scipio Africanus led his Roman army against Hannibal's Carthaginian clan.

GLADIATORIAL LEGENDS

THE T-10 UNOFFICIAL

EXAMPLE OF FAME

01	SPARTACUS	Legend who inspired fellow slaves to go into battle
02	LUCIUS RAECIUS FELIX	Had 12 gladitorial matches and won them all
03	COMMODUS	Thought he was the reincarnation of Hercules and regularly fought wild animals
04	PRISCUS	Famously fought with Verus for so long they both admitted defeat...
05	VERUS	...which lead to the pair being named joint victor by Titus
06	TITUS	This Roman Emperor wasn't shy of performing in the arena as a gladiator
07	MARCUS ATTILIUS	Was the first to defeat the previously unbeatable Lucius Raecius Felix
08	MARCUS CALPURNIUS FLAMMA	Was victor 21 times from his 34 battles
09	TETRAITES	Pottery has been unearthed depicting his victories in battle
10	ELAGABALUS	Another Emperor who didn't consider himself too high up to fight in the arena

XTREME FACT

SPARTACUS
The Roman soldier was enslaved and became a gladiator before escaping in 73 BC.

GODS OF SPORT

THE T-10 UNOFFICIAL

#	Name	ROLE	ORIGIN
01	NIKE	Goddess of victory	Greek mythology
02	ARTEMIS	Goddess of hunting	Greek
03	CHENG SAN-KUNG	Fishing	Chinese
04	TUNG LU	Skiing	Chinese
05	HERMES	Patron of athletics	Greek
06	APOLLO	Patron of archery	Greek
07	SATET	Archery	Egyptian
08	ELLI	Wrestling	Scandinavian
09	ULL	Skiing	Germany
10	HASTSEHOGAN	Racing	Navajo

CHECK IT OUT!

Apollo: French artist François-Léon Sicard sculpted this statue of Apollo in 1932. It stands in the Archibald Fountain in Australia's Hyde Park, Sydney.

119

TOP 10 OLDEST OLYMPIC-TYPE SPORTS

As you can see from the data, the origin of many sports that have become Olympic events pre-dates the actual beginning of the Olympic Games (776 BC) by thousands of years...

		YEARS AGO IT BEGAN
01	WRESTLING	
=	SPRINT RUNNING	
03	SWIMMING	17,300+
04	ARCHERY	17,300+
05	BOXING	8,000+
06	WEIGHTLIFTING	8,000+
=	ATHLETICS & GYMNASTICS	5,000+
=	ROWING	4,000+
=	HOCKEY	4,000+
=	EQUESTRIAN	4,000+

TOP 10 ANCIENT OLYMPIANS

		DISCIPLINE
01	MILO OF CROTON	Wrestling
02	ORSIPPUS OF MEGARA	Running
03	NERO	Chariot racing
04	DIAGORAS OF RHODES	Boxing
05	THEAGENES OF THASOS	Boxing
06	COROEBUS OF ELIS	Running
07	TIMOTHEOS OF CROTON	Wrestling
08	CYNISCA OF SPARTA	Chariot racing
09	LEONIDAS OF RHODES	Running
10	TIBERIUS	Chariot racing

THE 110 UNOFFICIAL

XTREME FACT

WRESTLING

Strangely, and sadly, the International Olympic Committee have decided to drop wrestling from the Olympics, starting from the 2020 Games.

CHECK IT OUT!

It wasn't always about prize money and golden cups. This ornate, decorated jug was given to the wrestling champions of the Panathenaic Games in Ancient Greece... Filled with olive oil!

OFF THE CHART

KUSHTI

3,000 years ago, the Indian style of wrestling called Kushti began. Here are Kushti competitors locked in battle at Shahupuri in Kolhapur, India on March 22, 2005. There is a website where practitioners and supporters of Kushti contribute: www. kushtiwrestling. blogspot.co.uk.

TOP 10 MOST SUCCESSFUL OLYMPIANS

Of all the disciplines and sporting experts, these 10 are the biggest Olympic champions...

#	Name	DISCIPLINE	COUNTRY	MEDALS
01	MICHAEL PHELPS	Swimming	USA	22
02	LARISA LATYNINA	Gymnastics	Russia	18
03	NIKOLAI ANDRIANOV	Gymnastics	Russia	15
04	BORIS SHAKHLIN	Gymnastics	Russia	13
=	EDOARDO MANGIAROTTI	Fencing	Italy	13
=	TAKASHI ONO	Gymnastics	Japan	13
07	PAAVO NURMI	Athletics	Finland	12
=	BJØRN DÆHLIE	Cross-country skiing	Norway	12
=	BIRGIT FISCHER	Canoeing	Germany	12
=	SAWAO KATO	Gymnastics	Japan	12

MEDALS 12

CHECK IT OUT!

Bjørn Dæhlie: clocking up 46 wins over his cross-country skiing career, Norwegian Bjørn is the most successful champion of the Winter Olympics in this sport, ever.

FASTEST MACHINES IN SPORT

There are so many sports that feature ferocious engines and skilled drivers, but these are the 10 that achieve the craziest speeds...

		SURFACE	TOP SPEED (KPH)	(MPH)
01	TOP FUEL DRAGSTER	Track	515	320
02	SPEEDBOAT	Water	511	317.5
03	AIRSHOW STUNT PLANE	Air	426	264.7
04	FORMULA ONE CAR	Circuit	370	230
05	MOTOR RALLY (NASCAR, ETC)	Circuit	342.4	212.8
06	SNOWMOBILE	Snow terrain	338	210
07	MOTORCYCLE	Circuit	312	194
08	JET SKI	Water	289.7	180
09	MONSTER TRUCK	Course	154.5	96
10	GO-KART	Circuit	128.7	80

SPEED
320
MPH

GRAND PRIX MOTORCYCLE MASTERS

Here we've combined all of the types of motorcycle championship wins (MotorGP, 350 cc, etc) to bring you the ultimate biking bosses...

		COUNTRY	TOTAL WINS
01	GIACOMO AGOSTINI	Italy	122
02	VALENTINO ROSSI	Italy	106
03	ÁNGEL NIETO	Spain	90
04	MIKE HAILWOOD	UK	76
05	MICHAEL DOOHAN	Australia	54
06	PHIL READ	UK	52
=	JORGE LORENZO	Spain	52
08	DANI PEDROSA	Spain	48
09	JIM REDMAN	Rhodesia	45
=	CASEY STONER	Australia	45

CHECK IT OUT!

Dani Pedrosa: here he is, swerving skillfully during the 2013 MotoGP in Valencia, Spain. In 2004, Dani became the youngest World Champion at just 19 years old.

XTREME FACT
TOP FUEL DRAGSTER

SPEED
317.5
MPH

Heard of the phrase "nitro" mentioned with fast cars? In Top Fuel Dragster racing, the fuel is made of 90 percent nitromethane and 10 percent methanol. It's a real-life nitro-boost!

CHECK IT OUT!

Speedboat: modern invention? Not so... Speedboats date back to 1886! German engineers Gottlieb Daimler and Wilhelm Maybach were the first to power a boat with a gasoline-based engine.

DEADLIEST CIRCUITS IN THE WORLD

TOP 10

Whether it's inside a four-wheeled vehicle hurtling around corners, or braving a motorcycle with neck-breaking acceleration, professional racing can be lethal...

		FATALITIES (DRIVERS)	FATALITIES (MECHANIC/SPECTATORS/WORKERS)	FATALITIES (TOTAL)
01	SNAEFELL MOUNTAIN COURSE	240	15	255
02	CIRCUIT DE LA SARTHE LE MANS	22	83 (+ 120 more have been injured)	105 (225 incl. injuries)
03	AUTODROMO NAZIONALE MONZA	52	36	88
04	INDIANAPOLIS MOTOR SPEEDWAY	42	35	77
05	NÜRBURGRING	73	3	76*
06	CIRCUIT DE SPA-FRANCORCHAMPS	47	4	51
07	DAYTONA INTERNATIONAL SPEEDWAY	34	-	34
08	THOMPSON INTERNATIONAL SPEEDWAY	5	-	5
09	CIRCUIT DE MONACO	4	-	4
10	ATLANTA MOTOR SPEEDWAY	3	-	3

*Allegedly more are killed every year as the circuit is open to the public, and many deaths are kept private by the families or not made public.

WINS 91

✗TREME FACT

MICHAEL SCHUMACHER

Germany's Michael Schumacher has won an amazing seven Formula One World Championships! His career has seen him in pole position 68 times.

TOP 10

F1 DRIVING LEGENDS

Formula One features some of the most incredible motor-vehicle technology around, plus, of course, some of the most talented drivers, like these multiple winners...

	Driver	COUNTRY	TOTAL WINS	RELATIVE SCALE:
01	MICHAEL SCHUMACHER	Germany	91	100%
02	ALAIN PROST	France	51	56%
03	AYRTON SENNA	Brazil	41	45%
04	FERNANDO ALONSO	Spain	32	35%
=	SEBASTIAN VETTEL	Germany	32	35%
06	NIGEL MANSELL	UK	31	34%
07	JACKIE STEWART	UK	27	30%
08	JIM CLARK	UK	25	27%
=	NIKI LAUDA	Austria	25	27%
10	JUAN MANUEL FANGIO	Argentina	24	26%

WINS 32

CHECK IT OUT!

Sebastian Vettel: 2010-13 consecutive World Champion, Vettel has always had racing in his blood. He started amateur karting at the tender age of three and a half!

XTREME FACT
JEFF GORDON

Fan of USA stock car racer Jeff Gordon? If you've followed many of his 720+ career races, you can join his official fan club, called the Jeff Gordon Network. See www.jeffgordon.com.

WINS
76

TOP 10 NASCAR LEGENDS
(CHAMPIONSHIP WINS)

Seems as if there's something special in the water in the Carolinas! Look how many amazing champs have come from those two States...

01 RICHARD PETTY
02 DAVID PEARSON
03 JEFF GORDON
04 BOBBY ALLISON
= DARRELL WALTRIP
06 CALE YARBOROUGH
07 DALE EARNHARDT, JR
08 JIMMIE JOHNSON
09 RUSTY WALLACE
10 LEE PETTY

FROM US STATE...	TOTAL NASCAR CHAMPIONSHIP WINS	RELATIVE SCALE:
North Carolina	200	100%
South Carolina	105	53%
California	87	44%
Florida	84	42%
Kentucky	84	42%
South Carolina	83	41%
North Carolina	76	38%
California	65	33%
Missouri	55	28%
North Carolina	54	27%

XTREME FACT
DALE EARNHARDT, JR

Born in North Carolina, Dale Earnhardt, Jr comes from a family of racing legends. His father, Dale Earnhardt, Sr, is in the NASCAR Hall of Fame, and both his grandfathers —Robert Gee and Ralph Earnhardt—built and drove stock cars, respectively.

NASCAR MANUFACTURING LEGENDS

TOP 10

If you didn't already know this, the US state of Michigan is steeped in a long history of car manufacturing, as shown by the headquarters of these car makers...

		HQ	SPRINT CUP SEASON WINS (ANNUAL)
01	CHEVROLET	Detroit, Michigan (USA)	38
02	FORD	Dearbon, Michigan (USA)	15
03	HUDSON	Detroit, Michigan (USA)	3
04	BUICK	Detroit, Michigan (USA)	2
05	DODGE	Auburn Hills, Michigan (USA)	2
06	OLDSMOBILE	Lansing, Michigan (USA)	1
07	PLYMOUTH	Auburn Hills, Michigan (USA)	1
08	PONTIAC	Detroit, Michigan (USA)	1
09	*	-	-
10	*	-	-

*Since the championships began in 1952, only eight manufacturers have taken the annual season title.

CHECK IT OUT!

Chevrolet: the company was founded 103 years ago in 1911 in Detroit, Michigan. Did you know it also makes watches? Co-founder Louis Chevrolet's father was a watchmaker.

WINS 38

STAT ATTACK
CHEVROLET

Founders........................Louis Chevrolet, William C. Durant

Founded................................1911
Emblem introduced........................1913
Countries operational..........................140
Worldwide unit sales per year........5 million

XTREME FACT DODGE

Dodge began in 1900 as a humble automobile spare parts company called Dodge Brothers, formed by John Francis Dodge and Horace Elgin Dodge. They both died in 1925, and the company was sold to investment bank Dillon, Read & Co. It has had five other owners since.

TOP 10 — F1 CHAMPION MANUFACTURERS

Behind every Formula One driving genius is a team of super-smart manufacturers who build the ultimate driving machines...

	MANUFACTURERS	COUNTRY	TOTAL CHAMPIONSHIP WINS
01	FERRARI	Italy	16
02	WILLIAMS	UK	9
03	McLAREN	UK	8
04	LOTUS	UK	7
05	RED BULL	Austria	3
06	COOPER	UK	2
=	BRABHAM	UK	2
=	RENAULT	France	2
09	VANWALL	UK	1
=	MATRA	France	1

XTREME FACT — FERRARI

These days, Ferrari employs almost 3,000 people worldwide. It was founded in 1929 by Enzo Ferrari, and 130,000 cars have been made and sold to date.

WINS 16

DANGER!

Car racing is an exciting sport, but it is also very dangerous. In Formula One alone, 49 drivers have been killed since the sport's inception.

OFF THE CHART

MANUFACTURERS	COUNTRY	TOTAL CHAMPIONSHIP WINS
BRM	UK	1
TYRRELL	UK	1
BENETTON	UK	1
BRAWN	UK	1

BOX OFFICE
282.5
MILLION DOLLARS

TOP 10 BIGGEST SPORTS MOVIES

The results are in, and it's clear that the screech of wheels, and exchanging blows in the ring, really resonates with moviegoers...

CHECK IT OUT!

Turbo's all-star cast includes the voices of Ryan Reynolds, Samuel L. Jackson, Michelle Rodriguez, and Snoop Dogg.

#	Title	SPORT	YEAR	BOX OFFICE ($ WORLDWIDE)
01	CARS 2	Car racing	2011	559,852,396
02	CARS	Car racing	2006	461,983,149
03	FAST & FURIOUS	Street racing	2009	363,164,265
04	THE BLIND SIDE	Football	2009	309,208,309
05	ROCKY IV	Boxing	1985	300,473,716
06	REAL STEEL	Robot boxing	2011	299,268,508
07	TURBO	Snail & car racing	2013	282,570,682
08	JERRY MAGUIRE	Football	1996	273,552,592
09	SPACE JAM	Basketball	1996	230,418,342
10	MILLION DOLLAR BABY	Boxing	2004	216,763,646

Source: IMDB.com

BEEN & SEEN

When you've seen these sporty movies with your own eyes, tick them off!

- ☐ DODGEBALL
- ☐ TURBO
- ☐ PLANES
- ☐ ROCKY BALBOA
- ☐ REMEMBER THE TITANS
- ☐ CARS 2
- ☐ REAL STEEL
- ☐ COOL RUNNINGS
- ☐ THE FAST & THE FURIOUS
- ☐ SPACE JAM

BIGGEST SPORTS DOCUMENTARIES

TOP 10

A great documentary really captures the emotion of its subject matter, and these 10 made a huge connection with us...

#	Title	SPORT	YEAR	BOX OFFICE ($ WORLDWIDE)
01	HOOP DREAMS	Basketball	1994	11,830,611
02	SENNA	F1 Racing	2010	8,212,430
03	THE ENDLESS SUMMER	Surfing	1966	5,000,000
04	WHEN WE WERE KINGS	Boxing	1996	4,647,606
05	RIDING GIANTS	Surfing	2004	3,216,111
06	THE ENDLESS SUMMER II	Surfing	1996	2,155,385
07	THE LIFE AND TIMES OF HANK GREENBERG	Baseball	1998	1,712,385
08	DOGTOWN AND Z-BOYS	Skateboarding	2002	1,523,090
09	PUMPING IRON II: THE WOMEN	Bodybuilding	1985	628,050
10	UNDEFEATED	Football	2012	562,218

Source: IMDb.com

XTREME FACT

SPACE JAM

1996 film *Space Jam* fused Looney Tunes cartoon characters (including Bugs Bunny and Daffy Duck) with NBA basketball legend Michael Jordan. It took almost three times its $80 million budget at the box office.

BOX OFFICE 230.4 MILLION DOLLARS

CHECK IT OUT!

When We Were Kings: director Leon Gast made this documentary about the October 30, 1974, heavyweight championship fight between Muhammad Ali and George Foreman, known as "The Rumble In The Jungle."

XTREME FACT

RIDING GIANTS

This documentary about the Hawaiian origins and allure of surfing was directed, co-written, and narrated by Los Angeles-born skateboarding and surfing legend Stacy Peralta. He also co-founded skateboard makers Powell Peralta.

BOX OFFICE 3.2 MILLION DOLLARS

TOP 10 BIGGEST SPORTS VIDEO GAMES

Without doubt, the gold medal for video gaming sports experiences goes to Nintendo and its Wii, which dominates this list...

#	Game	SPORT	RELEASED	PLATFORM(S)	UNIT SALES (MILLIONS)
01	WII SPORTS	Various	2006	WII	81.84
02	WII SPORTS RESORT	Various	2009	WII	32.24
03	WII FIT	Various	2007	WII	22.69
04	WII FIT PLUS	Various	2009	WII	21.43
05	MARIO & SONIC AT THE OLYMPIC GAMES	Various	2007-08	WII, DS	12.96
06	ZUMBA FITNESS	Some martial arts	2010	WII	6.53
07	FIFA SOCCER 12	Soccer	2011	PS3	6.48
08	KINECT SPORTS	Various	2010	XBOX 360	5.79
09	MADDEN NFL 2004	Football	2004	PS2	5.23
10	TONY HAWK'S PRO SKATER	Skateboarding	1999	PLAYSTATION	5.02

XTREME FACT

FIFA 12

The 2012 edition of the ever-popular soccer game franchise was made available on a whopping 12 different platforms, including iOS, Android, and Sony Ericsson Xperia Play for mobile gaming.

CHECK IT OUT!

Wii Sports: a hit with critics and gamers alike, *Wii Sports* has been an astounding success for Nintendo, becoming the best-selling video game of all time. This is especially impressive as it's not a multiple platform game, being made exclusively for the Wii. Sequel *Wii Sports Resort* was released in 2009, and *Wii Sports Club* followed in late 2013 for Nintendo's latest console, the Wii U.

OFF THE CHART

MADDEN NFL 13

Missing out on a place in the Top 10 is *Madden NFL 13* on the Xbox 360, with sales of 2.72 million units worldwide. The game features over 9,000 unique lines of commentary dialogue.

TOP 10 BOOKS ABOUT SPORT

		Author	Sport	Publication Year
01	RAW BLUE	Kirsty Eagar	SURFING	2009
02	THE BOY WHO SAVED BASEBALL	John H. Ritter	BASEBALL	2003
03	SLALOM	S. L. Rottman	SKIING	2004
04	BEYOND LUCKY	Sarah Aronson	SOCCER	2011
05	A BOY CALLED TWISTER	Anne Schraff	RUNNING	2000
06	FEVER PITCH	Nick Hornby	SOCCER	1992
07	THE BONE CAGE	Angie Abdou	SWIMMING, WRESTLING	2006
08	TAKE YOUR BEST SHOT	John Coy	BASKETBALL	2012
09	THE HOCKEY SWEATER	Roch Carrier	HOCKEY	1979
10	KARATE KATIE	Nancy E Krulik	KARATE	2006

X-PLORE RAW BLUE

Raw Blue won the 2010 Victorian Premier's Literary Award's Prize for Young Adult Fiction. Its author, Australian Kirsty Eager, also penned *Night Beach* and *Saltwater Vampires*. Visit www.kirsteagar.com.

XTREME FACT SLALOM

Slalom is a word with Norwegian origins. "Sla" means a hillside that has a slight incline, and "låm" is the word for the tracks left by skis.

TOP 10 PRICIEST SPORTS CONTRACTS

Wow. When Team T-10 looked into this, we knew baseball had some rich teams, but the sport clearly dominates the world of buying up players with truck-loads of gold...

VALUE
275 MILLION DOLLARS

		SPORT	TEAM	CONTRACT LENGTH	VALUE ($ MILLIONS)
01	ALEX RODRIGUEZ	Baseball	New York Yankees	(2008–17)	275
02	ALEX RODRIGUEZ	Baseball	Texas Rangers	(2001–10)	252
03	ALBERT PUJOLS	Baseball	Los Angeles Angels	(2012–21)	240
04	JOEY VOTTO	Baseball	Cincinnati Reds	(2014–23)	225
05	PRINCE FIELDER	Baseball	Detroit Tigers/Texas Rangers	(2012–20)	214
06	DEREK JETER	Baseball	New York Yankees	(2001–10)	189
07	JOE MAUER	Baseball	Minnesota Twins	(2011–18)	184
08	MARK TEIXEIRA	Baseball	New York Yankees	(2009–16)	180
=	FLOYD MAYWEATHER	Boxing	Showtime Sports*	(2013–15)	180
10	CC SABATHIA	Baseball	New York Yankees	(2009–15)	161

*TV network

XTREME FACT
JOEY VOTTO

Born on September 10, 1983, in Toronto, Canada, Cincinnati Reds' Joey Votto has surpassed 1,000 hits in his Canadian Major League Baseball career.

XTREME FACT
FLOYD MAYWEATHER

Undefeated boxer Floyd Mayweather has won eight world titles since he started his amateur career in 1993. With no losses, and no draws to date, Mayweather has also won 26 fights by knock-out.

VALUE
180 MILLION DOLLARS

CHECK IT OUT!

Alex Rodriguez: better known as "A-Rod," New York Yankees' Alex Rodriguez has nearly 3,000 hits to his name since he debuted professionally for the Seattle Mariners on July 8, 1994.

TOP 10

HIGHEST SOCCER TRANSFER FEES

Buying/transferring soccer players sees outrageous sums of money passing hands... And it seems like Real Madrid is playing their own game of "Soccer *Pokémon*" - obsessed with catching them all...

#	Player	From	Former Team	Transferred To	Fee (Millions) $	Fee (Millions) £
01	GARETH BALE	Wales	Tottenham Hotspur	Real Madrid	146	88
02	CRISTIANO RONALDO	Portugal	Manchester United	Real Madrid	126	76
03	ZINEDINE ZIDANE	France	Juventus	Real Madrid	100	61
04	ZLATAN IBRAHIMOVIĆ	Sweden	Inter Milan	Barcelona	92	55
05	RICARDO KAKÁ	Brazil	A. C. Milan	Real Madrid	91	54
06	EDINSON CAVANI	Uruguay	Napoli	Paris Saint-Germain	86	52
07	LUÍS FIGO	Portugal	Barcelona	Real Madrid	83	50
08	RADAMEL FALCAO	Colombia	Atlético de Madrid	AS Monaco	80	48
09	FERNANDO TORRES	Spain	Liverpool	Chelsea	77	46
10	NEYMAR DA SILVA SANTOS JÚNIOR	Brazil	Santos	Barcelona	76	45

VALUE
126
MILLION DOLLARS

X TREME FACT

GARETH BALE

Wales-born soccer star Gareth Bale may only be 25 years old, but he's already one of the most famous players around. His bank-busting transfer to Real Madrid occurred on September 1, 2013.

X TREME FACT

CRISTIANO RONALDO

Another star of Spanish team Real Madrid (since 2009) is Cristiano Ronaldo. Ever popular (and bankable), Alex Ferguson signed him to Manchester United in 2003 for £12.24 million (that's more than $20 million!).

OFF THE CHART

LIONEL MESSI

Talk about loyal... Lionel Messi has never been lured away from his Barcelona club for his entire 14+ years career (including his youth career). Messi is considered by fans and critics alike to be one of the best soccer players around today.

STAT ATTACK

METLIFE STADIUM

Location...................... East Rutherford, New Jersey, USA

Opened............................ April 10, 2010

Construction costs .... $1.6 billion

Highest attendance................... 81,285

Home to...................... New York Giants, New York Jets

VALUE 1.6 BILLION DOLLARS

CHECK IT OUT!

MetLife Stadium: here are the New York Giants running out onto the field at their home ground of MetLife Stadium. This shot was taken on November 10, 2013, for their game against the Oakland Raiders.

METLIFE STADIUM

TOP 10 MOST EXPENSIVE SPORTS STADIUMS/ARENAS EVER BUILT

Tickets for sporting and music events at the really big stadiums are always pretty pricey, but then take a look at how much these cost to actually build...

		COST OF BUILD ($)
01	METLIFE STADIUM	1.6 BILLION
02	YANKEE STADIUM	1.5 BILLION
03	COWBOYS STADIUM	1.33 BILLION
04	WEMBLEY STADIUM	1.25 BILLION
05	MADISON SQUARE GARDEN	1.1 BILLION
06	CITI FIELD	922 MILLION
07	ROGERS CENTRE	914 MILLION
08	LONDON OLYMPIC STADIUM	775 MILLION
09	SOLDIER FIELD	755 MILLION
10	EMIRATES STADIUM	750 MILLION

OFF THE CHART

DOHA PORT STADIUM

This amazing stadium in Qatar won't be ready until it hosts the 2022 FIFA World Cup, so this is just an artist's impression of how it will turn out. The design is inspired by its surrounding sea, and the shape depicts an aquatic creature.

LONGEST-RUNNING MOST POWERFUL SPORTS BRANDS

These are the 10 most valuable and commercially powerful sport-related companies on the planet, but we've mixed things up and ordered them by how long they've been running...

		TYPE	FOUNDED	YEARS IN OPERATION
01	REEBOK	Apparel/Footwear	1895	119
02	ADIDAS	Apparel/Footwear	1924	90
03	NIKE	Apparel/Footwear	1964	50
04	GATORADE	Beverage	1965	49
05	MSG	TV network	1969	45
06	ESPN	TV network	1979	35
07	SKY SPORTS	TV network	1991	23
=	EA SPORTS	Games developer	1991	23
09	UNDER ARMOUR	Apparel/Footwear	1996	18
10	YES NETWORK	TV network	2002	12

CHECK IT OUT!

Nike: the power of superstar brand endorsement! Here's American Olympic champion decathlete Ashton Eaton *(left)* and NFL New York Giants player Victor Cruz at the NikeFuel Forum in New York City on October 15, 2013.

XTREME FACT

EA SPORTS

EA Sports—a division of video game giants Electronic Arts, founded in 1982—continues to dominate the sports genre, with titles like *Grand Slam Tennis (left)*. The first sporty EA game was basketball-based *Jordan Vs Bird: One On One* released in 1988.

YOUR SHOUT

This section of the book is dedicated to testing your knowledge on the extreme world of sport...

YOUR TOP 10 PICK OF THE... SPORT

We've given you a mountain of lists and facts, so now it's your turn to tell us 10 best sports things...

01 ....

02 ....

03 ....

04 ....

05 ....

06 ....

07 ....

08 ....

09 ....

10 ....

ROUND 1: MULTIPLE CHOICE

01 Usain Bolt is the undisputed king of "fast twitch" sport. But what is his world record 100 m time?

A 9.29 SEC
B 9.58 SEC
C 9.87 SEC

02 What is the longest "slow twitch" sport on the planet at a gruelling 3,569.8 mi (5,745 km)?

A TOUR DE FRANCE
B ULTRAMARATHON
C IRON MAN TRIATHALON

03 Can you name the deadliest motor circuit in the world, with a staggering 255 fatalities?

A SNAEFELL MOUNTAIN COURSE
B NÜRBURGRING
C CIRCUIT DE MONACO

ROUND 2: QUESTION TIME

01 China's Yan Zhi Cheng holds the title of the highest jump in sport at a crazy 97 in (246 cm). Which sport does he compete in?

ANSWER: ....

ROUND 3:
PICTURE PUZZLES

Can you name the set of important muscles highlighted in this image?

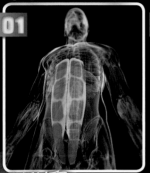

01

ANSWER:

Name the epic dog-sled race that takes place each year ending in Alaska...

02

ANSWER:

What is the name of this basketball legend that stared in the 1996 movie, *Space Jam*?

03

ANSWER:

ROUND 4:
WORDSEARCH

```
R A S W I M M I N G E S
H E F G J L I Y A C D Z
O B C W E B N R I W I D
F A N C T B V E A C S Y
X S R A O R E H B T C I
O E E R K S M C R Q U H
A B S E C Y A R N C S U
C A M I X C N A S C A R
N L E A V N I R W V E L
E L R A P I E X N G T I
Q U A D R A T H A L O N
W E N A T N I E S C E G
```

Take a look in the jumble of letters on the left, and see how many of these sports you can find inside:

SOCCER
BASEBALL
QUADRATHALON
HURLING
NASCAR
ARCHERY
SWIMMING
DISCUS

FIND THE ANSWERS ON PAGE 312

02 Guðjón Valur Sigurðsson *(right)* competes in the fifth oldest projectile sport ever. Can you name it?

03 Which very popular sport do a massive nine of the Top 10 Priciest Sports Contracts come from?

ANSWER:

SPORT
CAREER
QUIZ

Who would you rather meet?
- A USAIN BOLT
- B NBA BASKETBALL TEAM
- C PHIL JACKSON & ALEX FERGUSON

Which would you rather have as a pet?
- A SNAKE
- B AN ANT FARM
- C A DOG

Which of these movies would you most like to star in?
- A THE DARK KNIGHT
- B X-MEN
- C KARATE KID

For which of the following events would you rather get tickets?
- A WIMBLEDON
- B THE SUPER BOWL
- C NBA PLAY-OFFS

Which of the following activities would you prefer to do?
- A GO KARTING
- B PAINTBALLING
- C ROCK CLIMBING WITH A FRIEND

Which would you rather receive as a gift?
- A A SKATEBOARD
- B A FOOTBALL
- C A STOPWATCH

Which of the following statements best fits you?
- A I WORK BEST ON MY OWN
- B I'M A REAL TEAM PLAYER
- C I CAN SEE STRENGTHS IN PEOPLE

Find out which sport-related job is best suited to you on page 312

137

FORCES OF NATURE

TOP 10 DEADLIEST NATURAL DISASTERS OF ALL TIME

Examining all the different ways the planet can bring devastation into our lives, these are the 10 worst forms of nature turning nasty...

		LOCATION	YEAR	FATALITIES
01	VOLCANIC ERUPTION	Iceland	1783	6 MILLION (EST)
02	FLOOD	China	1931	2.5–3.7 MILLION
03	EARTHQUAKE	China	1556	820,000–830,000 (EST)
04	CYCLONE	Bangladesh (formerly East Pakistan)	1970	500,000
05	TSUNAMI	Over 13 countries (Indian Ocean)	2004	230,000–310,000
06	HEATWAVE	Europe	2003	70,000
07	AVALANCHE	Peru	1970	20,000
08	STORM	Venezuela	1999	15,100
09	BLIZZARD	Iran	1972	4,000
=	LIGHTNING	Greece	1856	4,000

XTREME FACT: INDIAN OCEAN TSUNAMI

In 2004, more than 230,000 people lost their lives during the destruction caused by this earthquake and subsequent tsunami. The force unleashed was like 1,500 atomic bombs simultaneously detonating. The movie *The Impossible* (2012) re-enacted the story of a family who were separated by the tsunami in Thailand.

OFF THE CHART

TORNADO

LOCATION: DAULTIPUR, SALTURIA, BANGLADESH
YEAR: 1989
FATALITIES: 1,300

This 1 mile (1.6 km)-wide tornado is the deadliest ever. It tore through 50 miles (80.5 km) of land, leaving 80,000 people without their homes.

DANGER!

Although volcanoes, earthquakes, landslides, and meteorites can cause tsunamis (Japanese for "port wave"), man-made explosions and bombs can, too.

TOP 10 BIGGEST NATURAL DISASTERS MOVIES

Mother Nature's wrath has inspired a ton of elemental carnage in the movie world. Check out which extreme conditions have made the biggest box office hits...

#	Movie	TYPE OF DISASTER	YEAR OF RELEASE	BOX OFFICE ($ WORLDWIDE)
01	2012	A natural apocalypse	2009	769,679,473
02	ARMAGEDDON	Giant asteroid on course for Earth	1998	553,709,788
03	THE DAY AFTER TOMORROW	Global warming causes a new ice age	2004	544,272,402
04	TWISTER	Tornadoes	1996	494,471,524
05	DEEP IMPACT	Comet collides with planet Earth	1998	349,464,664
06	THE PERFECT STORM	Huge waves	2000	328,718,434
07	WATERWORLD	Polar caps melt, covering Earth in water	1995	264,218,220
08	POSEIDON	150-ft wave capsizes cruise liner	2006	181,674,817
09	THE IMPOSSIBLE	2004 tsunami that devastated Thailand	2012	180,274,123
10	DANTE'S PEAK	Volcanic eruption in Columbia	1997	178,127,760

Source: IMDB.com

XTREME FACT

THE PERFECT STORM

This successful 2000 movie was based on the 1997 book of the same name by US author Sebastian Junger. The book is the true story of how a fishing boat crew coped with a violent storm in 1991, which went on to cause $200 million worth of damage and killed 13 people.

10 QUICK FIRE FACTS

THE PERFECT STORM

#	Fact
01	Released on June 30, 2000
02	Running time of 2 hours 9 minutes
03	Stars George Clooney, Mark Wahlberg, Diane Lane
04	Nominated for two Academy Awards: Visuals & Sound
05	Based on the crew of the *Andrea Gail*'s experience
06	Directed by German moviemaker Wolfgang Petersen
07	George Clooney was 39 years old on its release
08	Took $41,325,042 on its opening weekend
09	Was shown in 3,407 cinemas
10	Music was composed by James "*Titanic*" Horner

DANGER!

Volcanology is—you guessed it—the study of volcanoes. Volcanologists bravely get up close and study them to gather information that could save lives in the future.

XTREME FACT QUILOTOA

This is called a caldera (Spanish for "cooking pot"), which is very appropriate for this water-filled volcano. Quilotora is 1.86 mi (3 km) wide and located in the Ecuador section of the Andes mountain range. It hasn't erupted since 1799.

TOP 10 BIGGEST VOLCANIC ERUPTIONS

The amount of molten material that a volcano discharges is incredible. It scorches the sky and obliterates its surroundings...

	LOCATION	YEAR	AMOUNT OF VOLCANIC DISCHARGE (KM³)	(MI³)
01 UNKNOWN	The Tropics	1258	200-800	48-192
02 MOUNT TAMBORA	Lesser Sunda Islands (Indonesia)	1815	150	36
03 UNKNOWN	New Hebrides (Vanuatu)	1452-53	36-96	8.6-23
04 KOLUMBO	Santorini (Greece)	1650	60	14.4
05 HUAYNAPUTINA	Peru	1600	30	7.2
= LONG ISLAND (PAPUA NEW GUINEA)	New Guinea	1660	30	7.2
07 KRAKATOA	Indonesia	1883	21	5
= QUILOTOA	Ecuador	1280	21	5
09 SANTA MARIA	Guatemala	1902	20	4.8
10 MOUNT PINATUBO	Luzon (Philippines)	1991	6-16	1.4-3.8

XTREME FACT MOUNT TAMBORA

Huge amounts of magma filled a chamber inside the mountain over the course of several decades before the monster volcano finally exploded. It is believed that 11,000–12,000 were killed as a direct result of the eruption. However, an estimated 60,000 died through starvation and disease.

TOP 10
BIGGEST EARTHQUAKES (RICHTER)

The ground splits open, vibrations topple skyscrapers, and the oceans send forth violent waves. Earthquakes are terrifying examples of the planet's ability to destroy...

		DATE	MAGNITUDE (RICHTER SCALE)
01	VALDIVIA (CHILE)	MAY 22, 1960	9.5
02	ALASKA (USA)	MAR 27, 1964	9.2
03	SUMATRA (INDONESIA)	DEC 26, 2004	9.1-9.3
04	TŌHOKU REGION (JAPAN)	MAR 11, 2011	9.0
=	KAMCHATKA (RUSSIA)	NOV 4, 1952	9.0
06	SUMATRA (INDONESIA)	NOV 25, 1833	8.8-9.2
07	ECUADOR-COLOMBIA	JAN 31, 1906	8.8
=	MAULE (CHILE)	FEB 27, 2010	8.8
=	ARICA (CHILE)	SEP 16, 1615	8.8
10	KRAKATOA (INDONESIA)	AUG 26, 1883	8.75

CHECK IT OUT!

Alaska, 1964: this photo gives you an example of the sheer power of an earthquake—a street has been torn to pieces. It may have only lasted three minutes, but 143 people were killed in that time, plus $311 million worth of damage was inflicted.

XTREME FACT
MAULE (CHILE) 2010

Here, the Chilean Agriculture Ministry arc handing out much-needed supplies to residents of the seaside city of Constitución. In 2010, 525 were killed and nine percent of the population lost their homes. A blackout lasted for days and affected 93 percent of the area.

XTREME FACT

SPIRIT LAKE
WASHINGTON 1980

After Mount St. Helens erupted in 1980, Spirit Lake had to have special manmade drainage tunnels created. These maintain its water level and without them mass flooding could occur. The Lake's water surface level is a staggering 3,406 ft (1,038 m).

DANGER!

With tsunamis, it's not necessarily the height of the wave that's dangerous, it's the millions of gallons of water which engulf lands and homes.

TALLEST TSUNAMIS

These gigantic waves are often born from the forces of landslides and earthquakes. These are the locations of the tallest over the past four centuries...

		YEAR	HEIGHT OF TSUNAMI (M)	(FT)	RELATIVE SCALE:
01	LITUYA BAY, ALASKA (USA)	1958	524	1,719	100%
02	SPIRIT LAKE, WASHINGTON (USA)	1980	260	853	50%
03	VAJONT DAM (ITALY)	1963	250	820	48%
04	MOUNT UNZEN, KYŪSHŪ (JAPAN)	1792	100	328	19%
05	ISHIGAKI & MIYAKOJIMA ISLANDS (JAPAN)	1771	79.9	262	15%
06	LISBON (PORTUGAL)	1755	20.1	66	4%
07	MESSINA (ITALY)	1908	12.2	40	2%
08	HŌEI (JAPAN)	1707	9.8	32	2%
09	MEIJI-SANRIKU (JAPAN)	1896	9.1	30	2%
10	HAITI	2010	3.1	10	1%

CHECK IT OUT!

Ishigaki & Miyakojima Islands (Japan), 1771: nowadays, this beautiful and serene lagoon is a popular tourist location in Japan. So, it's hard to believe that back in 1771, one of the worst tsunamis ever wreaked havoc on the islands. It destroyed over 2,000 homes and killed 13,486 people.

XTREME FACT
BOREAS

Boreas, Greek god of the north wind, was not a "modern man," even by mythological standards. This artist's impression shows him kidnapping the Princess Oreithyia on a cloud because she turned down his proposal.

TOP 10 COOLEST ANCIENT WEATHER GODS

THE T-10 UNOFFICIAL

#		ROOTS	PLACE OF ORIGIN	KNOWN AS
01	WHAITIRI	Māori mythology	New Zealand, Polynesia	Goddess of thunder and lightning
02	YU SHI	Chinese mythology	China	God of rain
03	RA	Egyptian mythology	Egypt	God of the sun
04	BOREAS	Greek mythology	Greece	God of the north wind
05	AURA	Greek & Roman mythology	Greece, Italy	Goddess of the breeze
06	SHU	Egyptian mythology	Egypt	God of air and wind
07	THOR	Norse mythology	Iceland/Scandanavia	God of thunder and lightning
08	HUAYRA-TATA	Puruhá Quechuas & Aymaras beliefs	Bolivia, Peru	God of Hurricane Winds
09	ILMATAR	Finnish folklore	Finland	Goddess of the air
10	CHAAC	Mayan	Maya/South Americas	God of rain

CHECK IT OUT!

Thor: yes, indeed, the Thor you know from the movies and comics is based on the very same Norse god of thunder. He is also associated with "strength" and "protecting mankind," just like the movie version.

POWER PLANTS

TOP 10 MOST CARNIVOROUS PLANTS

Looks can be deceptive... The plants in this Top 10 may be kinda pretty, but each of them has a thirst for the blood of insects, arachnids, and even rats!

		LOCATION	TRAP TYPE	TRAPS & EATS
01	GIANT MALAYSIAN PITCHER PLANT	Malaysia (Borneo)	Pitfall/cup trap	Rats, mice, lizards, frogs, insects
02	COBRA LILY	California (USA)	Cobra-like pitcher trap	Flies, ants, beetles, crawling insects
03	COMMON BLADDERWORT	50 States (USA)	Aquatic hair-trigger bladder	Fish fry, tadpoles, round worms
04	WATERWHEEL PLANT	Africa, Asia, Australia, Europe	Aquatic hair-trigger bladder	Water fleas, tadpoles
05	WEST AUSTRALIAN PITCHER PLANT	Albany (Australia)	Pitfall/cup trap	Ants, small insects
06	GREEN PITCHER PLANT	N. Carolina, Georgia (USA)	Pitfall/cup trap	Wasps and other small insects
07	VENUS FLYTRAP	East Coast wetlands (USA)	Hair-trigger jaws/trap	Small insects and arachnids
08	CAPE SUNDEW	Cape of Good Hope (S. Africa)	Sticky tentacles	Small insects and arachnids
09	RAINBOW PLANT	Australia, Papua New Guinea, Indonesia	Sticky barbs	Small insects
10	YELLOW BUTTERWORT	Coast of Southeast USA	Sticky leaves	Flies and small insects

XTREME FACT
VENUS FLYTRAP

Don't like wasps? Then cheer for this killer plant! The Venus Fly Trap lures, then slowly dissolves and eats wasps, flies, spiders, bees—whatever gets trapped in those magnificent jaws.

CHECK IT OUT!

West Australian Pitcher Plant: this striking, carnivorous plant (about to ensnare a hoverfly for lunch in this photo) was one of the inspirations behind English author John Wyndham's classic 1951 novel, *The Day Of The Triffids*. In the dark tale, mysterious and intelligent plants—that can also WALK—begin attacking humans.

TOP 10 MOST POISONOUS PLANTS

They may come in all shapes and sizes, but be warned... Some also have the toxic power to kill!

#	PLANT	TOXICITY
01	ROSARY PEA	One seed could kill many people
02	STRYCHNINE TREE	One seed could kill a human
03	BELLADONNA/DEADLY NIGHTSHADE	A couple of berries could kill a human
04	CASTOR OIL/BEAN	Four seeds could kill a human
05	WATER HEMLOCK	Ingesting a small amount can be fatal
06	WOLFSBANE	Ingestion can kill a human & touching bare skin can cause extreme illness
07	DOLL'S EYES	Its berries can kill
08	ENGLISH YEW	Ingesting leaves or seeds can be fatal
09	JIMSON WEED	Its small seeds can kill if they are ingested
10	MANCHINEEL	Whole tree is highly toxic and it's potentially fatal to eat its fruit

XTREME FACT

ROSARY PEA

Amazingly, even though the toxicity of this plant is widely known, its seeds are often boiled and dried and used as beads/jewellery. When done correctly, this does remove the lethal toxin. Still, we'll stick to plastic beads, thanks very much!

TOP 10 BIGGEST WEIRD PLANTS IN MOVIES

In the movies, anything can happen... Peaceful plants can become heroes, or even uproot themselves and go on bloodthirsty rampages! Don't believe us? Look at this wild bunch...

#	PLANT	MOVIE(S)	YEAR	BOX OFFICE ($ WORLDWIDE)
01	WHOMPING WILLOW, MANDRAKES, DEVIL'S SNARE, MIMBULUS MIMBLETONIA, AND MORE	All eight *Harry Potter* films 2001-11	2001-11	7,709,205,984
02	PANDORAN NEURAL NETWORK	Avatar	2009	2,782,275,172
03	THE ENTS	Two and three of *The Lord Of The Rings* movies	2002-03	2,068,457,651
04	TALKING FLOWERS	Alice In Wonderland	2010	1,024,391,110
05	CARNIVOROUS PLANTS	Ice Age: Dawn Of The Dinosaurs	2009	886,686,817
06	MAN-EATING PLANTS	Oz The Great And The Powerful	2013	491,911,825
07	HALLUCINOGENIC PLANTS	Snow White And The Huntsman	2012	396,592,829
08	ENTIRE ECO-SYSTEM ON A FLOWER	Dr. Seuss' Horton Hears A Who!	2008	297,138,014
09	MAN-EATING PLANT	Jumanji	1995	262,797,249
10	PREDATORY, MOVING PLANTS	After Earth	2013	243,843,127

Source: IMDB.com

XTREME FACT

ALICE IN WONDERLAND

Imelda Staunton (Dolores Umbridge in the *Harry Potter* movies) provided the voices for the flowers in this 2010 movie.

POWER PLANTS

BEEN & SEEN

When you've seen these plants and trees with your eyes, tick them off!

- [ ] GIANT REDWOOD
- [ ] VENUS FLYTRAP
- [ ] CACTUS
- [ ] PITCHER PLANT
- [ ] ASH TREE
- [ ] PINE TREE
- [ ] WEEPING WILLOW
- [ ] PALM TREE
- [ ] ROSE
- [ ] TULIP

CHECK IT OUT!

Victorian Ash: fans of spooky tales, make sure you check out M. R. James's classic *The Ash-Tree*. It's the creepy story of cursed ancestry, accusations of witchcraft, and a very scary tree...

TOP 10 TALLEST TREES

Did you know that the subject of officially measuring trees is pretty controversial? Lots of fibs are being told out there! Here are the tallest accurately measured species...

		LOCATION	MAXIMUM KNOWN HEIGHT (M)	(FT)
01	GIANT REDWOOD	California (USA)	115.72	379.66
02	DOUGLAS SPRUCE	Oregon (USA)	99.76	327.3
03	VICTORIAN ASH	Tasmania (Australia)	99.6	327
04	SITKA SPRUCE	California (USA)	96.7	317
05	GIANT SEQUOIA	California (USA)	95.8	314
06	TASMANIAN BLUE GUM	Tasmania (Australia)	90.7	298
07	MANNA GUM	Tasmania (Australia)	89	292
08	YELLOW MERANTI	Sabah (Borneo)	88.3	290
09	ALPINE ASH	Tasmania (Australia)	87.9	288
10	KLINKI PINE*	Morobe Province (Papua New Guinea)	70+	230

RELATIVE SCALE: 100% 86% 86% 84% 83% 78% 77% 76% 76% 60%

*Was one of the tallest trees in 1941, but it's not been accurately measured. There are only nine officially recognised tallest trees.

XTREME FACT

GIANT REDWOOD

Want to impress your friends? Then tell them that the correct (latin) name for this massive species of tree is *Sequoiadendron giganteum*. It only lives naturally in the Californian Sierra Nevada mountains.

XTREME FACT

JAYA SRI MAHA BODHI

This fig tree is very special. It is a sapling from The Bodhi Tree that Buddha sat under and achieved Enlightenment (a state of "awakening" and awareness in Buddhism). It is the most ancient of all human-planted trees—given a sacred home in Anuradhapura, Sri Lanka, way, way back in 288 BC!

AGE 4,845 YEARS

TOP 10 OLDEST TREES ALIVE TODAY

Trees can outlive us humans by not hundreds, but thousands of years! Here are the old-timers that haven't died or been cut down and are still reaching for the stars...

#	Name	SPECIES	LOCATION	VERIFIED AGE (YEARS)
01	(UNNAMED)	Great Basin bristlecone pine	California (USA)	5,062
02	METHUSELAH	Great Basin bristlecone pine	California (USA)	4,845
03	(UNNAMED)	Patagonian cypress	Los Lagos (Chile)	3,642
04	THE PRESIDENT	Giant sequoia	Nevada (USA)	3,200
05	CB-90-11	Rocky Mountain Bristlecone Pine	Colorado (USA)	2,455
06	JAYA SRI MAHA BODHI	Sacred fig (from The Bodhi Tree)	North Central Province (Sri Lanka)	2,217
07	BENNETT JUNIPER	Western Juniper	Nevada (USA)	2,200
08	SHP 7	Foxtail Pine	Nevada (USA)	2,110
09	(UNNAMED)	Subalpine Larch	Alberta (Canada)	1,939
10	CRE 175	Rocky Mountain Juniper	New Mexico (USA)	1,889

HEIGHT 379.66 FT

CHECK IT OUT! Methuselah *(above)*: this awesome word/name comes from the Hebrew Bible and it is very appropriate for such an ancient age. The Bible says that Methuselah, who was Noah's (of the ark fame) grandad, lived to be 969. Imagine the birthday candles!

TOP 10 MOST ENDANGERED PLANTS

It's not just members of the animal kingdom that are under threat of extinction. Many plants and trees are endangered, too...

	LOCATION	NUMBER LEFT
01 HIBISCADELPHUS WOODII	Kalalau Valley (Hawaii)	Possibly extinct
= PSIADIA CATARACTAE	Mauritius	Possibly extinct
03 EUPHORBIA TANAENSIS	Witu Forest Reserve (Kenya)	Four
04 MAGNOLIA WOLFII	Risaralda (Columbia)	Less than five
05 FOREST COCONUT	Masoala Peninsula (Madagascar)	Less than 10
06 ROSA ARABICA	St. Katherine Mountains (Egypt)	10
07 QIAOJIA PINE	Yunnan (China)	Only 20 mature trees discovered
08 FICUS KATENDEI	Ishasha River (Uganda)	Less than 50
09 WEST AUSTRALIAN UNDERGROUND ORCHID	Western Australia (Australia)	Less than 100
10 BELIN VETCHLING	Antalya (Turkey)	Less than 1,000

XTREME FACT

UNDERGROUND ORCHID

Living up to its name, this plant remains below ground for its whole life.

TOP 10 COOLEST HEALING PLANTS

THE T-10 UNOFFICIAL

	MEDICAL QUALITY
01 ST. JOHN'S WORT	Helps treat mental health conditions like depression
02 PEPPERMINT	Congestion, headaches, aids digestion
03 BLACKBERRY	Leaves can help relieve diarrhea
04 LADY FERN	Its juices help ease pain of stinging nettles
05 WITCH HAZEL	Helps treats skin conditions, such as eczema
06 CATNIP	Relieves headaches, stomach pains, colds
07 DILL	Indigestion
08 HONEYSUCKLE	Its brewed flowers aid fever and flu symptoms
09 SNAPDRAGON	Helps treat burns
10 STRAWBERRY	Brewed leaves help sore throats

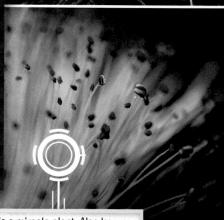

XTREME FACT

ST. JOHN'S WORT

This really is a miracle plant. Also known (appropriately) as Chase-Devil Weed, extracts from any of the 370 species of St. John's Wort help relieve depression for millions of people worldwide.

PLANTS WITH INCREDIBLE USES

TOP 10

THE T-10 UNOFFICIAL

#	Plant	CAN BE USED FOR...
01	OIL PALM	Biodiesel (fuel made from plants)
02	BAMBOO	Housing, tools, rafts
03	COTTON PLANT	Clothing
04	GIANT REED	Water pipes
05	GOAT WILLOW	Faux leather
06	SKUNK BUSH	Natural deodorant
07	GREASEWOOD	Basket-weaving
08	MUSK MALLOW	Natural insecticide
09	CANE REED	Musical instruments
10	HYACINTH ORCHID	Ink

Xtreme FACT
COTTON PLANT

Yes, cotton for clothes comes from the fluffy, completely natural substance formed on cotton plants!

Xtreme FACT
BAMBOO

Bamboo is another of the natural world's wonder plants. Check out this home, built almost entirely from bamboo, majestically standing above Inle Lake in Burma. Helpfully, this is one of the fastest-growing plants around.

MAGNIFICATION

TOP 10 BIGGEST COUNTRIES (LAND MASS)

Although our planet is mostly covered in water, there are still some huge areas of land that we've made our homes. Here are the 10 biggest chunks...

		SIZE (KM²)	SIZE (MI²)	RELATIVE SCALE:
01	RUSSIA	17,098,242	6,601,668	100%
02	CANADA	9,984,670	3,855,103	58%
03	CHINA	9,706,961	3,747,879	57%
04	USA	9,629,091	3,717,813	56%
05	BRAZIL	8,514,877	3,287,612	50%
06	AUSTRALIA	7,692,024	2,969,907	45%
07	INDIA	3,166,414	1,222,559	19%
08	ARGENTINA	2,780,400	1,073,518	16%
09	KAZAKHSTAN	2,724,900	1,052,100	16%
10	ALGERIA	2,381,741	919,595	14%

STAT ATTACK

RUSSIA

Size	6,601,668 sq mi (17,098,242 sq km)
Planet fraction	More than 1/8 of Earth's inhabited land masses
Population	143.5 million
Currency	Ruble
Time zones	Nine

TOP 10 BIGGEST TECTONIC PLATES

Our planet is made up of colossal moving pieces of rock that we call tectonic plates. Of the recognized 56 plates, these are the largest...

		TYPE	SIZE (KM²)	SIZE (MI²)
01	PACIFIC	Primary	103,300,000	39,884,353
02	NORTH AMERICA	Primary	75,900,000	29,305,154
03	EURASIA	Primary	67,800,000	26,177,726
04	AFRICA	Primary	61,300,000	23,668,062
05	ANTARCTICA	Primary	60,900,000	23,513,621
06	AUSTRALIA	Primary	47,000,000	18,146,801
07	SOUTH AMERICA	Primary	43,600,000	16,834,054
08	SOMALIA	Secondary	16,700,000	6,447,906
09	NAZCA	Secondary	15,600,000	6,023,194
10	INDIA	Secondary	11,900,000	4,594,616

DANGER! Earthquakes are common in areas of the planet with tectonic faults: the movement between such colossal pieces of land sends shock waves that can cause volcanoes to erupt, as well as tsunamis.

CHECK IT OUT!

This gargantuan "fault" or tear at Thingvellir National Park, near Reykjavik in Iceland, was created by the tectonic plates of North America and Eurasia drifting apart.

PANGEA

The beautiful word Pangea comes from the Greek *pan* meaning "entire" and *Gaia* meaning "Earth." Scientists believe that the single landmass of Pangea began to break apart around 200 million years ago. These pictures show how our planet has

changed from being one "supercontinent" to a series of land masses, split apart because of the moving crusts.

SIZE 3,855,103 MI²

XTREME FACT
CANADA

With an area of 3.8 million sq mi (9.98 million sq km), Canada may be the second biggest country in the world, but its total population is a LOT smaller than you'd think: just 34.9 million people!

XTREME FACT
AUSTRALIA

Similarly, Australia's huge size is mostly uninhabited areas of scorching deserts and tropical rainforests. There are 22.7 million people in this country, which is a tiny amount when you consider 8.3 million live in London, England!

SIZE 2,969,907 MI²

& ANOTHER THING!

Both Australia and India are currently moving northeast at 2-3 in (5-6 cm) a year.

153

TOP 10 LARGEST OCEANS & SEAS

A massive 72 percent of the Earth's surface is covered in water, which is a LOT of space for rivers, lakes, oceans, and seas (plus millions of little marine monsters)...

#		TYPE	SIZE (KM²)	SIZE (MI²)
01	PACIFIC	Ocean	166,266,876	64,196,000
02	ATLANTIC	Ocean	86,505,602	33,400,000
03	INDIAN	Ocean	73,555,662	28,400,000
04	SOUTHERN	Ocean	52,646,688	20,327,000
05	ARCTIC	Ocean	13,208,939	5,100,000
06	PHILIPPINE	Sea	5,179,976	2,000,000
07	CORAL	Sea	4,791,478	1,850,000
08	ARABIAN	Sea	3,861,672	1,491,000
09	SOUTH CHINA	Sea	2,973,306	1,148,000
10	CARIBBEAN	Sea	2,514,878	971,000

DANGER!

Maps of the world that were made between the 13th and 16th centuries often carried warnings of "here be dragons." This indicated uncharted territories, and often coincided with sightings of alleged sea monsters. It's important—and pretty shocking—to note that even today, 95 percent of our oceans remain unexplored...

XTREME FACT

INDIAN

This is the warmest ocean on Earth. It is also the site of a huge amount of fossil fuel—40 percent of our oil is produced from the Indian Ocean's riches.

XTREME FACT

ATLANTIC

Scientists currently believe this to be the second youngest of all our oceans, and they also think that it was formed 130 million years ago while Pangea continued to move and break up.

SIZE
28.4 MILLION MI²

LONGEST MOUNTAIN RANGES

When we think of mountains, we visualize snowy peaks, clouds, and brave climbers, but the longest mountain range is actually hidden deep beneath the waves...

		MOUNTAIN TYPE	LOCATION	LENGTH (KM)	LENGTH (MI)	RELATIVE SCALE:
01	MID-OCEANIC RIDGE	Oceanic	(Global)	65,000	40,389	100%
02	MID-ATLANTIC RIDGE	Oceanic	Atlantic Ocean	10,000	6,214	15%
03	ANDES	Land	South America	7,000	4,350	11%
04	ROCKIES	Land	North America	4,800	2,983	7%
05	TRANSANTARCTIC	Land	Antarctica	3,542	2,201	5%
06	GREAT DIVING RANGE	Land	Australia	3,059	1,901	5%
07	HIMALAYAS	Land	Asia	2,576	1,601	4%
08	SOUTHEAST INDIAN RIDGE	Oceanic	Indian Ocean	2,300	1,429	4%
09	SOUTHWEST INDIAN RIDGE	Oceanic	Rodrigues Island to Prince Edward Islands	1,931	1,200	3%
10	PACIFIC-ANTARCTIC RIDGE	Oceanic	South Pacific Ocean	1,029	639	2%

XTREME FACT ANDES

Here's just a glimpse of the magnificent Andes. This mountain range—with a top peak height of 22,841 ft (6,962 m)—cuts through no less than seven countries: Argentina, Bolivia, Chile, Colombia, Ecuador, Peru, and Venezuela.

LENGTH 4,350 MI

OFF THE CHART

JUAN DE FUCA RIDGE

Just missing out on a Top 10 spot is this 300 mi (482.8 km)-long oceanic mountain range. Here is a CGI (computer-generated image) of how it connects Canada and USA.

TOP 10

LONGEST COASTLINES

Team T-10 absolutely adores the ocean, and likes nothing better than being near it. So, naturally, we love these super-long coasts...

		LENGTH	
		(KM)	(MI)
01	CANADA	265,523	164,988.34
02	UNITED STATES	133,312	828,36.24
03	RUSSIA	110,310	68,543.46
04	INDONESIA	95,181	59,142.73
05	CHILE	78,563	48,816.78
06	AUSTRALIA	66,530	41,339.83
07	NORWAY	53,199	33,056.33
08	PHILIPPINES	33,900	21,064.48
09	BRAZIL	33,379	20,740.75
10	FINLAND	31,119	19,336.45

CHECK IT OUT!

Brazil: about 201 million people live here, in the fifth biggest country on Earth (and the largest country in South America).

TOP 10

CRAZIEST PHENOMENA ON EARTH

THE AWESOME FACTOR

THE T-10 UNOFFICIAL

01	"THE DOOR TO HELL"	230 ft (70 m)-wide crater has been burning for over 40 years
02	BERMUDA TRIANGLE	Countless ships and planes have vanished passing through it
03	NAZAC LINES	No one knows how or why these huge pictograms were made
04	AURORA BOREALIS	Charged particles high in the atmosphere create glowing swirls in the sky
05	"GODZILLA" (HEARD IN MONTREAL)	Several strange reports of monstrous stomping thumps in Sept 2011
06	BLOOD FALLS	Taylor Glacier has a flow of iron oxide-affected "blood" from it
07	ULURU	Ancient petroglyphs (carvings) and legends are a part of this iconic sandstone rock
08	SINK HOLES	A natural but very sci-fi-esque event: huge holes can appear overnight
09	STONEHENGE	How did the massive rocks get there? Why? What are they for?
10	KAUAI	Epic, supernatural-looking waterfalls and craters

XTREME FACT

SINK HOLES

This naturally occurring collapse of the Earth's surface can be pretty weird when it happens overnight. This one didn't cause any injuries, although bigger ones have—sink holes 2,000 ft (600 m) deep as they are wide.

Xtreme FACT
"THE DOOR TO HELL"

The fiery Darvaza Gas Crater in the Karakum Desert, Turkmenistan was caused by a drilling accident in 1971. When the rig collapsed, experts believed the resulting crater was releasing large amounts of methane gas. The gas was then lit to prevent if from poisoning the locals. It was assumed that, after a few days, it would all be burnt off. However, scientists still can't explain why it continues to burn over 40 years later, and hundreds of tourists flock to visit it every year.

X-PLORE
BERMUDA TRIANGLE

THE LOST SQUADRON

Here are members of the legendary "Lost Squadron" of USA Navy's Flight 19, who are said to have vanished in the Bermuda Triangle —often referred to as

"The Graveyard of the Atlantic"—on December 5, 1945. None of the crew from Flight 19's five TBM Avenger bombers, or the planes, have been found.

DANGER!
People who have experienced strangeness within the waters of the Triangle describe compasses failing or going crazy, and weather turning nasty without warning.

LARGEST CAVE SYSTEMS

TOP 10

There are many reasons why caves are awesome.
Batman has a cave. What more do you need?!

		LOCATION	LENGTH (KM)	(MI)
01	MAMMOTH CAVE	Kentucky (USA)	643.7	400
02	SISTEMA SAC ACTUN/ SISTEMA DOS OJOS	Quintana Roo (Mexico)	311	193.3
03	JEWEL CAVE	South Dakota (USA)	267.6	166.3
04	SISTEMA OX BEL HA	Quintana Roo (Mexico)	244.3	151.8
05	OPTYMISTYCHNA CAVE	Korolivka (Ukraine)	236	146.6
06	WIND CAVE	South Dakota (USA)	226.1	140.5
07	LECHUGUILLA CAVE	New Mexico (USA)	222.6	138.3
08	HÖLLOCH	Muotathal (Switzerland)	200.4	124.5
09	FISHER RIDGE CAVES	Kentucky (USA)	191.7	119.1
10	GUA AIR JERNIH	Sarawak (Malaysia)	189.1	117.5

LENGTH 400 MI

XTREME FACT
MAMMOTH CAVE

More than 483,000 people have visited this extraordinary cave system that is situated in a 52,830 acre park. The nearest city is called—you guessed it—Cave City.

CHECK IT OUT!

Jewel Cave: these limestone formations are called Organ Pipes for obvious reasons. Before you visit this cave, see the official website (www.nps.gov/jeca/index.htm) for downloadable challenges you can complete as you explore inside.

STAT ATTACK

LECHUGUILLA CAVE

Location	Carlsbad Caverns National Park, Eddy County, New Mexico, USA
Park size	46,766 acres
Wildlife	17 different species of bat
Known depth	1,604 ft (489 m)

CHECK IT OUT!

Jadeite: talk about ancient bling! Also, Jadeite axe heads, dating as far back as 10,000 BC, were dug up on the British Isles.

XTREME FACT

LECHUGUILLA CAVE

This incredible cave's name comes from a very unusual plant called *Agave lechuguilla* which only flowers once in its whole life, and dies afterward.

TOP 10 MOST EXPENSIVE PRECIOUS STONES

Diamonds are apparently a girl's best friend... Which is totally fine when you look at the prices of these OTHER precious gems...

APPROX VALUE PER CARAT (A UNIT OF MASS FOR GEMSTONES = 0.2 GRAM) IN US $

01	JADEITE	3 MILLION
02	RED DIAMOND	2–2.5 MILLION
03	SERENDIBITE	1.8–2 MILLION
04	BLUE GARNET	1.5 MILLION
05	GRANDIDIERITE	100,000
06	PAINITE	50,000–60,000
07	MUSGRAVITE	35,000
08	RED BERYL EMERALD	10,000
09	BLACK OPAL	2,355
10	JEREMEJEVITE	2,000

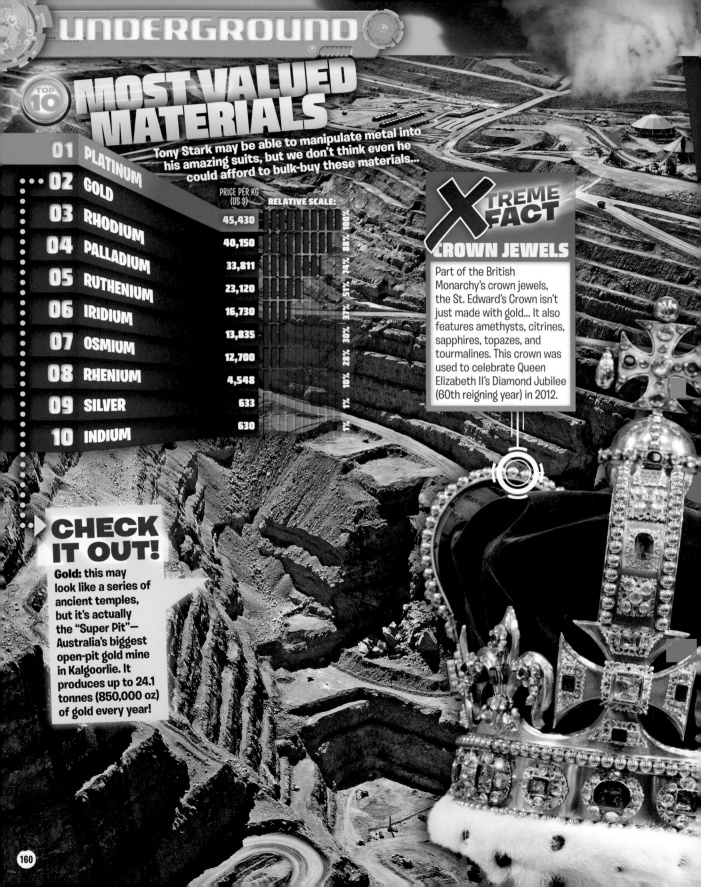

MOST VALUED MATERIALS

TOP 10

Tony Stark may be able to manipulate metal into his amazing suits, but we don't think even he could afford to bulk-buy these materials...

		PRICE PER KG (US $)
01	PLATINUM	45,430
02	GOLD	40,150
03	RHODIUM	33,811
04	PALLADIUM	23,120
05	RUTHENIUM	16,730
06	IRIDIUM	13,835
07	OSMIUM	12,700
08	RHENIUM	4,548
09	SILVER	633
10	INDIUM	630

RELATIVE SCALE: 100% 88% 74% 51% 37% 30% 28% 10% 1% 1%

XTREME FACT

CROWN JEWELS

Part of the British Monarchy's crown jewels, the St. Edward's Crown isn't just made with gold... It also features amethysts, citrines, sapphires, topazes, and tourmalines. This crown was used to celebrate Queen Elizabeth II's Diamond Jubilee (60th reigning year) in 2012.

CHECK IT OUT!

Gold: this may look like a series of ancient temples, but it's actually the "Super Pit"—Australia's biggest open-pit gold mine in Kalgoorlie. It produces up to 24.1 tonnes (850,000 oz) of gold every year!

TOP 10 MOST COMMON ELEMENTS

Our planet is made up of many wonderful things, but these are the 10 most common elements that contribute to the Earth's crust...

#	Element	% OF EARTH'S CRUST
01	OXYGEN	46.1%
02	SILICON	28.2%
03	ALUMINIUM	8.23%
04	IRON	5.63%
05	CALCIUM	4.15%
06	SODIUM	2.36%
07	MAGNESIUM	2.33%
08	POTASSIUM	2.09%
09	TITANIUM	0.59%
10	HYDROGEN	0.14%

XTREME FACT

SILICON

This is called a "macro photograph" (an extreme close-up) of a specimen of silicon, an extremely important element in the production of high-tech devices. That smartphone you enjoy? Your video games? Thank silicon for each and every one of them!

28.2% OF THE EARTH'S CRUST

XTREME FACT

ALUMINIUM

Recycling aluminium cans is not as modern an idea as you'd think. Although we started to be really proactive about it in the past 40 years, it was actually happening way back in 1900!

DID YOU KNOW?

Water is a compound, which means it is made up of more than one element: two hydrogen molecules, and one oxygen (hence H_2O), and our planet is covered with a LOT of H_2O...

154584331
5645445641-1545
514351-4564
213453434-4545433-4545435
5345435-4534354
42-46425
639363-535398
4933653-565
1253854-15862

YOUR SHOUT

This part of your book is dedicated to how much you know about nature...

YOUR PICK OF THE... NATURE

It's time for you to take T-10 control and tell us your ultimate top 10 forces of nature...

01

02

03

04

05

06

07

08

09

10

ROUND 1: MULTIPLE CHOICE

01 The biggest disaster movie of all time grossed $769 million at the box office. Can you tell us which one it is?

A TWISTER
B 2012
C ARMAGEDDON

02 The tallest tree on the planet is a Giant Redwood. Do you know how high it stands?

A 242.84 FT (74 M)
B 379.66 FT (115.72 M)
C 481.43 FT (146.73 M)

03 The Indian Ocean is the third largest ocean on the planet. What percentage of the world's oil comes from there?

A 5%
B 22%
C 40%

ROUND 2: QUESTION TIME

01 The Top 10 Longest Mountain Ranges includes both dizzyingly high snow-capped peaks and oceanic ridges at crushing depths. Of the 10, how many are on dry land?

ANSWER:

ROUND 3:
PICTURE PUZZLES

Jaya Sri Maha Bodhi is the oldest human-planted tree, but where is it located?

01

ANSWER:

Can you name this mineral? It is the most expensive stone in the world.

02

ANSWER:

Russia is the largest country on the planet, but can you name the sixth, seen here?

03

ANSWER:

ROUND 4:
WORDSEARCH

E	B	N	D	A	V	Y	R	I	U	K	A
W	E	C	B	N	I	Q	S	D	S	Z	S
A	S	V	N	C	A	N	A	D	A	T	E
Z	T	N	O	P	T	Q	U	E	U	C	N
N	O	R	W	A	Y	W	V	B	S	X	I
R	O	A	D	V	J	L	Y	C	T	E	P
C	B	N	R	R	A	C	B	H	R	O	P
A	B	M	I	W	U	C	X	I	A	E	I
V	N	E	F	R	W	S	C	L	L	T	L
G	A	D	W	O	B	E	S	E	I	O	I
X	I	N	D	O	N	E	S	I	A	E	H
A	W	O	M	C	M	B	E	A	A	M	P

Look in the jumble of letters to the left, and then see how many of these countries with the longest coastlines you can find within the mess:

CANADA

USA

RUSSIA

INDONESIA

CHILE

AUSTRALIA

NORWAY

PHILIPPINES

FIND THE ANSWERS ON PAGE 312

02 We all know Thor *(right)* from the Marvel movies. Can you name which natural phenomena this Norse god is associated with?

03 Kentucky, USA is home to one of the two largest cave systems on the planet. Can you name one of them?

ANSWER:

NATURE
CAREER
QUIZ

Which of these places would you rather spend a night?

☐ **A UNDER THE STARS**
☐ **B A TREEHOUSE**
☐ **C A SECRET HIDEOUT**

Of the following, which would you find the least frightening?

☐ **A SNOW BLIZZARD**
☐ **B KILLER VENUS FLY TRAPS**
☐ **C EARTH TREMORS**

Which of these movies do you like the most?

☐ **A TWISTER**
☐ **D DANTE'S PEAK**
☐ **C THE LORD OF THE RINGS: THE TWO TOWERS**

Which of the following would you rather own?

☐ **A AN ANEMOMETER** (MEASURES WIND SPEED)
☐ **B MICROSCOPE**
☐ **C SEISMOGRAPH** (MEASURES EARTH SHOCK WAVES)

Which of the following outdoor activities would you prefer to do?

☐ **A KITE FLYING IN THE RAIN**
☐ **B FACT FINDING IN A FOREST**
☐ **C EXPLORE CAVES AND TUNNELS**

Which place is most suited to you for a fun day out?

☐ **A AN OBSERVATORY**
☐ **B A NATURAL HISTORY MUSEUM**
☐ **C RIDE ON A SIMULATOR**

Which of the following statements best fits you?

☐ **A I LOVE BEING OUTSIDE**
☐ **B I THINK INSECT-EATING PLANTS ARE COOL**
☐ **C I LIKE DISASTER MOVIES**

Find out which nature-related job is best suited to you on page 312

MUSIC
MASH-UP

248.13.155
54893.52798514
785496.45641
156684129-48485555451I
1456156.5-1567897
69756132-48781415213
154584337-4156456
564545641-1545
514351-4564
213453434-4545433-4545435
5349435-4534354
42-45425
639363-535398
453363-565
1253854-15862
8632863-556
1456156I5-1567897
69756132-48781415213
154584337-4156456
564545641-1545
514351-4564
213453434-4545433
5349435-4534354-45343541

CHART TOPPERS

TOP 10 MOST DOWNLOADED SONGS EVER

Digital downloads have revolutionized how we enjoy music for more than a decade. These are the biggest digital sellers of all time...

#	TITLE	ARTIST(S)	UNITS SOLD
01	I GOTTA FEELING	THE BLACK EYED PEAS	8,438,000
02	ROLLING IN THE DEEP	ADELE	8,060,000
03	PARTY ROCK ANTHEM	LMFAO FT. LAUREN BENNETT & GOONROCK	7,821,000
04	SOMEBODY THAT I USED TO KNOW	GOTYE FT. KIMBRA	7,545,000
05	CALL ME MAYBE	CARLY RAE JEPSEN	7,304,000
06	THRIFT SHOP	MACKLEMORE & RYAN LEWIS	7,266,000
07	POKER FACE	LADY GAGA	7,054,000
08	LOW	FLO RIDA FT. T-PAIN	6,882,000
09	JUST DANCE	LADY GAGA FT. COLBY O'DONIS	6,860,000
10	WE ARE YOUNG	FUN. FT. JANELLE MONÁE	6,830,000

Source: Billboard

DOWNLOADS
7.05 MILLION

OFF THE CHART
WILL.I.AM
The Black Eyed Peas aside, Mr. i.am has also released four solo albums since 2001. #willpower (released April 19, 2013) featured the Top 10 Billboard hit, *This Is Love*, which sold more than 500,000 units worldwide.

XTREME FACT
LADY GAGA
Poker Face has also clocked in at over 175 million views on Lady Gaga's VEVO channel. The song was co-written by Gaga and Nadir Khayat, better known as superstar producer RedOne.

166

CHECK IT OUT!

Beyoncé: for her fifth solo album, Mrs. Jay Z made something that hasn't been done before... This self-titled collection has 14 tracks, each with an accompanying video, hence why Beyoncé described it as a "visual album."

TOP 10 MOST DOWNLOADED ALBUMS EVER

These 10 albums' digital audio files have been downloaded by music fans the most...

DOWNLOADS
1.02 MILLION

#	ALBUM	ARTIST(S)	UNITS SOLD
01	21	ADELE	3,009,000
02	SIGH NO MORE	MUMFORD & SONS	1,676,000
03	BABEL	MUMFORD & SONS	1,334,000
04	RECOVERY	EMINEM	1,300,000
05	NIGHT VISIONS	IMAGINE DRAGONS	1,157,000
06	RED	TAYLOR SWIFT	1,135,000
07	THE FAME	LADY GAGA	1,086,000
08	THE 20/20 EXPERIENCE	JUSTIN TIMBERLAKE	1,026,000
09	BEYONCÉ	BEYONCÉ	972,000
10	THE LUMINEERS	THE LUMINEERS	956,000

Source: Billboard

STAT ATTACK

JUSTIN TIMBERLAKE

Born .... January 31, 1981
Wife ....Jessica Biel
Debut solo album..... *Justified* (2002)
Previous 'N Sync era: 1995-2002
Website...... www.justintimberlake.com

DID YOU KNOW?

Beyoncé's debut with Destiny's Child was *Killing Time* on the *Men In Black* (1997) soundtrack, when she was only 15!

167

TOP 10 BIGGEST SELLING ARTISTS EVER

Of every musical genre—from country star to blisteringly heavy metaller—these are the 10 biggest artists of all time...

		UNITS SOLD	RELATIVE SCALE:
01	GARTH BROOKS		100%
02	THE BEATLES		94%
03	MARIAH CAREY	69,424,000	
04	METALLICA	65,111,000	78%
05	CÉLINE DION	54,209,000	78%
06	GEORGE STRAIT	54,129,000	75%
07	EMINEM	52,159,000	65%
08	TIM McGRAW	44,781,000	64%
09	ALAN JACKSON	44,469,000	60%
10	PINK FLOYD	41,844,000	58%
		40,361,000	55%
		38,508,000	

Source: Billboard

UNITS SOLD 44.4 MILLION

XTREME FACT: MARIAH CAREY

If you think Mariah's career sales are impressive, check this out: the singer's 1990 self-titled debut album has sold over 10 million copies worldwide. Not too bad for a first record!

CHECK IT OUT!

Eminem: the rapper from Detroit has released 10 albums since his debut release, *Infinite*, in 1996. His latest offering, *The Marshall Mathers LP 2*, contains the smash hit single *The Monster* which features Rihanna.

XTREME FACT

JAGGED LITTLE PILL

Alanis Morissette's third album is on *Rolling Stone*'s list of the 50 Greatest Female Artist Albums Of All Time. To celebrate its 10th anniversary, Morissette reinterpreted the album and released *Jagged Little Pill Acoustic* on June 13, 2005.

BEEN & SEEN

Listened to any of these classic albums? Tick them off the list as you do!

- [ ] **LOVE IS THE THING:** NAT KING COLE
- [ ] **BOYS FOR PELE:** TORI AMOS
- [ ] **FLOWERS IN THE DIRT:** PAUL McCARTNEY
- [ ] **THE COLOR AND THE SHAPE:** FOO FIGHTERS
- [ ] **GOD SHUFFLED HIS FEET:** CRASH TEST DUMMIES
- [ ] **COURT AND SPARK:** JONI MITCHELL
- [ ] **OK COMPUTER:** RADIOHEAD
- [ ] **THE BODYGUARD: ORIGINAL SOUNDTRACK** WHITNEY HOUSTON/VARIOUS
- [ ] **TRAGIC KINGDOM:** NO DOUBT
- [ ] **BAD:** MICHAEL JACKSON

TOP 10 — BIGGEST SELLING ALBUMS EVER

If you had to guess, which albums do you think would be on this list? From the SoundScan era (1991 onward), when album sales started to be tracked, it's these 10...

#	Album	ARTIST(S)	UNITS SOLD
01	METALLICA	METALLICA	15,948,000
02	COME ON OVER	SHANIA TWAIN	15,547,000
03	JAGGED LITTLE PILL	ALANIS MORISSETTE	14,895,000
04	1	THE BEATLES	12,281,000
05	MILLENNIUM	BACKSTREET BOYS	12,241,000
06	THE BODYGUARD: ORIGINAL SOUNDTRACK	WHITNEY HOUSTON/VARIOUS	12,085,000
07	SUPERNATURAL	SANTANA	11,792,000
08	HUMAN CLAY	CREED	11,674,000
09	LEGEND	BOB MARLEY & THE WAILERS	11,458,000
10	NO STRINGS ATTACHED	'N SYNC	11,152,000

Source: Billboard

CHECK IT OUT!

Metallica: Never underestimate a drummer... Lars Ulrich founded Metallica back in 1981, and he's still the metal band's skinsman.

CHECK IT OUT!

Bruno Mars: Honolulu, Hawaii-born popstar Bruno Mars had an amazing 2013. His *Unorthodox Jukebox* album was exactly that—a brave mix of styles—and it scored him five Grammy Awards and a win for Best Pop Vocal album. Mars has won 58 international awards.

TOP 10
BIGGEST SELLING ARTISTS OF 2013

2013 was an incredible year for music, with the biggest pop stars releasing some of the best albums of their careers. These were the 10 champions...

		UNITS SOLD
01	JUSTIN TIMBERLAKE	3,445,000
02	LUKE BRYAN	2,740,000
03	EMINEM	2,518,000
04	ONE DIRECTION	1,973,000
05	BLAKE SHELTON	1,720,000
06	BRUNO MARS	1,708,000
07	DRAKE	1,605,000
08	BEYONCÉ	1,573,000
09	MUMFORD & SONS	1,534,000
10	IMAGINE DRAGONS	1,434,000

Source: Billboard

XTREME FACT

ONE DIRECTION

The popular boyband had another all-conquering year in 2013. Their big screen debut tour movie, *One Direction: This Is Us,* took $68,532,898 at box offices worldwide.

10 QUICK FIRE FACTS

ONE DIRECTION

01	They are also known as 1D
02	The band members are Harry, Zayn, Niall, Liam, and Louis
03	The group was formed on a hit TV show in the UK
04	They were the 2010 *The X Factor* finalists
05	They are signed to Simon Cowell's label Syco
06	They were named 2012's "Top New Artist" by Billboard
07	Their 2014 stadium tour was called *Where We Are*
08	The official website is www.onedirectionmusic.com
09	The group's Twitter handle is @onedirection
10	They have more than 27 million Facebook "Likes"

UNITS SOLD
1.35 MILLION

▶ CHECK IT OUT!

Here's To The Good Times: since its December 4, 2012 release, Florida Georgia Line's debut album has torn up charts everywhere. Less than a year later, on August 1, 2013, it was already a platinum seller (one million copies)! VERY good times...

TOP 10

BIGGEST SELLING ALBUMS OF 2013

Combining the sales from digital downloads, CDs, vinyls, special editions—the LOT—these were 2013's greatest album sales' successes...

#	Album	ARTIST(S)	UNITS SOLD
01	THE 20/20 EXPERIENCE	JUSTIN TIMBERLAKE	2,427,000
02	THE MARSHALL MATHERS LP 2	EMINEM	1,727,000
03	CRASH MY PARTY	LUKE BRYAN	1,521,000
04	NIGHT VISIONS	IMAGINE DRAGONS	1,402,000
05	UNORTHODOX JUKEBOX	BRUNO MARS	1,399,000
06	HERE'S TO THE GOOD TIMES	FLORIDA GEORGIA LINE	1,350,000
07	NOTHING WAS THE SAME	DRAKE	1,344,000
08	BEYONCÉ	BEYONCÉ	1,301,000
09	BASED ON A TRUE STORY	BLAKE SHELTON	1,109,000
10	MAGNA CARTA... HOLY GRAIL	JAY Z	1,099,000

Source: Billboard

UNITS SOLD
1.34 MILLION

✗TREME FACT

NOTHING WAS THE SAME

Clocking in at just under an hour long (59:26), Canadian Drake's third album contains no less than SIX huge singles, featuring megastar guest appearances from Jay Z, 2 Chainz, and Big Sean.

171

BIGGEST SELLING CD ALBUMS OF 2013

For music fans who prefer to collect artists' work on CD (compact disc), these were the bestsellers across every genre...

TOP 10

#	Album	ARTIST(S)	UNITS SOLD
01	THE 20/20 EXPERIENCE	JUSTIN TIMBERLAKE	1,381,000
02	CRASH MY PARTY	LUKE BRYAN	1,065,000
03	THE MARSHALL MATHERS LP 2	EMINEM	950,000
04	HERE'S TO THE GOOD TIMES	FLORIDA GEORGIA LINE	902,000
05	UNORTHODOX JUKEBOX	BRUNO MARS	871,000
06	BLAME IT ALL ON MY ROOTS	GARTH BROOKS	771,000
07	BASED ON A TRUE STORY...	BLAKE SHELTON	765,000
08	MIDNIGHT MEMORIES	ONE DIRECTION	714,000
09	PRISM	KATY PERRY	686,000
10	DUCK THE HALLS: A ROBERTSON FAMILY CHRISTMAS	THE ROBERTSONS	677,000

Source: Billboard

CHECK IT OUT!

Prism: Ms. Perry... You knocked it out of the park with your fourth record! Released on October 18, 2013, *Prism* is her fastest-selling album, and secured the number one spot in Canada, Australia, New Zealand, the UK, and Ireland. Plus, the lead single *Roar* marked the eighth US number one single for her.

BIGGEST SELLING VINYL ALBUMS OF 2013

Vinyl has been making a comeback for the past decade, and its popularity is spreading, especially with Record Store Day becoming a planet-wide tradition each April...

TOP 10

#	Album	ARTIST(S)	UNITS SOLD
01	RANDOM ACCESS MEMORIES	DAFT PUNK	49,000
02	MODERN VAMPIRES OF THE CITY	VAMPIRE WEEKEND	34,000
03	REFLEKTOR	ARCADE FIRE	31,000
04	BABEL	MUMFORD & SONS	27,000
=	SIGH NO MORE	MUMFORD & SONS	27,000
=	...LIKE CLOCKWORK	QUEENS OF THE STONE AGE	27,000
=	FOR EMMA, FOREVER AGO	BON IVER	23,000
07	THE LUMINEERS	THE LUMINEERS	22,000
08	TROUBLE WILL FIND ME	THE NATIONAL	22,000
=	THE 20/20 EXPERIENCE	JUSTIN TIMBERLAKE	21,000
10			

Source: Billboard

▶XTREME FACT ...LIKE CLOCKWORK

Prior to writing and recording *...Like Clockwork*, Queens Of The Stone Age's frontman/captain Josh Homme actually died briefly on the operating table in 2011, during complications to do with a knee operation.

X-PLORE
JUSTIN TIMBERLAKE
THE 20/20 EXPERIENCE

TRACK LISTING:
DISC 1
1. Pusher Love Girl
2. Suit & Tie
3. Don't Hold The Wall
4. Strawberry Bubblegum
5. Tunnel Vision
6. Spaceship Coupe
7. That Girl
8. Let The Groove Get In
9. Mirrors
10. Blue Ocean Floor

DISC 2
1. Gimme What I Don't Know (I Want)
2. True Blood
3. Cabaret
4. TKO
5. Take Back The Night
6. Murder
7. Drink You Away
8. You Got It On
9. Amnesia
10. Only When I Walk Away
11. Not A Bad Thing
12. Pair Of Wings

Xtreme Fact

MAGNA CARTA... HOLY GRAIL

This is Jay Z's twelfth studio album! It's also bursting with A-list guest appearances, like wife Beyoncé, Jerome "J-Roc" Harmon, Nas, Frank Ocean, Rick Ross, Timbaland, Justin Timberlake, AND Pharrell Williams.

TOP 10
BIGGEST SELLING DIGITAL ALBUMS OF 2013

Do you mainly download your music? Then this chart will be of special interest to you...

#	Album	ARTIST(S)	UNITS SOLD
01	THE 20/20 EXPERIENCE	JUSTIN TIMBERLAKE	1,026,000
02	BEYONCÉ	BEYONCÉ	972,000
03	NIGHT VISIONS	IMAGINE DRAGONS	833,000
04	THE MARSHALL MATHERS LP 2	EMINEM	777,000
05	NOTHING WAS THE SAME	DRAKE	689,000
06	THE HEIST	MACKLEMORE & RYAN LEWIS	658,000
07	MAGNA CARTA... HOLY GRAIL	JAY Z	640,000
08	PITCH PERFECT: ORIGINAL SOUNDTRACK	VARIOUS	559,000
09	BABEL	MUMFORD & SONS	556,000
10	UNORTHODOX JUKEBOX	BRUNO MARS	524,000

Source: Billboard

CHECK IT OUT!

The 20/20 Experience: JT scooped three trophies at the 2014 People's Choice Awards, including ones for best male artist and best album.

X TREME FACT
THRIFT SHOP

This massive hit was actually released back in 2012 on August 27. But being featured on two big movie trailers in 2013 —Owen Wilson comedy *The Internship* and Dwayne Johnson crime caper *Pain & Gain*—helped boost its popularity.

UNITS
6.14
MILLION

TOP 10

BIGGEST SELLING DIGITAL SONGS OF 2013

We've covered all aspects of albums, so now it's time for some stats about the most significant singles of 2013! Digital downloads, you're up...

#	Song	ARTIST(S)	UNITS
01	BLURRED LINES	ROBIN THICKE FT. T.I. & PHARRELL	6,498,000
02	THRIFT SHOP	MACKLEMORE & RYAN LEWIS FT. WANZ	6,148,000
03	RADIOACTIVE	IMAGINE DRAGONS	5,496,000
04	CRUISE	FLORIDA GEORGIA LINE	4,691,000
05	ROYALS	LORDE	4,415,000
06	ROAR	KATY PERRY	4,410,000
07	JUST GIVE ME A REASON	P!NK FT. NATE RUESS	4,321,000
08	CAN'T HOLD US	MACKLEMORE & RYAN LEWIS FT. RAY DALTON	4,260,000
09	WHEN I WAS YOUR MAN	BRUNO MARS	3,928,000
10	STAY	RIHANNA FT. MIKKY EKKO	3,854,000

Source: Billboard

OFF THE CHART
MILEY CYRUS

Although Miley Cyrus misses out on this Top 10, her singles *We Can't Stop* and *Wrecking Ball* both sold in excess of three million copies.

TOP 10 MOST POPULAR MUSIC GENRES OF 2013

What genre of music do you adore? Team T-10 loves rock and metal the most, so we're pleased to see the riff-masters are still going very strong...

#	Genre	% OF TOTAL SALES
01	ROCK	
02	R&B	
03	ALTERNATIVE	34.8
04	COUNTRY	17.5
05	METAL	17.4
06	RAP	13.8
07	SOUNDTRACK	10.2
08	ELECTRONIC	8.7
09	CLASSIC	4.0
10	LATIN	3.0
		2.8
		2.9

CHECK IT OUT!

Alternative: this genre still takes a big chunk of total sales. Chester Bennington (*right*) now fronts Stone Temple Pilots, as well as Linkin Park—still his "day job."

17.4%
OF TOTAL SALES

TOP 10 BEST NUMBER ONES OF THE 2000s

THE T10 UNOFFICIAL

#	Song	Royals
01	LORDE	ROYALS
02	LOCKED OUT OF HEAVEN	BRUNO MARS
03	CALL ME MAYBE	CARLY RAE JEPSEN
04	TEENAGE DREAM	KATY PERRY
05	SINGLE LADIES (PUT A RING ON IT)	BEYONCÉ
06	HEY YA!	OUTKAST
07	UMBRELLA	RIHANNA FT. JAY Z
08	HOLLABACK GIRL	GWEN STEFANI
09	THE MONSTER	EMINEM FT. RIHANNA
10	FALLIN'	ALICIA KEYS

Source: Billboard

XTREME FACT

HOLLABACK GIRL

This, the third single from Gwen "No Doubt" Stefani's 2004 debut solo album *Love. Angel. Music. Baby.* was co-written by Pharrell Williams, the vocalist on Daft Punk's *Get Lucky* among a million other projects!

175

TOP 10 MOST PLAYED SONGS OF 2013

A big listener of a radio station? Then chances are you would've heard these 10 dominating the airwaves throughout 2013...

#	SONG	ARTIST(S)	DETECTIONS
01	BLURRED LINES	ROBIN THICKE FT. T.I. & PHARRELL	673,000
02	MIRRORS	JUSTIN TIMBERLAKE	568,000
03	STAY	RIHANNA FT. MIKKY EKKO	519,000
04	WHEN I WAS YOUR MAN	BRUNO MARS	517,000
05	LOCKED OUT OF HEAVEN	BRUNO MARS	514,000
06	HO HEY	THE LUMINEERS	502,000
07	RADIOACTIVE	IMAGINE DRAGONS	493,000
08	JUST GIVE ME A REASON	P!NK FT. NATE RUESS	479,000
09	CAN'T HOLD US	MACKLEMORE & RYAN LEWIS FT. RAY DALTON	464,000
10	SUIT & TIE	JUSTIN TIMBERLAKE FT. JAY Z	462,000

Source: Billboard

10 QUICK FIRE FACTS

RIHANNA

#	
01	Her full name is Robyn Rihanna Fenty
02	Her date of birth is February 20, 1988
03	She was born in Saint Michael, Barbados
04	She lives in New York City, USA
05	Received "Icon Award" at the 2013 American Music Awards
06	Her fragrance "Reb'l Fleur" was released in 2011
07	She has appeared in four movies since 2006
08	Her official website is www.rihannanow.com
09	Her Twitter handle is @rihanna
10	She has more than 85 million Facebook "Likes"

DETECTIONS
519 THOUSAND

CHECK IT OUT!

Stay: Rihanna's 2013 began with the single *Stay*, released on January 7. Guest vocalist on the track, Mikky Ekko, also co-wrote and co-produced the song. Rihanna has released seven albums in as many years since 2005.

STREAMS
171.2
MILLION

CHECK IT OUT!

Radioactive: released on May 3, 2013, this awesome Imagine Dragons song was actually being pushed for radio play way back in April 2012 and again that October. It just goes to show that a great song will eventually find its audience.

XTREME FACT

HARLEM SHAKE

It may have become the internet meme sensation of 2013, but Baauer's debut single *Harlem Shake* was actually released on May 22, 2012. It peaked at number 4 on the US Billboard chart.

TOP 10 MOST STREAMED SONGS OF 2013

Combining the totals from the official video streams AND the audio streams, these are the 10 songs that planet earth listened to the most online in 2013...

#	SONG	ARTIST(S)	STREAMS
01	HARLEM SHAKE	BAAUER	489,674,000
02	GANGNAM STYLE	PSY	279,949,000
03	THRIFT SHOP	MACKLEMORE & RYAN LEWIS FT. WANZ	256,954,000
04	WRECKING BALL	MILEY CYRUS	187,648,000
05	RADIOACTIVE	IMAGINE DRAGONS	171,286,000
06	WE CAN'T STOP	MILEY CYRUS	155,356,000
07	BLURRED LINES	ROBIN THICKE FT. T.I. & PHARRELL	138,790,000
08	CAN'T HOLD US	MACKLEMORE & RYAN LEWIS FT. RAY DALTON	135,758,000
09	SAIL	AWOLNATION	134,483,000
10	STARTED FROM THE BOTTOM	DRAKE	125,465,000

Source: Billboard

DID YOU KNOW?

Katy Perry's 2010 album *Teenage Dream* spawned five digital number one singles—a record!

STAT ATTACK
THE LUMINEERS
Debut album: .... The Lumineers
Release date:................... April 3, 2012
Tracks:.. 11
Running time:........................... 42:15
Label............................Dualtone Records

DETECTIONS
247 THOUSAND

XTREME FACT
HO HEY
Don't recognize the title? You know the song... *"I belong to you, you belong to me, you're my sweetheart,"* but this was a total sleeper hit. Released on June 4, 2012, it slowly became popular at the end of 2012 and for all of 2013.

MOST PLAYED POP SONGS OF 2013

Although Team T-10 loves the world of rock, we totally adore awesome pop songwriting, too. There are some great ones here...

Source: Billboard

#	Song	Artist(s)	Detections
01	HO HEY	THE LUMINEERS	247,000
02	JUST GIVE ME A REASON	P!NK FT. NATE RUESS	225,000
03	DAYLIGHT	MAROON 5	214,000
04	CATCH MY BREATH	KELLY CLARKSON	203,000
05	TRY	P!NK	195,000
06	HOME	PHILLIP PHILLIPS	191,000
=	GONE, GONE, GONE	PHILLIP PHILLIPS	191,000
08	WHEN I WAS YOUR MAN	BRUNO MARS	180,000
09	I WILL WAIT	MUMFORD & SONS	167,000
10	STAY	RIHANNA FT. MIKKY EKKO	164,000

CHECK IT OUT!
Just Give Me A Reason: what a FUN collaboration! Sorry, we couldn't resist... Frontman of Fun., Nate Ruess, lent his vocal skills to this, P!nk's 29th single. The other guy in the song's video? That's P!nk's husband, off-road trucker and motorcross legend Carey Hart.

MOST PLAYED ROCK/ALTERNATIVE SONGS OF 2013

The alternative music scene always sees sonically fascinating artists emerge. Here are the 10 that mattered the most on the radio in 2013...

#		ARTIST(S)	DETECTIONS
01	RADIOACTIVE	IMAGINE DRAGONS	132,000
02	SAFE AND SOUND	CAPITAL CITIES	88,000
03	SWEATER WEATHER	THE NEIGHBOURHOOD	83,000
04	DEMONS	IMAGINE DRAGONS	81,000
05	MADNESS	MUSE	80,000
06	MOUNTAIN SOUND	OF MONSTERS AND MEN	76,000
07	OUT OF MY LEAGUE	FITZ AND THE TANTRUMS	73,000
08	LITTLE BLACK SUBMARINES	THE BLACK KEYS	65,000
09	HO HEY	THE LUMINEERS	61,000
=	I WILL WAIT	MUMFORD & SONS	61,000

Source: Billboard

CHECK IT OUT!

Little Black Submarines: seven albums and 19 singles later, Ohio duo Dan Auerbach and Patrick Carney, aka The Black Keys, released this, their 20th single. It was a smash hit.

MOST PLAYED R&B SONGS OF 2013

The smooth beats and grooves of R&B are quite a dominating force on the radio, and these songs got plenty of airplay in 2013...

#		ARTIST(S)	DETECTIONS
01	ADORN	MIGUEL	158,000
02	BLURRED LINES	ROBIN THICKE FT. T.I. & PHARRELL	122,000
=	BAD	WALE FT. TIARA THOMAS	122,000
04	POWER TRIP	J. COLE FT. MIGUEL	119,000
05	LOVE AND WAR	TAMAR BRAXTON	118,000
06	POUR IT UP	RIHANNA FT. VARIOUS ARTISTS	117,000
07	HOW MANY DRINKS?	MIGUEL FT. KENDRICK LAMAR	105,000
08	BODY PARTY	CIARA	97,000
09	SUIT & TIE	JUSTIN TIMBERLAKE FT. JAY Z	96,000
10	POETIC JUSTICE	KENDRICK LAMAR FT. DRAKE	92,000

Source: Billboard

XTREME FACT

ADORN

California-born singer and producer extraordinaire Miguel put his massive hit *Adorn* out first on a mixtape, *Art Dealer Chic, Vol. 1.* Then it became the song that led his fans to his huge 2012 album, *Kaleidoscope Dream.*

CHECK IT OUT!

Britney Spears: over her 16 years so far in the pop spotlight, Britney Spears has released eight albums and received countless awards, including the 2014 People's Choice Award for best pop artist.

TOP 10 MUSICIANS WITH THE MOST TWITTER FOLLOWERS

Pop stars love to tweet, and we love to follow their daily antics. Here are the Twitter handles that we hold onto the most dearly...

		TWITTER HANDLE	FOLLOWING	FOLLOWERS
01	KATY PERRY	@KATPERRY	133	50,813,148
02	JUSTIN BIEBER	@JUSTINBIEBER	124,431	49,835,156
03	LADY GAGA	@LADYGAGA	134,942	41,042,058
04	TAYLOR SWIFT	@TAYLORSWIFT13	125	39,305,061
05	BRITNEY SPEARS	@BRITNEYSPEARS	404,725	36,066,431
06	RIHANNA	@RIHANNA	999	34,262,517
07	JUSTIN TIMBERLAKE	@JTIMBERLAKE	66	30,844,525
08	JENNIFER LOPEZ	@JLO	355	26,723,537
09	SHAKIRA	@SHAKIRA	125	24,059,514
10	P!NK	@PINK	302	22,454,032

FOLLOWERS 50.8 MILLION

XTREME FACT
KATY PERRY

On February 1, 2014, Katy Perry made social media history. She became the first celebrity to reach a staggering 50 million followers on Twitter. Her celebratory tweet was: "Oh yeah AND we grew to 50 million Katycats! Eh, regular day at the office."

TOP 10
OFFICIAL MUSIC VIDEOS WITH THE MOST YOUTUBE VIEWS

When an artist has a brilliant music video, it can be a career-maker —especially if it goes viral. These are the all-conquering 10 right now...

		ARTIST(S)	DATE UPLOADED	VIEWS
01	GANGNAM STYLE	PSY	JUL 15, 2012	1,913,938,569
02	BABY	JUSTIN BIEBER FT. LUDACRIS	FEB 19, 2010	994,612,318
03	ON THE FLOOR	JENNIFER LOPEZ FT. PITBULL	MAR 3, 2011	733,708,354
04	LOVE THE WAY YOU LIE	EMINEM FT. RIHANNA	AUG 5, 2010	666,322,223
05	PARTY ROCK ANTHEM	LMFAO FT. LAUREN BENNETT & GOONROCK	MAR 8, 2011	647,433,102
06	GENTLEMAN	PSY	APR 13, 2013	645,789,081
07	WAKA WAKA (THIS TIME FOR AFRICA)	SHAKIRA FT. FRESHLYGROUND	JUN 4, 2010	618,433,985
08	BAD ROMANCE	LADY GAGA	NOV 23, 2009	569,417,533
09	AI SE EU TE PEGO	MICHEL TELÓ	JUL 25, 2011	555,184,172
10	WRECKING BALL	MILEY CYRUS	SEP 9, 2013	553,093,259

VIEWS
666.3 MILLION

BEEN & SEEN

When you've seen these music vids, tick them off the list!

- [ ] KYLIE MINOGUE: **INTO THE BLUE**
- [ ] LIT: **MY OWN WORST ENEMY**
- [ ] RIHANNA: **DIAMONDS**
- [ ] SEVENDUST: **DECAY**
- [ ] CARLY RAE JEPSEN: **CALL ME MAYBE**
- [ ] SOUNDGARDEN: **BY CROOKED STEPS**
- [ ] DAFT PUNK: **GET LUCKY**
- [ ] SOPHIE ELLIS BEXTOR: **YOUNG BLOOD**
- [ ] KATY PERRY: **ROAR**
- [ ] BRUNO MARS: **LOCKED OUT OF HEAVEN**

CHECK IT OUT!

Love The Way You Lie: this track scored rapper Eminem five Grammy nominations, and its music video featured *Lost* and *The Lord Of The Rings*' star Dominic Monaghan, as well as *Transformers*' leading lady, Megan Fox.

XTREME FACT
GANGNAM STYLE

Video-sharing internet service YouTube may have begun in 2005, but it wasn't until December 21, 2012, that a video —*Gangnam Style* by Psy—registered an unbelievable one BILLION views.

MOST SUBSCRIBED VEVO CHANNEL

Do you subscribe to any music artists' VEVO channel? Check to see if any of them have made it into this Top 10...

SUBSCRIBERS 4.82 MILLION

#	Artist	SUBSCRIBERS
01	RIHANNA	
02	ONE DIRECTION	13,014,980
03	EMINEM	12,381,833
04	KATY PERRY	11,472,748
05	JUSTIN BIEBER	10,685,971
06	TAYLOR SWIFT	8,749,532
07	MILEY CYRUS	7,292,296
08	AVICII	6,156,419
09	DAVID GUETTA	4,944,952
10	NICKI MINAJ	4,912,820
		4,829,272

CHECK IT OUT!

Taylor Swift: her VEVO channel was launched May 11, 2009, and the Pennsylvania-born pop-rock star has uploaded 61 videos to date. These include behind-the-scenes footage and awards' events, too.

SUBSCRIBERS 7.29 MILLION

XTREME FACT

NICKI MINAJ

Nicki Minaj has racked up 1,639,431,124 views of her VEVO videos since she started her channel on April 1, 2010. Her 2011 single *Super Bass* remains her most popular, with 399,749,812 views.

& ANOTHER THING!

One of the most popular video services, VEVO is still a young company—founded just a few years ago on December 8, 2009.

XTREME FACT
GIRL ON FIRE

New Yorker pianist/popster Alicia Keys certainly knows how to debut a great song... *Girl On Fire* was performed at the 2012 MTV Video Music Awards on September 6, 2012 (just after its September 4, release), with US 2012 Olympic Games gold medalist Gabby Douglas performing gymnastics.

XTREME FACT
DAVID GUETTA

The French dance artist has been topping charts since 2002, and not just with his own work. A frequent co-writer/producer, he crafted *Fashion!* with Lady Gaga for her 2013 album, *Artpop*.

MOST POPULAR RINGTONES OF 2013

So, you like the song, you've downloaded it and viewed the video, and now the world can hear your tune of choice with every call you receive! These were 2013's top-rated...

#	Title	ARTIST(S)
01	CRUISE	FLORIDA GEORGIA LINE
02	THRIFT SHOP	MACKLEMORE & RYAN LEWIS FT. WANZ
03	BOYS 'ROUND HERE	BLAKE SHELTON FT. PISTOL ANNIES & FRIENDS
04	GANGNAM STYLE	PSY
05	BLURRED LINES	ROBIN THICKE FT. T.I. & PHARRELL
06	GIRL ON FIRE	ALICIA KEYS FT. NICKI MINAJ
07	WAGON WHEEL	DARIUS RUCKER FT. LADY ANTEBELLUM
08	JUST GIVE ME A REASON	P!NK FT. NATE RUESS
09	LOCKED OUT OF HEAVEN	BRUNO MARS
10	PONTOON	LITTLE BIG TOWN

DID YOU KNOW?

Finnish programmer Vesa-Matti Paananen was responsible for the first-ever ringtone service in 1997.

"LIKES"
83.5
MILLION

ADAM LEVINE

OFF THE **CHART**

Maroon 5 frontman Adam Levine has got a little way to go before he's eligible for this Top 10, with just 3,892,140 "Likes." His band is doing very well, though, with 29,159,660 "Likes"!

"LIKES"
3.8
MILLION

TOP 10

MOST FACEBOOK "LIKES" (SOLO ARTISTS)

We like LOADS of music artists, but which ones do you think Team T-10 "Like"? And which of the most popular 10 do you "Like"?

		"LIKES"	RELATIVE SCALE:	
01	RIHANNA	85,513,645		100%
02	SHAKIRA	83,512,638		98%
		82,575,456		97%
03	EMINEM	70,587,268		83%
04	MICHAEL JACKSON	64,436,345		75%
05	KATY PERRY	63,426,438		74%
		63,252,650		74%
06	JUSTIN BIEBER	56,981,410		67%
07	LADY GAGA	56,079,567		66%
		56,065,466		65%
08	BEYONCÉ			
09	SELENA GOMEZ			
10	BOB MARLEY			

X TREME FACT

SHAKIRA

Aside from her epic pop career, which began with her 1991 debut *Magia*—when she was only 14 years old—Columbian Shakira is also a judge on USA's *The Voice*. She featured in the 2012-13 fourth season, and in 2014, returned for the sixth season.

CHECK IT OUT!

Anneke van Giersbergen: the ever-awesome Dutch singer-songwriter has had a massive 15 career studio albums to date. These include five solo records, the latest album being 2013's *Drive*.

TOP 10

MOST AWESOME FEMALE ARTISTS EVER

THE T-10 UNOFFICIAL

01	TORI AMOS
02	NINA SIMONE
03	ANNEKE VAN GIERSBERGEN
04	PALOMA FAITH
05	JOAN ARMATRADING
06	IMOGEN HEAP
07	ALISON MOSSHART
08	BJÖRK
09	P!NK
10	JONI MITCHELL

XTREME FACT

ALISON MOSSHART

Alison really rocks, being the frontwoman of not one, but TWO bands: The Kills (with Kate Moss's husband Jamie Hince) and The Dead Weather (featuring Jack White and Queens Of The Stone Age's Dean Fertita).

TOP 10
GREATEST FRONTMEN OF ALL TIME

BAND

#	NAME	BAND
01	FREDDIE MERCURY	QUEEN
02	SIMON NEIL	BIFFY CLYRO
03	DAVE GROHL	FOO FIGHTERS
04	MATT BELLAMY	MUSE
05	DEVIN TOWNSEND	DEVIN TOWNSEND PROJECT
06	MIKE SHINODA & CHESTER BENNINGTON	LINKIN PARK
07	CHRIS CORNELL	SOUNDGARDEN
08	BRANDON BOYD	INCUBUS
09	JUSTIN HAWKINS	THE DARKNESS
10	EDDIE VEDDER	PEARL JAM

CHECK IT OUT!

Dave Grohl: he truly is rock royalty, being the drummer in Nirvana (1990-94), singer and guitarist in Foo Fighters (1994-present), AND he was Animool in *The Muppets* (2011)!

XTREME FACT

BRANDON BOYD

Eight studio albums with Incubus since 1995, frontman Brandon Boyd has also managed to produce some books, including: *White Fluffy Clouds: Found Inspiration Moving Forward* (2003), *From The Murks Of The Sultry Abyss* (2007), and *So The Echo* (2013).

"LIKES"
28.6
MILLION

MOST FACEBOOK "LIKES" (BANDS/GROUPS)

We've covered the solo stars, so let's not leave the music world's bands and groups out of the "Like" party...

"LIKES"

		"LIKES"
01	LINKIN PARK	60,087,783
02	BLACK EYED PEAS	47,659,958
03	THE BEATLES	39,205,625
04	METALLICA	35,252,313
05	GREEN DAY	32,760,495
06	LMFAO	32,618,325
07	COLDPLAY	32,073,875
08	MAROON 5	29,159,660
09	PARAMORE	28,609,466
10	AC/DC	28,515,579

"LIKES"
32.7
MILLION →

CHECK IT OUT!

Green Day: formed in 1987, the three-piece line-up of Billie Joe Armstrong (lead vocals, guitars), Mike Dirnt (bass guitar, vocals), and Tré Cool (drums, vocals) has remained unchanged since 1990. The band even adapted their 2004 album *American Idiot* into a stage musical that had 422 performances on Broadway between 2010-11.

TOP 10

HIGHEST EARNING SOLO ARTIST OF 2013

Dollar-dollar bills, y'all! Here are the solo stars from across every musical genre who "did quite well" in 2013...

		2013 EARNINGS ($)
01	MADONNA	
02	BRUCE SPRINGSTEEN	34,577,308
03	ROGER WATERS	33,443,606
04	KENNY CHESNEY	21,160,131
05	TIM MCGRAW	19,148,525
06	JASON ALDEAN	18,329,167
07	JUSTIN BIEBER	17,578,651
08	ADELE	15,944,293
09	CELINE DION	13,906,635
10	BRAD PAISLEY	12,927,494
		12,848,724

Source: Billboard

CHECK IT OUT!

Madonna: Madge has certainly not had what you'd call a lazy career... Some 12 studio albums, a crazy 77 singles, and music aside, Madonna has even managed to find the time to star in 19 movies, and direct a further two!

2013 EARNINGS **13.9** MILLION DOLLARS

2013 EARNINGS **34.5** MILLION DOLLARS

X TREME FACT

ADELE

Adele attended the UK's BRIT School for Performing Arts & Technology in Croydon. Other famous graduates of the school include Imogen Heap, Jessie J, Katie Melua, Leona Lewis, Amy Winehouse, and young actor Tom Holland.

XTREME FACT

COLDPLAY

Coldplay unveiled a brand new, non album song called *Atlas* on September 6, 2013, which was featured on *The Hunger Games: Catching Fire* soundtrack. Of the album's 12 songs, only Coldplay's and three others were featured in the movie.

2013 EARNINGS
9.47 MILLION DOLLARS

TOP 10 HIGHEST EARNING BANDS/GROUPS OF 2013

Prog-rock legends and indie darlings both did well in the biggest bucks' list of 2013...

		2013 EARNINGS ($)	RELATIVE SCALE:
01	VAN HALEN	20,184,709	100%
02	DAVE MATTHEWS BAND	18,903,334	94%
03	COLDPLAY	17,300,144	86%
04	LADY ANTEBELLUM	12,968,992	64%
05	NICKELBACK	11,121,419	55%
06	RASCAL FLATTS	10,777,282	53%
07	TRANS-SIBERIAN ORCHESTRA	9,959,362	49%
08	RED HOT CHILI PEPPERS	9,477,807	47%
09	THE ROLLING STONES	9,276,084	46%
10	RUSH	8,719,834	43%

Source: Billboard

STAT ATTACK

RED HOT CHILI PEPPERS

Formed	1983
Total studio albums	10
Total singles	46
Most famous song	*Under The Bridge* (1992)
Latest album	*I'm With You* (2011)

XTREME FACT

RED HOT CHILI PEPPERS

Heard of movie composer Cliff Martinez? Well, way before his Hollywood scoring success, he was the Red Hot Chili Peppers' original drummer, and is featured on the band's first two albums.

TOUR GROSSED 77.4 MILLION DOLLARS

Xtreme Fact

JUSTIN BIEBER

He may have had a successful 2013 *Believe* Tour, but many of his fans and their parents were not smiling... Bieber was two hours late on stage for a London show in March, and a crazy THREE hours late in July for Iowa's gig!

TOP 10 MOST SUCCESSFUL SOLO TOURS OF 2013

Pop stars of the world unite in this top 10! Here are the ones that made their bank managers the most happy in 2013...

		TOTAL SHOWS	TOTAL GROSS ($)
01	P!NK	114	147,947,543
02	RIHANNA	87	137,982,530
03	TAYLOR SWIFT	66	115,379,331
04	BEYONCÉ	59	104,358,899
05	KENNY CHESNEY	44	90,932,957
06	ROGER WATERS	27	81,305,650
07	JUSTIN BIEBER	65	77,423,264
08	MADONNA	16	76,752,277
09	PAUL McCARTNEY	21	69,584,403
10	ANDRÉ RIEU	70	49,983,266

10 QUICK FIRE FACTS

JUSTIN BIEBER

01	He was born March 1, 1994
02	He was born in London, Ontario, Canada
03	Can play the drums, piano, and guitar
04	Has released three albums since 2010
05	His 2011 Christmas album was *Under The Mistletoe*
06	Has won 135 international awards
07	In 2013, had a cameo appearance in *The Simpsons*
08	Appeared in Katy Perry's 2012 movie *Part Of Me*
09	Has made two concert movies, *Never Say Never* and *Believe*
10	Starred in two episodes of *CSI* in 2010 and 2011

CHECK IT OUT!

Iron Maiden: bassist Steve Harris started the band in 1975, and the UK metal gods are still going strong. Frontman Bruce Dickinson is even a qualified pilot, and has flown his band around the world on tour in their private plane!

TOUR GROSSED 44.9 MILLION DOLLARS

TOP 10 MOST SUCCESSFUL BAND/GROUP TOURS OF 2013

Countless acts tour our planet's venues every year. In 2013, these were the 10 that made the most...

		TOTAL SHOWS	TOTAL GROSS ($)
01	BON JOVI	90	205,158,370
02	BRUCE SPRINGSTEEN AND THE E STREET BAND	53	147,608,938
03	THE ROLLING STONES	23	126,182,391
04	DEPECHE MODE	54	99,972,733
05	ONE DIRECTION	81	78,311,383
06	JAY Z & JUSTIN TIMBERLAKE	14	69,753,905
07	FLEETWOOD MAC	45	61,899,473
08	MAROON 5	60	54,354,974
09	DAVE MATTHEWS BAND	61	52,960,667
10	IRON MAIDEN	34	44,980,749

X TREME FACT

KENNY CHESNEY

A true titan of American country music, Kenny Chesney has played a mammoth tour every consecutive year since 2001 to date. Across his 12 studio albums, singer Kenny has released 44 singles.

DID YOU KNOW?

Iron Maiden has won 22 of 32 international awards, including Metal Hammer's Best Event in 2012.

TOP 10 MOST SUCCESSFUL MUSIC BIOPICS

Some music stars have had Hollywood's finest portray them on the big screen...

01	WALK THE LINE
02	RAY
03	LA VIE EN ROSE
04	COAL MINER'S DAUGHTER
05	LA BAMBA
06	AMADEUS
07	THE SOLOIST
08	SHINE
09	SELENA
10	THE BUDDY HOLLY STORY

ABOUT THE LIFE OF...	YEAR	BOX OFFICE ($ WORLDWIDE)
JOHNNY CASH	2005	186,438,883
RAY CHARLES	2004	124,731,534
ÉDITH PIAF	2007	86,274,793
LORETTA LYNN	1980	67,182,787
RITCHIE VALENS	1987	54,215,416
MOZART	1984	51,973,029
NATHANIEL AYERS	2009	38,332,994
DAVID HELFGOTT	1996	35,892,330
SELENA QUINTANILLA	1997	35,281,794
BUDDY HOLLY	1978	14,363,400

Source: IMDB.com

BOX OFFICE 186.4 MILLION DOLLARS

XTREME FACT — WALK THE LINE

Based on the life and times of country star Johnny Cash, *Walk The Line* picked up 25 awards, including 14 Best Actress awards for co-star Reese Witherspoon as his second wife, June Carter Cash.

BOX OFFICE 124.7 MILLION DOLLARS

XTREME FACT — RAY

Tragically, rhythm and blues legend Ray Charles, whose life Jamie Foxx depicted, died in June 2004 (aged 73), just months before the movie's October release.

CHECK IT OUT!

Price Tag: the video for Jessie J's second single has had over 306 million views on her VEVO channel.

TOP 10 SONGS ABOUT MONEY

THE T-10 UNOFFICIAL

#	SONG	ARTIST(S)
01	DOLLARS & CENTS	RADIOHEAD
02	CAN'T BUY ME LOVE	THE BEATLES
03	MONEY (IN GOD WE TRUST)	EXTREME
04	PRICE TAG	JESSIE J
05	MONEYTALKS	AC/DC
06	RICH	YEAH YEAH YEAHS
07	MONEY, MONEY, MONEY	ABBA
08	I NEED A DOLLAR	ALOE BLACC
09	MONEY FOR NOTHING	DIRE STRAITS
10	MATERIAL GIRL	MADONNA

CHECK IT OUT!

Dollars & Cents: the eighth track on Radiohead's fifth album, *Amnesiac* (2001), is a record Team T-10 adore. Speaking of money, the album has sold in excess of 900,000 copies.

193

TOP 10 TOURS WITH THE MOST SHOWS THIS DECADE (SO FAR...)

This list has nothing to do with profits... It's about stamina! Here are the 10 artists who've rocked the most shows in their most successful tours, and P!nk is the overall champion...

#	Artist	TOUR	DATES	TOTAL SHOWS
01	ROGER WATERS	THE WALL LIVE	2010–13	219
02	LADY GAGA	THE MONSTER BALL	2009–11	201
03	METALLICA	WORLD MAGNETIC	2008–10	187
04	P!NK	FUNHOUSE/SUMMER CARNIVAL	2009–10	185
05	COLDPLAY	VIVA LA VIDA	2008–10	170
06	AC/DC	BLACK ICE	2008–10	168
07	EAGLES	LONG ROAD OUT OF EDEN	2008–11	161
08	P!NK	THE TRUTH ABOUT LOVE	2013–14	142
09	BRUCE SPRINGSTEEN AND THE E STREET BAND	WRECKING BALL	2012–13	133
10	U2	360°	2009–11	110

TOTAL SHOWS 170

CHECK IT OUT!

U2: during their nearly 40-year-long career, the Irish band has completed 14 major tours.

& ...ANOTHER THING!

U2 have not changed their line-up since the band first formed back in 1976!

XTREME FACT

COLDPLAY

This epic tour supported their 2008 album, *Viva La Vida Or Death And All His Friends*. Some of the opening acts on the tour included Jay Z, The Flaming Lips, and Elbow. The tour reached over 25 countries and included cities from Nashville to Barcelona.

TOTAL SHOWS 110

TOP 10

HIGHEST GROSSING BAND/GROUP TOURS OF THIS DECADE (SO FAR...)

There may be hundreds of new bands emerging each year, but it's still the classics that are cleaning up on the tour front...

		BAND/GROUP	DATES	GROSS ($ MILLIONS)	RELATIVE SCALE:
01	360°	U2	2009–11	736,421,584	100%
02	BLACK ICE	AC/DC	2008–10	441,121,000	60%
03	WRECKING BALL	BRUCE SPRINGSTEEN AND THE E STREET BAND	2012–13	355,600,000	48%
04	LONG ROAD OUT OF EDEN	EAGLES	2008–11	251,112,882	34%
05	WORLD MAGNETIC	METALLICA	2008–10	217,245,629	30%
06	THE CIRCLE	BON JOVI	2010	201,000,000	27%
07	PROGRESS LIVE	TAKE THAT	2011	185,175,360	25%
08	MYLO XYLOTO	COLDPLAY	2011–12	147,188,828	20%
09	BON JOVI LIVE	BON JOVI	2011	142,977,988	19%
10	VIVA LA VIDA	COLDPLAY	2008–2010	126,000,000	17%

GROSS 201 MILLION DOLLARS

CHECK IT OUT!

The Circle: across six legs, New Jersey rockers Bon Jovi spent almost all of 2010 playing 85 live shows. A glittering array of bands provided support slots, including Train, Fuel, and OneRepublic. Bon Jovi's setlist featured 25 songs from the band's 31-year-long and 12-album career.

HIGHEST GROSSING SOLO TOURS OF THIS DECADE (SO FAR...)

Some may think it's a man's world, but not so when it comes to solo tours! Check out the amazing women who appear TWICE in this Top 10...

#	Title	ARTIST	DATES	GROSS ($ MILLIONS)
01	THE WALL	ROGER WATERS	2010–13	458,673,798
02	MDNA	MADONNA	2012	305,158,363
03	THE MONSTER BALL	LADY GAGA	2009–11	227,400,000
04	THE MRS CARTER SHOW	BEYONCÉ	2013–14	188,600,000
05	BORN THIS WAY BALL	LADY GAGA	2012–13	181,100,000
06	THE TRUTH ABOUT LOVE	P!NK	2013–14	170,600,000
07	FUNHOUSE	P!NK	2009–10	149,278,271
08	DIAMONDS	RIHANNA	2013	140,118,252
09	RED	TAYLOR SWIFT	2013–14	131,000,000
10	SPEAK NOW	TAYLOR SWIFT	2011–12	123,101,131

GROSS **458** MILLION DOLLARS

XTREME FACT
THE WALL

Roger Waters, formerly of Pink Floyd, decided to tour his band's epic and beloved 1979 album again, with a 13-piece band backing him. *The Wall Live* was on the road for three years between September 2010 and September 2013, with the tour (costing $60 million) putting on 219 performances.

CHECK IT OUT!

Funhouse: Alecia Moore (better known as powerhouse pop-punkster P!nk) is the clear winner of solo tours between 2009 and 2014—both her smash hit tours total 327 shows!

XTREME FACT

THE MONSTER BALL

New Yorker Lady Gaga's (real name Stefani Joanne Angelina Germanotta) second global tour lasted 18 months, concluding May 6, 2011, after 201 shows.

GROSS 227 MILLION DOLLARS

CHECK IT OUT!

The Phantom Of The Opera: here's one of the most successful tenors on Broadway, Hugh Panaro (*right*). This is from *The Phantom Of The Opera*'s 25th anniversary performance, held at New York City's Majestic Theatre on January 26, 2013.

TOP 10 MOST SUCCESSFUL STAGE MUSICALS

Actors who can sing and dance and smash it live again and again? Yes, that is the amazing world of stage musicals! Combining the titan's of Broadway and London's West End, we've got...

		LONDON (UK) SHOWS	BROADWAY (USA) SHOWS	TOTAL
01	THE PHANTOM OF THE OPERA	11,000+	10,700	21,700+
02	LES MISÉRABLES	11,500+	6,680	18,180+
03	CATS	8,949	7,485	16,434
04	CHICAGO	6,187	7,100	13,287
05	THE LION KING	6,000+	6,700+	12,700+
06	BLOOD BROTHERS	10,013	839	10,852
07	MAMMA MIA!	5,700+	5,000+	10,700+
08	OH! CALCUTTA!	2,305	5,959	8,264
09	STARLIGHT EXPRESS	7,406	761	8,167
10	A CHORUS LINE	912	6,896	7,808

DID YOU KNOW?

Hugh Panaro (*above*) has over 55 stage credits to his name!

TOP 10 LARGEST FESTIVALS

The wall of sound. The atmosphere from the crowd and the environment. The food trucks that are EVERYWHERE. Yes, there is nothing like a music festival...

#	Festival	LOCATION	ATTENDANCE (PER DAY)
01	GLASTONBURY	UK	175,000
02	ROSKILDE	DENMARK	110,000
=	ROCK WERCHTER	BELGIUM	110,000
04	ROCK AL PARQUE	COLOMBIA	88,600
05	T IN THE PARK	SCOTLAND	85,000
06	EXIT	SERBIA	75,000
=	COACHELLA	USA	75,000
=	READING/LEEDS	UK	75,000
09	SZIGET	HUNGARY	65,000
10	PUKKELPOP	BELGIUM	62,500

XTREME FACT

GLASTONBURY

The popularity of the UK's Glastonbury Festival has been increasing rapidly over the past decade. The 2013 festival saw all of its 135,000 tickets sold in just one hour and 40 minutes—a new record!

ATTENDANCE PER DAY
175 THOUSAND

CHECK IT OUT!

Coachella: here's 2 Chainz at Coachella 2013. The festival featured more than 150 acts performing over two weekends, and tickets for the 2014 event sold out in less than three hours. This festival seriously rocks!

X-PLORE
DONAUINSELFEST

In a world where many of the major music festivals get more and more expensive each year, it's nice to know that the

Donauinselfest is FREE! This open-air music festival is held on Donauinsel, an island in Vienna, Austria. With visitors reaching the three million mark, more than 1,500 people volunteer to help run the event.

&... ANOTHER THING!

The island of Donauinsel is very long and VERY narrow... It's 13.1 mi (21.1 km) long and a maximum of 689 ft (210 m) across!

TOP 10
BEST FESTIVALS FROM AROUND THE WORLD

THE T-10 UNOFFICIAL

		LOCATION
01	COACHELLA	USA
02	DOWNLOAD	UK
03	MASTERS OF ROCK	CZECH REPUBLIC
04	SOUNDWAVE	AUSTRALIA
05	SUMMER SONIC	JAPAN
06	DONAUINSELFEST	AUSTRIA
07	RHYTHM & VINES	NEW ZEALAND
08	LAKE OF STARS	AFRICA
09	WORLD DJ	SOUTH KOREA
10	CASTLE PALOOZA	IRELAND

XTREME FACT
DOWNLOAD

The first ever Download Festival was held in 2003, in the same Donington Park motorsport circuit location where the Monsters Of Rock festival ran from 1980 to 1996. Linkin Park performed their 2000 debut album *Hybrid Theory* in full at Download 2014.

YOUR SHOUT

This section of the book is dedicated to testing you on the sights and stats of the music world...

YOUR PICK OF THE... MUSIC

It's over to you now... Fill this chart up with your ultimate top 10 music-related likes!

01
02
03
04
05
06
07
08
09
10

ROUND 1: MULTIPLE CHOICE

01 The most downloaded song of all time is the Black Eyed Peas' *I Gotta Feeling*, but how many units has it sold?

A 6,739,000
B 8,438,000
C 12,482,000

02 The Lumineers' smash hit of 2013 was the most played pop song of the year. Can you name the track?

A HO HEY
B I WILL WAIT
C CATCH MY BREATH

03 Which pop act tops our Most Subscribed Vevo Channel with over 12 million followers?

A EMINEM
B ONE DIRECTION
C RIHANNA

ROUND 2: QUESTION TIME

01 Which material girl has spent over 30 years in the music business, had 12 studio albums, 77 singles, been involved in 21 movies... And earned the most money among her peers in 2013?

ANSWER:

ROUND 3:
PICTURE PUZZLES

Can you tell us who this hairdo belongs to? It's almost as tall as the Empire State building!

01

ANSWER:

Which multimillion-selling metal band do these guitar-shredding arms play for?

02

ANSWER:

Name this popular floor-shaking DJ that had the most streamed song of 2013...

03

ANSWER:

ROUND 4:
WORDSEARCH

Check out the jumbled letters on the left and then see how many of these music artists you can find:

```
A S D A C I L L A T E M
H D I D B H S E F Z J A
C I R I H A N N A E R G
B M E A D V B E W N I R
B I X I K A V M F E N C
U G C E W E G I N A P J
I U O A D V N N A F P J
A E T D Y U I E S A S D
Z L A E A S E M U M Y B
C D E L T Y U O E A D F
I F E E C N O Y E B T Y
A D H E R T B M A F H O
```

EMINEM

DRAKE

BEYONCE

RIHANNA

METALLICA

ADELE

MIGUEL

PSY

FIND THE ANSWERS ON PAGE 313

02 Can you name the star that had the hit, *Just Give Me A Reason* with Nate Ruess *(right)* in 2013? The song had over 225,000 hits...

03 Can you name Justin Timberlake's album that sits at number one in our Top 10 Biggest Selling Albums of 2013 list?

ANSWER:

MUSIC
CAREER QUIZ

In which of these locations would you most like to live?

- ☐ **A BY A BEACH**
- ☐ **B ON A RANCH**
- ☐ **C IN A CITY**

Who would you rather hang out with?

- ☐ **A JUSTIN TIMBERLAKE**
- ☐ **B WILL.I.AM**
- ☐ **C SIMON COWELL**

Which of these would you rather get as a gift?

- ☐ **A A MICROPHONE**
- ☐ **B HEADPHONES**
- ☐ **C A TABLET DEVICE**

If your single got to number one, what would you do?

- ☐ **A THROW A HUGE PARTY WITH ALL YOUR FRIENDS**
- ☐ **B START THINKING ABOUT THE SECOND SINGLE**
- ☐ **C POST A TWEET AND FACEBOOK COMMENT**

What is the best thing about a party?

- ☐ **A THE KARAOKE**
- ☐ **B PLANNING IT**
- ☐ **C DESIGNING THE INVITES**

When do you feel most comfortable?

- ☐ **A WHEN I'M ON STAGE**
- ☐ **B WORKING BEHIND A DESK**
- ☐ **C WHEN I HAVE LOTS OF PEOPLE AROUND**

Which of the following statements best fits you?

- ☐ **A I LOVE PERFORMING**
- ☐ **B MY MP3 PLAYER IS ALWAY ON**
- ☐ **C I'M VERY SOCIABLE**

Find out which music-related job is best suited to you on page 313

EPIC STRUCTURES

1354541
35,2/2,145432?3
455892698/4-4545425
633363-535398
4533693-565
12538541-15862
8632863-5565
248-1553-45435-4534354
42-4584337-4156456
561-5445641-1545
5143511-4564
2134-3434-4545433
12128415-455
54935-62798514
785456-45641
15668412r5-48485555451l
14561561S-1567897
89756132-48781415213
15863-4552255862
1553055055-5
42377802-4545435
5345435-4534354
42-4584337-4156456
5645445641-1545

TOP 10 FASTEST ROLLER COASTERS

Calling all speed-freaks out there! These are the fastest roller coasters on the planet, so start planning your visits now to experience acceleration like never before...

		LOCATION	TOP SPEED (KPH)	TOP SPEED (MPH)
01	FORMULA ROSSA	Ferrari World (United Arab Emirates)	240	149
02	KINGDA KA	Six Flags Great Adventure (USA)	206	128
03	TOP THRILL DRAGSTER	Cedar Point (USA)	190	118
04	DODONPA	Fuji-Q Highland (Japan)	172	107
05	RING°RACER	Nürburgring (Germany)	169	105
06	TOWER OF TERROR II	Dreamworld (Australia)	167	104
=	SUPERMAN: ESCAPE FROM KRYPTON	Six Flags Magic Mountain (USA)	167	104
08	STEEL DRAGON 2000	Nagashima Spa Land (Japan)	153	95
09	MILLENNIUM FORCE	Cedar Point (USA)	150	93
10	LEVIATHAN	Canada's Wonderland (Canada)	148	92

CHECK IT OUT!

Kingda Ka: not only is this the world's second fastest roller coaster, it is also the king of heights, being the tallest roller coaster ever built. At a staggering 456 ft (139 m) high, this steel beast gives 18 brave riders (each run) a drop of 417 ft (127 m).

SPEED 107 MPH

XTREME FACT
DODONPA

Every hour, 1,000 strong-stomached thrill-seekers make their way around the 3,901 ft (1,189 m) of Dodonpa's track for a super-intense 55 seconds.

SPEED 128 MPH

STAT ATTACK
KINGDA KA

First opened.......................May 21, 2005
Designer.............Werner Stengel (Germany)
Ride theme.............Giant mythical tiger
Duration.................................50.6 sec
Length.........................3,118 ft (950 m)

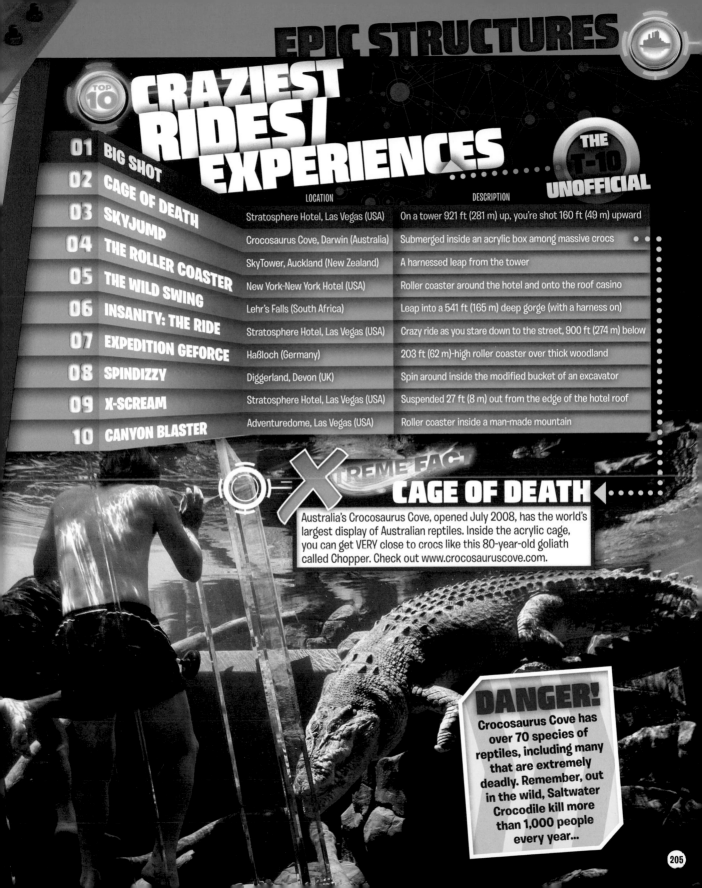

TOP 10 CRAZIEST RIDES/ EXPERIENCES

THE T-10 UNOFFICIAL

#		LOCATION	DESCRIPTION
01	BIG SHOT	Stratosphere Hotel, Las Vegas (USA)	On a tower 921 ft (281 m) up, you're shot 160 ft (49 m) upward
02	CAGE OF DEATH	Crocosaurus Cove, Darwin (Australia)	Submerged inside an acrylic box among massive crocs
03	SKYJUMP	SkyTower, Auckland (New Zealand)	A harnessed leap from the tower
04	THE ROLLER COASTER	New York-New York Hotel (USA)	Roller coaster around the hotel and onto the roof casino
05	THE WILD SWING	Lehr's Falls (South Africa)	Leap into a 541 ft (165 m) deep gorge (with a harness on)
06	INSANITY: THE RIDE	Stratosphere Hotel, Las Vegas (USA)	Crazy ride as you stare down to the street, 900 ft (274 m) below
07	EXPEDITION GEFORCE	Haßloch (Germany)	203 ft (62 m)-high roller coaster over thick woodland
08	SPINDIZZY	Diggerland, Devon (UK)	Spin around inside the modified bucket of an excavator
09	X-SCREAM	Stratosphere Hotel, Las Vegas (USA)	Suspended 27 ft (8 m) out from the edge of the hotel roof
10	CANYON BLASTER	Adventuredome, Las Vegas (USA)	Roller coaster inside a man-made mountain

XTREME FACT
CAGE OF DEATH

Australia's Crocosaurus Cove, opened July 2008, has the world's largest display of Australian reptiles. Inside the acrylic cage, you can get VERY close to crocs like this 80-year-old goliath called Chopper. Check out www.crocosauruscove.com.

DANGER!

Crocosaurus Cove has over 70 species of reptiles, including many that are extremely deadly. Remember, out in the wild, Saltwater Crocodile kill more than 1,000 people every year...

BIGGEST ROLLER COASTER DROPS

If you love these theme park rides, you'll know that feeling when the coaster peaks before it plummets down! These are the highest roller-drops...

#	Ride	LOCATION	HIGHEST DROP (M)	(FT)
01	KINGDA KA	Six Flags Great Adventure (USA)	127.4	418
02	TOP THRILL DRAGSTER	Cedar Point (USA)	121.9	400
03	TOWER OF TERROR II	Dreamworld (Australia)	100	328
04	SUPERMAN: ESCAPE FROM KRYPTON	Six Flags Magic Mountain (USA)	100	328
05	STEEL DRAGON 2000	Nagashima Spa Land (Japan)	93.6	307
06	LEVIATHAN	Canada's Wonderland (Canada)	93.3	306
07	INTIMIDATOR 305	King's Dominion (USA)	91.4	300
=	MILLENNIUM FORCE	Cedar Point (USA)	91.4	300
09	SHAMBHALA	PortAventura (Spain)	78	256
10	GOLIATH	Six Flags Magic Mountain (USA)	77.7	255

CHECK IT OUT!

Steel Dragon 2000: costing more than $50 million, here is a photo of Steel Dragon's highest point. It's also the tallest roller coaster in the world to still use a traditional chain-lift system.

THE T-10 UNOFFICIAL

COOLEST RIDES

#	Ride	THEME PARK	LOCATION
01	REVENGE OF THE MUMMY	Universal Studios Hollywood	California (USA)
02	WONDER MOUNTAIN'S GUARDIAN	Canada's Wonderland	Ontario (Canada)
03	JURASSIC PARK	Universal Studios Hollywood	California (USA)
04	WIZARDING WORLD OF HARRY POTTER	Universal Orlando Resort	Florida (USA)
05	BUZZSAW	Dreamworld	Queensland (Australia)
06	SPACE MOUNTAIN	Disneyland Park	California (USA)
07	THE SMILER	Alton Towers Resort	Staffordshire (UK)
08	STAR TOURS – THE ADVENTURES CONTINUE	Disneyland Park	California (USA)
09	THE TWILIGHT ZONE TOWER OF TERROR	Disney California Adventure Park	California (USA)
10	TRANSFORMERS: THE RIDE	Universal Studios Hollywood	California (USA)

XTREME FACT

THE TWILIGHT ZONE TOWER OF TERROR

This ride is based on the iconic TV series *The Twilight Zone* that first aired way back in 1959. Versions of the ride exist in four locations, including Tokyo, Japan.

EPIC STRUCTURES

MOST POPULAR THEME PARKS

TOP 10

We all love to spend time with our family and friends at adventure parks, but these are the 10 that are visited the most each year...

#	Park	LOCATION	ANNUAL ATTENDANCE
01	**MAGIC KINGDOM** (Walt Disney World Resort)	Lake Buena Vista, Florida (USA)	17,536,000
02	**DISNEYLAND** (Disneyland Resort Anaheim)	California (USA)	15,963,000
03	**TOKYO DISNEYLAND**	Tokyo (Japan)	14,847,000
04	**TOKYO DISNEYSEA**	Tokyo (Japan)	12,656,000
05	**DISNEYLAND PARK** (Disneyland Paris)	Marne-la-Vallée (France)	11,200,000
06	**EPCOT** (Walt Disney World Resort)	Lake Buena Vista, Florida (USA)	11,063,000
07	**DISNEY'S ANIMAL KINGDOM** (Walt Disney World Resort)	Lake Buena Vista, Florida (USA)	9,998,000
08	**DISNEY'S HOLLYWOOD STUDIOS** (Walt Disney World Resort)	Lake Buena Vista, Florida (USA)	9,912,000
09	**UNIVERSAL STUDIOS JAPAN**	Osaka (Japan)	9,700,000
10	**ISLANDS OF ADVENTURE** (Universal Orlando Resort)	Orlando, Florida (USA)	7,981,000

XTREME FACT

ISLANDS OF ADVENTURE

Universal's Islands Of Adventure features this Incredible Hulk Coaster. It goes 67 mph (108 kph), but before you experience the 2 min 15 sec thrill-ride, you line-up inside Bruce Banner's lab!

CHECK IT OUT!

Tokyo Disneyland: this opened on April 15, 1983. Its 115 acres of awesomeness are spread across seven lands: World Bazaar, Adventureland, Westernland, Critter Country, Fantasyland, Toontown, and Tomorrowland. Tokyo-tastic!

ANNUAL ATTENDANCE
7.98 MILLION

X TREME FACT

MICHIGAN STADIUM

Although "The Big House" (as it's known) opened in 1927, a massive renovation scheme took place in 2010 that cost $226 million.

CAPACITY
109,901

TOP 10 BIGGEST INNER CITY STADIUMS

These amazing structures are purpose-built to bring us live sport and music on a massive scale, with hundreds of thousands of seats and giant-sized screens....

X TREME FACT

ESTADIO AZTECA

Estadio Azteca took four years to build, largely due to the extremely hard volcanic rock that the land is made of. It's 9.3 mi (15 km) south of Mexico City.

		LOCATION	CAPACITY
01	RUNGNADO MAY DAY STADIUM	Pyongyang (North Korea)	150,000
02	SALT LAKE STADIUM	Kolkata (India)	120,000
03	MICHIGAN STADIUM	Michigan (USA)	109,901
04	BEAVER STADIUM	Pennsylvania (USA)	106,572
05	ESTADIO AZTECA	Mexico City (Mexico)	105,000
06	NEYLAND STADIUM	Tennessee (USA)	102,455
07	OHIO STADIUM	Ohio (USA)	102,329
08	BRYANT-DENNY STADIUM	Alabama (USA)	101,821
09	DARRELL K ROYAL - TEXAS MEMORIAL STADIUM	Austin (Texas)	100,119
10	MELBOURNE CRICKET GROUND	Victoria (Australia)	100,018

TOP 10 MOST AWESOME SKATEPARKS

THE T-10 UNOFFICIAL

		LOCATION
01	MARSEILLE SKATEPARK	Marseille (France)
02	SOUTHBANK UNDERCROFT	London (UK)
03	SMP SKATEPARK	Shanghai (China)
04	SPRING TEXAS SKATEPARK	Texas (USA)
05	VANCOUVER SKATE PLAZA	Vancouver (Canada)
06	NORTH BRIGADE SKATEPARK	Cologne (Germany)
07	MICROPOLIS SKATEPARK	Helsinki (Finland)
08	LIVINGSTON SKATEPARK	Livingston, Scotland (UK)
09	JINDALEE SKATEPARK	Queensland (Australia)
10	VENICE SKATEPARK	California (USA)

XTREME FACT

SOUTHBANK UNDERCROFT

London's Southbank Undercroft, next to the River Thames, has seen skateboarders and BMXers honing their skills for 35 years. In 2012, plans were proposed to demolish the culturally historic area and turn it into stores. As of 2014, the site remains one of the UK's best and most loved skateparks.

▶CHECK IT OUT!

Venice Skatepark: what a place to skate—on a beach, just a stone's throw from the Pacific Ocean! Aside from the deep "pool" sections, there are plenty of steps and rails, with easier sections for beginners.

STAT ATTACK

VENICE SKATEPARK

Location........Venice Beach, California (USA)
Opened...........................March 2009
Cost ....$2 million
Website............www.veniceskatepark.com
Web features...........Live camera feed

TOP 10 FASTEST WATER SLIDES

There's no better way to cool off than a dip in a pool... And nothing more fun than to end up in one via the world's fastest slides!

		COUNTRY	TOP SPEED (KPH)	(MPH)
01	VERRÜCKT	USA	125.5	78
02	INSANO	Brazil	105	65.2
03	SPACEMAKER	Italy	100	62.1
04	KILIMANJARO	Brazil	91	56.5
05	SUMMIT PLUMMET	USA	89	55.3
06	JUMEIRAH SCEIRAH	United Arab Emirates	80	49.7
=	POWER TOWER	USA	80	49.7
08	CLIFFHANGER	USA	56.3	35
09	SCORPION'S TAIL	USA	54.9	34.1
10	WILDEBEEST	USA	39.5	24.5

OFF THE CHART

WAIMAUKU WATER SLIDE

Not the fastest, but the longest at 2,132.5 ft (650 m)! It was made in Waimauku, Auckland (New Zealand) on February 23, 2013, by Jimi Hunt and Dan Drupstee so 2,000 people could slide down it for charity (www.livemoreawesome.com).

TOP 10 BIGGEST CINEMA SCREENS EVER

All of Team T-10 are obsessed with movies, so imagine how quickly our jaws hit the floor when we discovered these Godzilla-sized cinema screens...

		LOCATION	TOTAL AREA (M²)	(FT²)
01	LOVELL RADIO TELESCOPE*	Cheshire (UK)	4,560.367	49,087
02	NOKIA N8* (PROJECTED)	Malmö (Sweden)	1,428	15,371
03	PINEWOOD STUDIOS*	Middlesex (UK)	1,337.73	14,399
04	IMAX DARLING HARBOUR	Sydney (Australia)	1,056.24	11,369
05	IMAX MELBOURNE	Melbourne (Australia)	736	7,922.2
06	OSLO SPEKTRUM*	Oslo (Norway)	676	7,273.2
07	TOKYO DOME	Tokyo (Japan)	647	6,970
08	MEYDAN IMAX	Dubai (United Arab Emirates)	638	6,867.4
09	PRASADS IMAX	Hyderabad (India)	635.46	6,840
10	HOYTS SYLVIA PARK CINEMA	Auckland (New Zealand)	376.57	4,053.4

*Temporary screen erected for one-night event.

XTREME FACT

LOVELL RADIO TELESCOPE*

On October 5, 2007, cinematic history was made when the Lovell Radio Telescope got turned into a movie screen—the biggest EVER! The event was to celebrate the 50th anniversary of the telescope, and moving images of space exploration were projected on to it, along with a laser show.

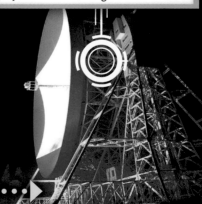

TOP 10 BIGGEST AQUARIUMS

Exploring, studying, and learning from the wonders of the marine world can be incredibly important, as long as the oceanic life is given the right conditions...

#		COUNTRY	TOTAL WATER (MILLIONS)	
			(L)	(US GAL)
01	GEORGIA AQUARIUM	USA	23.85	6.3
02	DUBAI AQUARIUM & UNDERWATER ZOO	UAE	10	2.64
03	OKINAWA CHURAUMI AQUARIUM	Japan	7.5	1.98
04	THE OCEANOGRÀFIC OF THE CITY OF ARTS AND SCIENCES	Spain	7	1.85
05	TURKUAZOO	Turkey	5	1.32
06	MONTEREY BAY AQUARIUM	USA	4.54	1.2
07	USHAKA MARINE WORLD	South Africa	3.71	0.98
08	SHANGHAI OCEAN AQUARIUM	China	3.48	0.92
09	AQUARIUM OF GENOA	Italy	3.29	0.87
10	THE AQUARIUM OF WESTERN AUSTRALIA	Australia	3.03	0.8

XTREME FACT

OKINAWA CHURA AQUARIUM

This massive aquarium opened on November 1, 2002. It features 65,000 aquatic creatures! There are 650 different species on display, including the biggest of all the sharks, the majestic plankton-eating Whale Shark.

WATER 1.98 MILLION US GAL

CHECK IT OUT!

Georgia Aquarium: some 120,000 creatures are studied and observed by visitors to the Atlanta attraction. It is heavily involved with several conservation and research initiatives.

TOP 10

MOST POPULAR ART MUSEUMS

Art in all its forms can teach us so much, and make us experience a wealth of emotions. Of all the art museums in the world, these received the most visitors...

		LOCATION	ANNUAL VISITORS (MILLIONS)
01	THE PALACE MUSEUM	Beijing (China)	15.3
02	THE LOUVRE	Paris (France)	9.7
03	METROPOLITAN MUSEUM OF ART	New York (USA)	6.1
04	THE BRITISH MUSEUM	London (UK)	5.6
05	TATE MODERN	London (UK)	5.3
06	THE NATIONAL GALLERY	London (UK)	5.2
07	VATICAN MUSEUMS	Vatican City (Italy)	5.1
08	NATIONAL PALACE MUSEUM	Taipei (Taiwan)	4.4
09	NATIONAL GALLERY OF ART	Washington DC (USA)	4.2
10	CENTRE POMPIDOU	Paris (France)	3.8

XTREME FACT
LOUVRE

The Louvre is one of the most famous buildings in France. Centuries before it became a museum (in 1793), the Louvre Palace was a fortress used by Philip II way, way back in the 12th century.

TOP 10

MOST EXPENSIVE PUBLIC ART DISPLAYS

THE T-10 UNOFFICIAL

		ARTIST(S)	LOCATION	COST ($)
01	THE MASTABA	Christo & Jeanne-Claude	Al Gharbia, Abu Dhabi (United Arab Emirates)	340 MILLION
02	THE GATES	Christo & Jeanne-Claude	Central Park, New York (USA)	21 MILLION
03	NEW YORK CITY WATERFALLS	Olafur Eliasson	New York (USA)	15.5 MILLION
04	YOUR RAINBOW PANORAMA	Olafur Eliasson	Aarhus (Denmark)	10.7 MILLION
05	PHX SKY TRAIN PROJECT	Various	Sky Train, Phoenix Airport, Arizona (USA)	5.6 MILLION
06	MAMAN	Louise Bourgeois	Ottawa (Canada)	3.2 MILLION
07	MUTE MEADOW	Vong Phaophanit & Claire Oboussier	Derry/Londonderry (N Ireland)	1.6 MILLION
08	ANGEL OF THE NORTH	Antony Gormley	Gateshead, Tyne and Wear (UK)	1 MILLION
09	ASCALON	Marcus Canning & Christian de Vietri	Perth (Australia)	500,000
10	RADIUS	Ed Carpenter	Ann Arbor, Michigan (USA)	150,000

XTREME FACT
NEW YORK CITY WATERFALLS

Danish artist Olafur Eliasson's impressive waterfalls installation was in full flow every day between 7 am and 10 pm, from June 26 to October 13, in 2008.

CHECK IT OUT!

Angel Of The North: at a staggering 66 ft (20 m) tall, with outstretched 177 ft (54 m) wings, British artist Antony Gormley's steel Angel is a stunning sight to behold.

TOP 10 BIZARRE BUILDINGS IN ANIMATION

THE T-10 UNOFFICIAL

	FROM	PRODUCTION TYPE	YEAR(S) OF RELEASE
01 HOWL'S MOVING CASTLE	*Howl's Moving Castle*	Movie	**2004**
02 THE CAT'S LAIR	*ThunderCats*	TV series	**1985–89, 2011–12**
03 VICTOR'S HOME	*Frankenweenie*	Movie	**2012**
04 PLANET EXPRESS HQ	*Futurama*	TV series	**1999–2013**
05 SYNDROME'S LAIR	*The Incredibles*	Movie	**2004**
06 THE BATHHOUSE	*Spirited Away*	Movie	**2001**
07 MR. BURNS' MANOR	*The Simpsons*	TV series/movie	**1987–PRESENT**
08 THE CASTLE IN THE SKY	*Laputa: Castle In The Sky*	Movie	**1986**
09 THE BANANA CABANA	*Almost Naked Animals*	TV series	**2011–PRESENT**
10 CARL'S FLYING HOME	*Up*	Movie	**2009**

CHECK IT OUT!

Howl's moving castle *(above)*: Japanese filmmakers Studio Ghibli adapted this from the novel *Howl's Moving Castle* (1986) by English writer Diana Wynne Jones. When Ghibli films are released in the West, well-known actors provide the English-language dialogue. Howl is voiced by none other than Christian "Batman" Bale!

NUMBER OF LEGO BRICKS
5.3 MILLION

MAGNIFICATION

X TREME FACT

X-WING FIGHTER

Here it is in all its 5,335,200 LEGO-piece glory! This most excellent *Star Wars* X-Wing Starfighter was built in the LEGO model shop in Kladno, Czechoslovakia, and carefully transported for display in Times Square, New York City (USA).

TOP 10

BIGGEST LEGO STRUCTURES IN THE WORLD

Did you know that Team T-10 used to work with The LEGO Company many moons ago? Now you do! Here are the constructions that feature the most bricks used ever...

		LOCATION	YEAR	(M/M²)	SIZE (FT/FT²)	NUMBER OF LEGO BRICKS
01	AIRCRAFT: X-WING STARFIGHTER	New York (USA)	2013	13.44	44 (Wingspan)	5,335,200
02	PLACE: AMOSKEAG MILLYARD	New Hampshire (USA)	2006	204²	2,200² (Area)	3,000,000
03	INSECT: MILLIPEDE MADE BY 20,000 CHILDREN	Bangkok (Thailand)	2003	1,052	3,451 (Length)	2,477,140
04	CHAIN: LONG CHAIN OF LEGO	Prague (Czech Republic)	1998	578	1,896.3 (Length)	1,500,834
05	STATUE: SITTING BULL	LEGOLAND Billund (Denmark)	1974	7.6	24.93 (Height)	1,500,000
06	CASTLE: WITH 2,100 MINIFIGURE RESIDENTS	Museum in Ohio (USA)	2008	12.2	40 (Length)	1,400,000
07	FACADE: SCHOOL/CHILDREN'S FACILITY	London (UK)	2010	250²	2,691² (Area)	1,263,801
08	PICTURE: TRACTOR TRAILER IMAGE	Museum in Ohio (USA)	2007	85.84²	924² (Area)	1,200,000
09	TOWER: BUILT BY 1,800 VOLUNTEERS	Limmen (The Netherlands)	2010	30.52	100.13 (Height)	700,000+
10	CAR: SUPER-SIZED TECHNIC CAR	Chicago (USA)	1996	4.75	15.6 (Length)	650,000

OFF THE CHART

LEGO TOWER IN PRAGUE

This is an impressive 106.6 ft (32.5 m)-tall tower made in Prague, Czech Republic, on Sept 8, 2012. It was created using an amazing 450,000 LEGO bricks.

MOST LEGO BRICKS IN A MODEL SET

TOP 10

Now you've seen those insanely large LEGO constructions, here are the Top 10 biggest LEGO sets that you can actually buy and build yourself...

		YEAR RELEASED	NUMBER OF LEGO BRICKS
01	TAJ MAHAL	2008	5,922
02	STAR WARS: ULTIMATE COLLECTOR'S MILLENNIUM FALCON	2007	5,197
03	TOWER BRIDGE	2010	4,287
04	STAR WARS: DEATH STAR	2008	3,803
05	STAR WARS: DEATH STAR II	2005	3,449
06	EIFFEL TOWER	2007	3,428
07	GRAND CAROUSEL	2009	3,263
08	STAR WARS: ULTIMATE COLLECTOR'S SUPER STAR DESTROYER	2011	3,152
09	STAR WARS: ULTIMATE COLLECTOR'S IMPERIAL STAR DESTROYER	2002	3,096
10	STATUE OF LIBERTY	2000	2,882

10 QUICK FIRE FACTS

LEGO

01	Use to have a magazine called *LEGO Adventures*
02	Began making the bricks in 1949
03	Invented by Ole Kirk Christiansen
04	560 billion LEGO pieces have been made
05	HQ is based in Billund, Denmark
06	Comes from the Danish "leg godt" = "play well"
07	*The LEGO Movie* was released February 1, 2014...
08	...and took $69,050,279 on its US opening weekend
09	*The LEGO Movie 2* is set for a 2017 release
10	Official website is www.LEGO.com

NUMBER OF LEGO BRICKS
35 THOUSAND

OFF THE CHART

STAR WARS: REBEL ATTACK CRUISER

This very special LEGO model of a *Star Wars* Rebel Attack Cruiser was built by LEGO Master Builder Erik Varszegi, using 35,000 bricks. A one time project, it measured 8 ft (2.45 m) long, and was certified by *Star Wars* creator George Lucas. In Dec 2005, it raised $32,602 for Habitat for Humanity International's Hurricane Relief Efforts.

TOP 10

TALLEST BUILDINGS

As technology improves, architects seem to be getting more and more adventurous with buildings, especially with height! There are some HUGE new entries in this Top 10...

		LOCATION	YEAR COMPLETED	FLOORS	HEIGHT (M)	HEIGHT (FT)
01	SKY CITY	China	2014	202	838	2,749
02	BURJ KHALIFA	United Arab Emirates	2010	163	828	2,717
03	SHANGHAI TOWER	China	2014	128	632	2,073
04	MAKKAH ROYAL CLOCK TOWER HOTEL	Saudi Arabia	2012	120	601	1,972
05	LOTTE WORLD TOWER	South Korea	2015	123	555	1,821
06	ONE WORLD TRADE CENTER	USA	2014	104	541	1,775
07	TAIPEI 101	Taiwan	2004	101	508	1,666
08	SHANGHAI WORLD FINANCIAL CENTER	China	2008	101	492	1,614
09	INTERNATIONAL COMMERCE CENTER	China	2010	108	484	1,588
10	PETRONAS TWIN TOWERS	Malaysia	1998	88	452	1,483

Source: Council on Tall Buildings and Urban Habitat

HEIGHT 1,775 FT

XTREME FACT

ONE WORLD TRADE CENTER

This building ($3.9 billion) opened in 2014. It was part of a rebuild and a memorial scheme to remember the lives of those lost from the attacks and destruction of the World Trade Towers on September 11, 2001.

XTREME FACT

SHANGHAI TOWER

Construction began on this $2.2 billon tower back on November 29, 2008. It stands in Lujiazui, in the Pudong region of Shanghai, which is one of the main financial districts.

CHECK IT OUT!

Shanghai World Financial Center: After 11 years of construction, and a total cost $1.2 billion, the Shanghai World Financial Center opened its new doors in 2008.

TOP 10 LARGEST PRIVATE RESIDENTS

When money is no object, the house you decide to make your home can end up being outrageously massive...

		LOCATION	OWNER	OWNER'S OCCUPATION	SIZE (M²)	(FT²)
01	BILTMORE HOUSE	North Carolina (USA)	William AV Cecil	Owner, The Biltmore Company	16,623	178,928
02	OHEKA CASTLE	New York (USA)	Gary Melius	Developer	10,126	109,000
03	FAIRFIELD	New York (USA)	Ira Rennert	Investor	6,168.3	66,395
04	XANADU 2.0	Washington (USA)	Bill Gates	Co-founder, Microsoft	6,131.6	66,000
05	MAISON DE L'AMITIE	Florida (USA)	Dmitry Rybolovlev	Owner, AS Monaco Soccer Club	5,739	61,774
06	51 WINDING BROOK DRIVE	New York (USA)	John Breyo	Founder/Former CEO, Ayco Co	5,704.5	61,403
07	ESCHMAN MEADOWS	Ohio (USA)	Tami Longaberger	The Longaberger Company	5,295.5	57,000
08	THE MANOR	California (USA)	Petra Ecclestone	Model/Fashion designer	5,249	56,501
09	WALKER McCUNE MANSION	Arizona (USA)	Hormel family	Hormel Foods Corporation	4,905.3	52,800
10	7 MONTAGEL WAY	Alabama (USA)	Larry House	Former CEO, MedPartners	4,645.2	50,001

XTREME FACT

BILTMORE HOUSE

Biltmore House's 8,000-acre estate is teeming with antiquities, including Napoleon's famous chess set and original Renoir paintings. It was built by art collector George Washington Vanderbilt II (Nov 14, 1862–Mar 6, 1914).

STAT ATTACK

BILTMORE HOUSE

Built	1889-95
Architect	Richard Morris Hunt
Rooms	250
Opened to the public	March 1930
National historic landmark	Since 1964

MOST EXPENSIVE BRIDGES

They may help us travel with ease across rivers, chasms, or simply built-up areas, but they cost a LOT of money...

		LOCATION	COST ($ BILLIONS)
01	HONSHŪ-SHIKOKU BRIDGE PROJECT (17 BRIDGES)	Japan	48
02	STRAIT OF MESSINA BRIDGE*	Italy	8.6
03	SAN FRANCISCO-OAKLAND BAY BRIDGE	USA	6.3
04	ØRESUND BRIDGE	Denmark/Sweden	5.7
05	AKASHI-KAIKYŌ BRIDGE	Japan	5
06	NEW INTERNATIONAL TRADE CROSSING	USA/Canada	2.2
07	JIAOZHOU BAY BRIDGE	China	1.5
08	DURANGO-MAZATLÁN HIGHWAY & BALUARTE BRIDGE	Mexico	1.46
09	INCHEON BRIDGE	South Korea	1.4
10	VASCO DA GAMA BRIDGE	Portugal	1.3

*To be completed by 2016

LONGEST FOOTBRIDGES

Walking is not just a fantastic way to keep physically fit, it also calms the mind. So a walk across these super-long bridges would be fun and very good for you...

		LOCATION	LENGTH (M)	(FT)
01	POUGHKEEPSIE BRIDGE	Poughkeepsie, New York (USA)	2,060	6,758
02	CHAIN OF ROCKS BRIDGE	Mississippi River (USA)	1,632	5,354
03	SHELBY STREET BRIDGE	Tennessee (USA)	960	3,150
04	HŌRAI BRIDGE	Shizuoka Prefecture (Japan)	897.4	2,944
05	NEWPORT SOUTHBANK BRIDGE	Ohio River (USA)	813.8	2,670
06	KURILPA BRIDGE	Queensland (Australia)	470	1,542
07	MILLENNIUM BRIDGE	London (UK)	370	1,214
08	ESPLANADE RIEL	Manitoba (Canada)	197	646.3
09	WILLIMANTIC FOOTBRIDGE	Connecticut (USA)	193.6	635
10	DAVENPORT SKYBRIDGE	River Drive, Iowa (USA)	175.3	575

LENGTH
1,214
FT

COST
6.3
BILLION DOLLARS

CHECK IT OUT!

San Francisco-Oakland Bay Bridge: nearly a quarter of a million cars use the Bay Bridge every day. Although the East span opened on September 2, 2013, the West span has been in use since 1936.

CHECK IT OUT!

Millennium Bridge: this steel suspension bridge was called the "wobbly bridge" when it opened in 2000, due to it swaying under foot. After being closed for two years, and the wobbliness solved, since 2002 it has been solid as a rock and very popular.

XTREME FACT
KURILPA BRIDGE

This footbridge opened on October 4, 2009, and it still retains the record of being the biggest "hybrid tensegrity" bridge in the world. That unusual word means special struts are compressed, but don't touch, to bear the load.

LENGTH
1,542
FT

XTREME FACT

BEIJING SUBWAY

How many lines does your local subway have? Beijing's has 17, with the possibility of visiting a crazy 270 stations! Daily usage? Up to 11 million people ride this subway every day.

LENGTH
283.35 MI

TOP 10 LARGEST UNDERGROUND RAIL SYSTEMS

Zipping around on underground trains is one of the best ways to see cities that have great sights spread far and wide. Here are the longest ever made...

	LOCATION	STATIONS	TOTAL LENGTH (KM)	(MI)
01 SEOUL METROPOLITAN SUBWAY	Seoul (South Korea)	397	526.3	327.03
02 SHANGHAI METRO	Shanghai (China)	300	462	287.07
03 BEIJING SUBWAY	Beijing (China)	270	456	283.35
04 LONDON UNDERGROUND	London (UK)	270	402	249.79
05 NEW YORK CITY SUBWAY	New York City (USA)	468	373	231.77
06 S-BAHN BERLIN	Berlin (Germany)	166	331	205.67
07 MOSCOW METRO	Moscow (Russia)	188	313.1	194.55
08 METRO DE MADRID	Madrid (Spain)	300	293	182.06
09 MEXICO CITY METRO	Mexico City (Mexico)	195	226	140.43
10 PARIS MÉTRO	Paris (France)	303	219.9	136.64

CHECK IT OUT!

Moscow Metro: this was the first ever underground rail system created for the country. It's also like a time capsule, with the original marble walls and mosaics still contained there.

STAT ATTACK

MOSCOW METRO

Opened	May 15, 1935
Lines	12
Stations	188
Daily usage	9 million
Expansion plans	To be completed by 2020

MOST STRIKING STATUES

THE T-10 UNOFFICIAL

	MADE BY	LOCATION	UNIQUE DETAILS
01 GHOST GIRL	Kevin Francis Gray	London (UK)	Emotionally affecting marble statue of a woman with a shower of glass bead tears
02 ANOTHER PLACE	Antony Gormley	Liverpool (UK)	100 life-sized iron nude selfs of Gormley stare out to the sea at Crosby Beach
03 TERRA MEGIDO	Alexey Morosov	St. Petersberg (Russia)	Serene women riding Segways
04 MICHAEL JACKSON	Unknown	Best (Netherlands)	32 ft (10 m) steel and fibreglass statue. Nine were built to promote the *HIStory* album
05 BRUCE LEE	Ivan Fijolić	Mostar (Bosnia)	Life-sized Silver Surfer-esque shiny statue of the martial arts legend
06 MR DARCY	Toby Crowther	London (UK)	Giant-sized version of the *Pride & Prejudice* character in a lake
07 CRAWLING BABIES	David Černý	Prague (Czech Republic)	Bronze babies "crawling" up and down the Žižkov Television Tower
08 VERITY	Damien Hirst	Ilfracombe (UK)	A 66 ft (20 m) bronze pregnant woman, half showing the body's inner organs/workings
09 DAVID BECKHAM	H&M	Various, worldwide	Giant silver versions of the famous soccer star to promote underwear
10 CHILD EATER	Hans Gieng	Bern, Switzerland	Nobody knows why this creepy statue/fountain was made back in 1546

MOST RECENT YOUNG ARCHITECTS OF THE YEAR

Launched in 2004, we love that these awards exist as they recognize young talent! Like designing buildings? You could be a future winner...

	MOST STRIKING BUILD TO DATE	YEAR
01 JOSEP CAMPS & OLGA FELIP	Museum of Energy Asco	2013
02 COFFEY ARCHITECTS	Scala	2012
03 JONATHAN HENDRY ARCHITECTS	Intimate Garden Rooms	2011
04 SERIE ARCHITECTS	BMW Olympic Pavilion	2010
05 DAVID KOHN ARCHITECTS	Carrer Avinyó	2009
06 HACKETT HALL McKNIGHT	PSNI Memorial Garden	2008
07 CARMODY GROARKE	Studio East	2007
08 NORD	Køge Culture House	2006
09 LYNCH ARCHITECTS	Barking Abbey Green	2005
10 QUERKRAFT	ML Museum Liaunig	2004

Source: Young Architect Of The Year Awards

XTREME FACT

CARMODY GROARKE

Here is a beautiful example of Carmody Groarke's design skills: pop-up dining establishment Studio East in London. In Nov 2013, Groarke collaborated with set designer Shona Heath for the exhibition *Isabella Blow: Fashion Galore!*

TOP 10 BIGGEST STADIUMS OF THE FUTURE (COMPLETION DUE 2015)

Sports and music fans around the world, listen up: even MORE awesome stadiums are on their way! These are the biggest 10 that are due to open their doors in 2015...

		LOCATION	PROPOSED CAPACITY
01	NEW ZENIT STADIUM	Saint Petersburg (Russia)	69,501
02	BAKU OLYMPIC STADIUM	Baku (Azerbaijan)	68,000
03	GRAND STADE D'ALGER	Baraki (Algeria)	60,000
04	JAKARTA BMW STADIUM	Jakarta (Indonesia)	50,000
05	NEW KONYA STADIUM	Konya (Turkey)	42,276
06	NEW GAZIANTEP STADIUM	Gaziantep (Turkey)	36,400
07	NEW ESKİŞEHIR STADIUM	Eskişehir (Turkey)	34,930
08	NEW SAMSUN 19 MAYIS	Samsun (Turkey)	33,919
09	NEW ANTALYA STADIUM	Antalya (Turkey)	33,000
10	CSKA MOSCOW STADIUM	Moscow (Russia)	30,000

PROPOSED CAPACITY 68,000

CHECK IT OUT!

Baku Olympic Stadium: along with a super high-tech retractable roof, the Baku Stadium will also feature a crazy 3,617 car parking spaces to help accommodate the 68,000 people that will fill its seats for soccer matches and concerts.

STAT ATTACK

BAKU OLYMPIC STADIUM

Location..... Boyuk Shor, Baku, Azerbaijan
Construction started.......... June 6, 2011
Set to open 2015
Built by............... Tekfen Construction
Mainly used by.................Azerbaijan's national soccer team

MOST FUTURISTIC
FUNCTIONAL BUILDINGS

TOP 10

THE T-10 UNOFFICIAL

		LOCATION
01	THÉÂTRE AGORA	Lelystad (Netherlands)
02	FESTIVAL HALL	Erl (Austria)
03	YEOSU EXPO VILLAGE	Yeosu (South Korea)
04	SELFRIDGES SHOPPING MALL	Birmingham (UK)
05	BICENTENNIAL CONSERVATORY	Adelaide (Australia)
06	GALAXY SOHO	Beijing (China)
07	KHAN SHATYR	Astana (Kazakhstan)
08	THE SHARD	London (UK)
09	ORDOS MUSEUM	Inner Mongolia (China)
10	WALT DISNEY CONCERT HALL	California (USA)

XTREME FACT
THÉÂTRE AGORA

This awesome 1,059,440 ft^3-building also has dressing rooms, various foyers, a stage tower, a café, and a restaurant. The futuristic exterior is made of a mix of flat steel sections, corrugated metals, with an orange and yellow mesh.

XTREME FACT
SELFRIDGES SHOPPING MALL

Designed by Future Systems in 2003, this stunning shopping mall in Birmingham, UK, has been given the affectionate term of "blob-itecture," and we can see why!

CHECK IT OUT!

Khan Shatyr: translating as the "Royal Marquee," this alien-esque tent shelters grounds that are bigger than 10 sports stadiums. It even stars on one of Kazakhstan's national postage stamps.

TOP 10 OLDEST CHURCHES/CATHEDRALS

There are many different spiritual beliefs and religions all over the world.
Here are the most ancient buildings of worship that we know about...

	LOCATION	OLDEST ELEMENTS
01 THE BASILICA OF OUR LADY IN TRASTEVERE	Rome (Italy)	221-227 AD
02 DURA-EUROPOS CHURCH	Dura-Europos (Syria)	BETWEEN 233-256 AD
03 MEGIDDO CHURCH	Tel Megiddo (Israel)	3RD CENTURY
04 MOTHER CATHEDRAL OF HOLY ETCHMIADZIN	Vagharshapat (Armenia)	301-303 AD
05 OLD SAINT PETER'S BASILICA	Vatican City (Italy)	319-333 AD
06 PANAGIA EKATONTAPILIANI	Paros (Greece)	326 AD
07 CATHEDRAL OF SAINT PETER	Trier (Germany)	329-346 AD
08 MONASTERY OF SAINT ANTHONY	Suez Governorate (Egypt)	356 AD
09 CHURCH OF THE HOLY APOSTLES PETER AND PAUL	Novi Pazar (Serbia)	4TH CENTURY
10 CHURCH OF SAINT PETER	Mount Starius (Turkey)	4TH TO 5TH CENTURY

XTREME FACT

MOTHER CATHEDRAL OF HOLY ETCHMIADZIN

Since 2000, this is recognized as a World Heritage Site by UNESCO (United Nations Educational, Scientific and Cultural Organization).

TOP 10 HISTORICAL GHOST SIGHTINGS

THE T-10 UNOFFICIAL

	LOCATION	ALLEGED GHOSTLY REPORTS
01 EDINBURGH VAULTS	Edinburgh (Scotland)	Many, including voices and scratches appearing on visitors
02 BEECHWORTH ASYLUM	Victoria (Australia)	Several of the deceased patients
03 DUCKETT'S GROVE	Carlow (Ireland)	Banshee, a phantom horse and cart, and more
04 UNION CEMETERY	Connecticut (USA)	"The White Lady," as well as ghostly mists and lights
05 LIGHTHOUSE HOTEL	Truro (Canada)	Gunshots, screaming, beds and furniture moving violently
06 GREAT WALL OF CHINA	Jia-yu Pass of Gansu to Shan-hai Pass (China)	Ghostly marching footsteps
07 MARGAM CASTLE	Port Talbot (Wales)	Deceased enraged gamekeeper, giggling children
08 AKERSHUS FORTRESS	Oslo (Norway)	Norway's most haunted place, including a vicious dog
09 MALACAÑANG PALACE	Manila (Philippines)	Former politicians and leaders
10 VALLEY OF THE KINGS	Theban Hills (Egypt)	Ghostly pharaoh riding a chariot with horses

VALLEY OF THE KINGS

TALLEST HISTORICAL STATUES

TOP 10

Their subject matters may be of significant historical (and often spiritual) figures, but the architectural feats that created these are truly modern marvels...

#	Name	SUBJECT MATTER	LOCATION	HEIGHT (M)	HEIGHT (FT)
01	SPRING TEMPLE BUDDHA	Vairocana Buddha	Henan (China)	153	502
02	LAYKYUN SETKYAR	Guatama Buddha	Myanmar (Burma)	130	426.51
03	USHIKU DAIBUTSU	Amitabha Buddha	Ushiku (Japan)	120	394
04	GUANYIN OF THE SOUTH SEA OF SANYA	Guanyin	Hainan (China)	108	354.33
05	EMPERORS YAN & HUANG	Emperors of China: Yan & Huang	Henan (China)	106	348
06	CRISTO-REI	Jesus	Almada (Portugal)	103	338
07	MOTHER OF THE MOTHERLAND	Warrior statue war memorial	Kiev (Ukraine)	102	335
08	SENDAI DAIKANNON	Guanyin	Sendai (Japan)	100	328
09	AWAJI KANNON	Guanyin	Hyōgo Prefecture (Japan)	100	328
10	QIANSHOU QIANYAN GUANYIN OF WEISHAN	Guanyin	Hunan (China)	99	325

HEIGHT 305 FT

XTREME FACT
CRISTO-REI

You may think this epic structure is solid stone... But you'd be wrong. Within this religious monument lies areas such as a chapel, a library, and even a bar.

HEIGHT 338 FT

OFF THE CHART

STATUE OF LIBERTY

Liberty Enlightening The World (its full name) was gifted to USA from France to reflect freedom and democracy. Designed by Frédéric Auguste Bartholdi and dedicated on October 28, 1886, it became a national monument in 1924.

ANCIENT MYTHICAL PLACES

THE T-10 UNOFFICIAL

#		THE TALE BEHIND THE REALM
01	XIBALBA	An underworld in Mayan mythology
02	SHAMBHALA	A magical, secret realm in Asia from Buddhism
03	THE ELYSIAN FIELDS	Greek mythology's resting place for good souls
04	CAMELOT	The legendary castle and home to King Arthur, central figure of the Arthurian myth
05	EL DORADO	Possibly a hidden city of gold in South America
06	ATLANTIS	A continent that sank into the Atlantic Ocean a long time ago
07	MOUNT OLYMPUS	Home to the gods of Greek mythology
08	ASGARD	Norse mythology's home to the god of thunder (Thor) and others
09	TARTARUS	An underworld place for evil souls in Greek mythology
10	NIBIRU	Ancient Babylonians talk about this planet by name

10 QUICK FIRE FACTS

MOUNT OLYMPUS

01	It's the highest mountain in Greece
02	The highest peak is 9,573 ft (2,918 m) up
03	Has 52 peaks in total
04	In mythology, home to 12 gods
05	First accent took place on August 2, 1913...
06	...by Christos Kakalos, Frederic Boissonnas, & Daniel Baud-Bovy
07	Found between Macedonia and Thessaly
08	Several mythological tales are set on Olympus
09	Is part of a National Park
10	10,000 people climb it every year

XTREME FACT
MOUNT OLYMPUS

This home of the mythical Greek gods has been depicted in the movie world many times. *Batman Begins*' Liam Neeson has played Olympus leader Zeus in *Clash Of The Titans*, AND *Wrath Of The Titans*.

XTREME FACT
TARTARUS

The 2011 movie *Immortals* featured a scene where Zeus destroyed Tartarus. It took $226,904,017 at the box office.

CHECK IT OUT!

Ping An Finance Center: it may be based in China, but this was designed by American firm KPF (Kohn Pedersen Fox Associates), one of the biggest architectural firms in the world. Ping An Finance Center will have 76 elevators for its 115 floors.

HEIGHT 2,165 FT

TOP 10 TALLEST BUILDS UNDER CONSTRUCTION

Loads of massive buildings are currently being built all over world. Of those with completion years already set, this lot are the biggest...

		COUNTRY	YEAR DUE FOR COMPLETION	FLOORS	HEIGHT (M)	HEIGHT (FT)
01	KINGDOM TOWER	Saudi Arabia	2019	163	828	2,717
02	PING AN FINANCE CENTER	China	2016	115	660	2,165
03	SIGNATURE TOWER JAKARTA	Indonesia	2020	113	638	2,093
04	WUHAN GREENLAND CENTER	China	2017	125	636	2,087
05	MENARA WARISAN MERDEKA	Malaysia	2018	118	600	1,969
06	GOLDIN FINANCE 117	China	2016	128	597	1,959
07	PEARL OF THE NORTH	China	2018	111	565	1,854
08	THE CTF GUANGZHOU	China	2017	111	530	1,739
=	PERTAMINA TOWER	Indonesia	2018	99	530	1,739
=	TIANJIN CHOW TAI FOOK BINHAI CENTER	China	2016	97	530	1,739

CHECK IT OUT!

Kingdom Tower: this is actually a model of the forthcoming Kingdom Tower. It was used in a press conference in Riyadh (the capital of Saudi Arabia) on August 2, 2011.

227

WELCOME TO
HILL VALLEY
2015

SKYWAY 3

ACCESS 12E
20' MAX HT
4 HOVER LANES
NO HOVER

CHECK IT OUT!

Hill Valley: for *Back To The Future Part II*, production designer Rick Carter and his team spent months planning how to make the 2015 version of the quaint Hill Valley imposing and futuristic.

XTREME FACT
CITIES IN INCEPTION

You may think that all of the sprawling, shifting cities in *Inception* were CGI (computer-generated imagery), but not so. Writer/director Christopher Nolan likes to use physical, real effects as much as possible, so many were big-scale miniatures, with visual effects only tallying to around 500 shots.

TOP 10 FICTIONAL FUTURISTIC CITIES

THE T-10 UNOFFICIAL

		DESCRIPTION	DESCRIBED/FEATURED IN
01	BREGNA	Dystopian city set in the year 2415	*Aeon Flux* (1991 animated TV series, 2005 movie, comic books)
02	METROPOLIS	Sprawling industrial city in 2026	*Metropolis* (1927 movie)
03	SAN FRANCISCO	2388 version of the American city	*Star Trek Into Darkness* (2013 movie)
04	NEW NEW YORK	New York City in the 31st century	*Futurama* (1999–2013 animated TV series, comic books)
05	SEVERAL LOCATIONS	2020 version of Earth where alien Kaiju attack	*Pacific Rim* (2013 movie)
06	THE ALLIANCE PARLIAMENT	City-sized government on the planet Londinium	*Firefly* (2002–03 TV series), *Serenity* (2005 movie, comic books)
07	SEVERAL LOCATIONS	Cities created in the subconsciousness of characters	*Inception* (2010 movie)
08	IACON	Capital city of Cybertron	*Transformers* (1984–87 animated TV series and 1987 movie, comic books)
09	BOSTON	2036 version where The Observers control humanity	*Fringe* (2008–13 TV series, comics and other books)
10	HILL VALLEY	2015 version of Marty McFly's 1985 hometown	*Back To The Future Part II* (1989 movie)

MOST EXPENSIVE SPACE PROJECTS

Exploring the stars is very important, but it's also insanely expensive. Here are the 10 projects that have a launch date in the future, or those that are still ongoing...

#		FUTURE PLANS	COST ($ BILLIONS)
01	INTERNATIONAL SPACE STATION	May continue being developed until 2028	150*
02	BEIDOU NAVIGATION SATELLITE SYSTEM	Continued development to 2020	65.3
03	HUBBLE SPACE TELESCOPE	May continue usage until 2020	10
04	JAMES WEBB SPACE TELESCOPE	Launch date 2018	4
05	CASSINI-HUYGENS (SATURN EXPLORER)	Mission ends 2017	3.26
06	ORION MULTI-PURPOSE CREW VEHICLE (MPCV)	First manned mission 2020	2.6
07	MARS SCIENCE LABORATORY	Ongoing	2.5
08	ALPHA MAGNETIC SPECTROMETER	Continuing to at least 2021	2
09	JUPITER ICY MOON EXPLORER (JUICE)	Launch date 2022	1.3
10	JUNO (JUPITER EXPLORATORY CRAFT)	Will arrive at Jupiter 2016	1

*Including the necessary space shuttle flights/visits

X-PLORE

JAMES WEBB SPACE TELESCOPE

Launching in 2018, the JWST (James Webb Space Telescope) is a massive infrared telescope. Its mission? To seek out the first galaxies that were formed... Pretty important then! JWST will make its home in an orbit approx 0.93 million miles (1.5 million km) from Earth. Check out www.jwst.nasa.gov.

COST 150 BILLION DOLLARS

XTREME FACT

INTERNATIONAL SPACE STATION

Since November 2, 2000, the ISS has been occupied by humans from 15 different nations! Although it technically weighs nothing in space's vacuum, the ISS is actually quite a hefty 992.080 lb (450,000 kg)!

YOUR SHOUT

This book has been structured so that these two pages can challenge what you know about... Structures!

YOUR PICK OF THE... STRUCTURES

You've read the facts and studied the lists... Now tell us your ultimate top 10 fave structures!

01 ....
02 ....
03 ....
04 ....
05 ....
06 ....
07 ....
08 ....
09 ....
10 ....

ROUND 1: MULTIPLE CHOICE

01 How fast does Formula Rossa in Ferrari World, the world's fastest roller coaster, go?

A 149 MPH (240 KPH)
B 104 MPH (167 KPH)
C 92 MPH (148 KPH)

02 Which country has four of the world's tallest buildings including the tallest, Sky City, standing at 2,749 ft (838 m)?

A USA
B SAUDI ARABIA
C CHINA

03 What is the name of the biggest inner city stadium on the planet? It's in North Korea and seats 150,000 spectators...

A ESTADIO AZTECA
B RUNGNADO MAY DAY STADIUM
C NEYLAND STADIUM

ROUND 2: QUESTION TIME

01 The biggest LEGO structure in the world contained 5,335,200 pieces and was displayed in Times Square, New York City (USA). Which *Star Wars* craft was it of?

ANSWER:
_____

ROUND 3:
PICTURE PUZZLES

In which European capital city is this skateboard and BMX riders' haven?

01

ANSWER:

Can you name this museum that sees 9.7 million visitors pass through it each year?

02

ANSWER:

Where does the Cristo-Rei in Portugal stand in our Top 10 Tallest Historical Statues' list?

03

ANSWER:

ROUND 4:
WORDSEARCH

Take a look in the jumble of letters to the left and see how many of these structures you can find:

```
S A Q U A R I U M R E G
O R F A V M E G D I R B
N E D W V K E J N S X Q
O N E S V M U Q R K B E
C A S T L E A X B Y E Y
I S B A A M O C V S W Q
X C E D R S K D A C O W
D B N I R T W E I R C A
A E R U X A O J W A Y Z
S B E M F T P W U P I B
H E O W C U H S E E V Q
B U Q E C E O S V R G E
```

SKYSCRAPER

BRIDGE

TOWER

STATUE

CASTLE

STADIUM

AQUARIUM

ARENA

FIND THE ANSWERS ON PAGE 313

02 The American skyscraper on the right is number six on our Top 10 Tallest Buildings list. Can you name it?

03 Which country has two in the top five most expensive bridges in the world, with a combined cost of $53 billion?

ANSWER:

STRUCTURES
CAREER QUIZ

In which of these buildings would you most like to live?

- **A** AN AWARD-WINNING HOUSE
- **B** TOP OF A SKYSCRAPER
- **C** A CONVERTED CHURCH

Which material would you use to build it with?

- **A** BRICKS
- **B** STEEL
- **C** WOOD

Which of these movie locations would you most like to have access to?

- **A** STARK TOWER
- **B** THE BAT CAVE
- **C** HOGWARTS

Which of these subjects are you best at?

- **A** MATHEMATICS
- **B** ART & DESIGN
- **C** HISTORY

Which of the following activities would you prefer to do?

- **A** A CITY TOUR
- **B** GO TO A CARNIVAL
- **C** VISIT A CASTLE

Which place is most suited to you for a fun day out?

- **A** AN ART GALLERY
- **B** THE CIRCUS
- **C** A MUSEUM

Which of the following statements best fits you?

- **A** I LOVE TO DRAW
- **B** I DO EXTREME SPORTS
- **C** I COULD READ ALL DAY

Find out which structures-related job is best suited to you on page 313

THE BIG SCREEN

TOP 10 BIGGEST MOVIES OF ALL TIME

		YEAR	BOX OFFICE ($ WORLDWIDE)	RELATIVE SCALE:
01	AVATAR	2009	2,782,275,172	
02	TITANIC	1997	2,186,772,302	
03	THE AVENGERS	2012	1,518,594,910	
04	HARRY POTTER AND THE DEATHLY HALLOWS: PART 2	2011	1,341,511,219	
05	IRON MAN 3	2013	1,215,439,994	
06	TRANSFORMERS: DARK OF THE MOON	2011	1,123,794,079	
07	THE LORD OF THE RINGS: THE RETURN OF THE KING	2003	1,119,929,521	
08	SKYFALL	2012	1,108,561,013	
09	THE DARK KNIGHT RISES	2012	1,084,439,099	
10	PIRATES OF THE CARIBBEAN: DEAD MAN'S CHEST	2006	1,066,179,725	

Relative scale percentages: 100%, 79%, 55%, 48%, 44%, 40%, 40%, 40%, 39%, 38%

Source: IMDB.com

Superheroes and adventurers still have a huge impact on the Top 10 most successful movies ever made...

XTREME FACT
THE DARK KNIGHT RISES

Moviemaker Christopher Nolan's final chapter of his *Dark Knight* trilogy won several awards. These included an American Film Institute (AFI) Movie Of The Year Award 2012, and a Saturn Award for Best Supporting Actress for Anne Hathaway.

BOX OFFICE 1.08 BILLION DOLLARS

CHECK IT OUT!

Skyfall: the 23rd Eon Productions' 007 saga is the most successful Bond movie. Shooting began in London on November 7, 2011, and took 128 days. Including the 2012 Olympic Games' short film, *Happy And Glorious*, Daniel Craig has played the secret agent four times.

MOST BANKABLE STARS

There are thousands of actors, but which are the 10 that pull in the most dollars for their movies? These guys...

		TOTAL MOVIES	TOTAL BOX OFFICE ($ BILLIONS)*
01	TOM HANKS	42	4.26
02	MORGAN FREEMAN	52	3.95
03	HARRISON FORD	38	3.85
04	EDDIE MURPHY	38	3.81
05	SAMUEL L. JACKSON	61	3.72
06	TOM CRUISE	34	3.29
07	BRUCE WILLIS	57	3.17
08	ROBIN WILLIAMS	46	3.16
09	JOHNNY DEPP	40	3.07
10	ROBERT DOWNEY, JR	49	3.00

*U.S. domestic

Source: IMDB.com

TOTAL BOX OFFICE
3.72 BILLION DOLLARS

XTREME FACT

JOHNNY DEPP

Most known for playing very "out there" characters, Johnny Depp's portrayal of Tonto in *The Lone Ranger* (2013) marked the actor's fifth collaboration with director Gore Verbinski (as well as *Rango* and the first three *Pirates* movies).

XTREME FACT

SAMUEL L. JACKSON

Master of all things super-cool, Samuel L. Jackson has played Nick Fury eight times in Marvel movies. The character has a very complex past, but the most amazing thing is that he is basically immortal.

TOP 10 MOST MOVIES IN A FRANCHISE

When it comes to successful movie franchises, the world of comics comes out top, yet again...

		TOTAL MOVIES
01	MARVEL COMICS	39
02	SHERLOCK HOLMES	37
03	JAMES BOND	26
04	DC COMICS	22
05	POKÉMON	13
06	STAR TREK	12
07	STAR WARS	8
=	HARRY POTTER	8
=	PLANET OF THE APES	8
10	FAST & FURIOUS	7

BEEN & SEEN

Tick off which of these ace Marvel Comics movies you've seen!

- [ ] GUARDIANS OF THE GALAXY
- [ ] THE AVENGERS
- [ ] IRON MAN
- [ ] IRON MAN 2
- [ ] IRON MAN 3
- [ ] CAPTAIN AMERICA: THE FIRST AVENGER
- [ ] CAPTAIN AMERICA: THE WINTER SOLDIER
- [ ] THOR
- [ ] THOR: THE DARK WORLD
- [ ] THE INCREDIBLE HULK

CHECK IT OUT!

Marvel Comics: although Marvel Comics' characters also include the X-Men (Fox Studios) and Spider-Man (Sony Studios), 2015's *The Avengers: Age Of Ultron* is Marvel Studios' 11th action-packed movie that shares characters and story developments.

TOTAL MOVIES 8

XTREME FACT

STAR WARS

Not counting 2008's animated adventure *Star Wars: The Clone Wars*, US composer John Williams has created the score for every *Star Wars* movie since the first one in 1977, with the J. J. Abrams-directed *Star Wars: Episode VII* (2015) being his latest.

XTREME FACT
CHRISTOPHER NOLAN

From humble beginnings, British moviemaker Christopher Nolan has gone on to be one of the most successful directors ever. His first feature-length movie, *Following* (1998), was made at a cost of just $6,000, but took an amazing $240,495 at the box office.

TOTAL BOX OFFICE 3.55 BILLION DOLLARS

TOP 10 MOST BANKABLE MOVIEMAKERS

Which directors do you love? Have they made the Top 10 of the most profitable moviemakers of all time?

		TOTAL MOVIES	WORLDWIDE BOX OFFICE ($ BILLIONS)
01	STEVEN SPIELBERG	27	9.01
02	JAMES CAMERON	9	6.20
03	PETER JACKSON	11	5.49
04	MICHAEL BAY	10	4.67
05	ROBERT ZEMECKIS	16	4.09
06	CHRIS COLUMBUS	14	3.85
07	TIM BURTON	16	3.76
08	GORE VERBINSKI	9	3.72
09	RON HOWARD	21	3.62
10	CHRISTOPHER NOLAN	8	3.55

Source: IMDB.com

CHECK IT OUT!

Steven Spielberg: remember that dinosaur-esque wail heard in the ocean at the end of *Jaws* (1975)? It's the same sound sample Spielberg used for the destructive finale of his debut *Duel* (1971).

237

BOX OFFICE 262 MILLION DOLLARS

XTREME FACT

THE AMAZING SPIDER-MAN

The character of Dr. Curt "The Lizard" Connors has had a curious journey on the big screen. Dylan Baker played him in *Spider-Man 2* (2004) and *Spider-Man 3* (2007), but he never got transformed into The Lizard. Rhys Ifans got that delight when he played him in *The Amazing Spider-Man* (2012).

TOP 10 BIGGEST 3D MOVIES OF ALL TIME

As 3D movie technology gets better and better, projects like *Gravity* are making them more immersive and eye-popping. Here are the 10 most successful to date...

		YEAR	BOX OFFICE (3D ONLY) ($ MILLIONS)*	RELATIVE SCALE:
01	AVATAR	2009	760,507,625	100%
02	THE AVENGERS	2012	623,357,910	82%
03	TOY STORY 3	2010	415,004,880	55%
04	IRON MAN 3	2013	409,013,994	54%
05	HARRY POTTER AND THE DEATHLY HALLOWS: PART 2	2011	381,011,219	50%
06	DESPICABLE ME 2	2013	368,061,265	48%
07	TRANSFORMERS: DARK OF THE MOON	2011	352,390,543	46%
08	ALICE IN WONDERLAND	2010	334,191,110	44%
09	THE HOBBIT: AN UNEXPECTED JOURNEY	2012	303,003,568	40%
10	THE AMAZING SPIDER-MAN	2012	262,030,663	34%

*U.S. domestic

CHECK IT OUT!

***Despicable Me 2*:** one of the most profitable animated movies ever, this had a budget of $76 million and has taken a total of more than $950 million!

XTREME FACT

THE DARK KNIGHT RISES

The first teaser trailer for *The Dark Knight Rises* featured an epic, progressive shot of Gotham crumbling, resulting in the Batman logo, made from the skyscrapers' alignment.

TOP 10 MOST EXCITING TEASER TRAILERS OF ALL TIME

THE T-10 UNOFFICIAL

		WHY THE TEASER ROCKS
01	BACK TO THE FUTURE	Shot like a sneakers or car commercial
02	CLOVERFIELD	Statue of Liberty head crashing through the street
03	SUPER 8	Something is punching its way out of a train crate
04	THE DARK KNIGHT RISES	Gotham City crumbling away from a bat symbol above
05	STAR TREK	Reveals a team of people building the USS Enterprise
06	THE AVENGERS: AGE OF ULTRON	Gave a very stylish glimpse of Ultron... (see Xtreme Fact)
07	SPIDER-MAN	A helicopter ends up trapped in a massive spider web
08	INCEPTION	Tantilizing scenes where the laws of physics are broken
09	GODZILLA	Shots of insane carnage ending with a look at Godzilla
10	THE DARK KNIGHT	Voice-over of The Joker's creepy accent

XTREME FACT

THE AVENGERS: AGE OF ULTRON

A simple, but brilliant idea was used for the *Age Of Ultron* teaser: we saw Iron Man's helmet gradually being dented, damaged, and affected, until it was revealed that it had changed into Ultron's adamantium-infused helmet.

BOX OFFICE 746 MILLION DOLLARS

TOP 10 BIGGEST CGI ANIMATED MOVIES

The most modern way to create an animated story is with CGI (computer-generated imagery), and here are the 10 biggest hits...

		YEAR	BOX OFFICE ($ WORLDWIDE)
01	TOY STORY 3	2010	1,063,171,911
02	DESPICABLE ME 2	2013	970,761,885
03	FINDING NEMO	2013	936,743,261
04	SHREK 2	2004	919,838,758
05	ICE AGE: DAWN OF THE DINOSAURS	2009	886,686,817
06	ICE AGE: CONTINENTAL DRIFT	2012	877,244,782
07	SHREK THE THIRD	2007	798,958,162
08	SHREK FOREVER AFTER	2010	752,600,867
09	MADAGASCAR 3: EUROPE'S MOST WANTED	2012	746,921,274
10	MONSTERS UNIVERSITY	2013	743,559,607

Source: IMDB.com

CHECK IT OUT!

Despicable Me 2: the sequel to 2010's *Despicable Me* was so successful that it spawned 2015's *Minions*, with those little yellow critters becoming the stars.

BOX OFFICE 970 MILLION DOLLARS

TOP 10 LOVABLE ANIMATED CHARACTERS

THE T-10 UNOFFICIAL

XTREME FACT

MADAGASCAR 3: EUROPE'S MOST WANTED

The third movie in the *Madagascar* franchise of Alex, Marty, Melman, and Gloria is also the most successful. Batman fans—guess who scored the movie? None other than *The Dark Knight* trilogy's composer, Hans Zimmer! A special comic book prequel was also released, *Madagascar 3: Long Live The King!*

#	Character	Movie
01	TOOTHLESS	HOW TO TRAIN YOUR DRAGON
02	VANELLOPE	WRECK-IT RALPH
03	SPARKY	FRANKENWEENIE
04	SCRAT	ICE AGE
05	BOLT	BOLT
06	UNICRON	TRANSFORMERS: THE MOVIE
07	WALL•E	WALL•E
08	SULLY	MONSTERS, INC.
09	THUMPER	BAMBI
10	LITTLEFOOT	THE LAND BEFORE TIME

Source: IMDB.com

XTREME FACT

ICE AGE: CONTINENTAL DRIFT

This, the fourth *Ice Age* movie, is the second (after 2009's *Dawn Of The Dinosaurs*) to be shot in Digital 3D, the same technology used for the likes of *Avatar*. It was also the highest-grossing animated movie in 2012 (its release year).

CHECK IT OUT!

Toothless: this is one of Team T-10's most loved characters! He's a type of dragon known as a Night Fury, and stars in the first movie, as well as *How To Train Your Dragon 2* (2014), and three shorts: *Legend Of The Boneknapper Dragon* (2010), *Book Of Dragons* (2011), and *Gift Of The Night Fury* (2011).

TOP 10 BIGGEST STOP-MOTION ANIMATED MOVIES

Stop-motion animation takes a huge amount of time and patience: moving a model a tiny bit, taking a still image, and then repeating this for months...

#		YEAR	BOX OFFICE ($ WORLDWIDE)
01	CHICKEN RUN	2000	224,834,564
02	WALLACE & GROMIT: THE CURSE OF THE WERE-RABBIT	2005	192,610,372
03	CORALINE	2009	124,596,398
04	THE PIRATES! IN AN ADVENTURE WITH SCIENTISTS!	2012	123,054,041
05	CORPSE BRIDE	2005	117,195,061
06	PARANORMAN	2012	107,139,399
07	FRANKENWEENIE	2012	81,491,068
08	THE NIGHTMARE BEFORE CHRISTMAS	1993	75,082,668
09	FANTASTIC MR. FOX	2009	46,471,023
10	JAMES AND THE GIANT PEACH	1996	28,946,127

Source: IMDB.com

BOX OFFICE 107 MILLION DOLLARS

XTREME FACT

PARANORMAN

Made by stop-motion animation experts Laika, and three years in the making, *ParaNorman* was the first stop-motion movie to use full-color 3D printers (which actually print three-dimensional objects) for the movie's various models and their expressions.

TOP 10: BIGGEST CELL/TRADITIONAL ANIMATION MOVIES

The oldest, most traditional style of animation—hand-drawn and painted/shaded plastic cells—has produced some of the most beloved movies ever...

#	Title	Year	Box Office ($ worldwide)
01	THE LION KING	1994	987,483,777
02	THE SIMPSONS MOVIE	2007	527,071,022
03	ALADDIN	1992	504,050,219
04	TARZAN	1999	448,191,819
05	BEAUTY AND THE BEAST	1991	424,967,620
06	POCAHONTAS	1995	346,079,773
07	WHO FRAMED ROGER RABBIT	1988	329,803,958
08	THE HUNCHBACK OF NOTRE DAME	1996	325,338,851
09	MULAN	1998	304,320,254
10	LILO & STITCH	2002	273,144,151

Source: IMDB.com

CHECK IT OUT!

The Simpsons Movie: it may have been released in 2007, but the vocal talents behind Springfield's characters were signed on to do the movie in 2001! After 100 revisions of the ideas, animation began in 2006.

STAT ATTACK

CORPSE BRIDE

Directed by .... Mike Johnson & Tim Burton

Starring ....Johnny Depp (Victor Van Dort), Helena Bonham Carter (Emily)

Music by .... Danny Elfman

Running time ....77 mins

TOP 10: BIGGEST ANIME MOVIES

The Japanese world of anime features some of the most imaginative characters, worlds, and stories ever seen in the history of animation...

#	Title	Year	Box Office ($ worldwide)
01	SPIRITED AWAY	2002	274,925,095
02	HOWL'S MOVING CASTLE	2005	235,184,110
03	PONYO	2009	201,750,937
04	POKÉMON: THE FIRST MOVIE	1999	163,644,662
05	PRINCESS MONONOKE	1999	159,375,308
06	THE SECRET WORLD OF ARRIETTY	2012	145,570,270
07	POKÉMON: THE MOVIE 2000	1999	133,949,270
08	POKÉMON 3: THE MOVIE	2010	68,673,565
09	TALES FROM EARTHSEA	2001	68,411,275
10	FROM UP ON POPPY HILL	2013	61,037,844

Source: IMDB.com

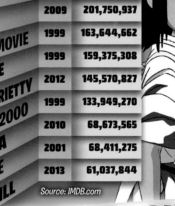

CHECK IT OUT!

Spirited Away: Studio Ghibli's 12th production took more money at the Japanese box office than *Titanic* (1997)!

TOP 10 BIGGEST SUPERHERO FRANCHISES

Of all the superhero movies ever released, check out the most powerful 10 franchises on the planet today...

		NO. OF MOVIES	BOX OFFICE ($ WORLDWIDE)
01	BATMAN		
02	IRON MAN		
03	SPIDER-MAN	9	4,728,742,151
04	THOR	5	3,943,142,457
05	WOLVERINE	5	3,248,563,075
06	HULK	4	2,598,384,528
07	CAPTAIN AMERICA	7	2,304,925,865
08	X-MEN	4	2,027,382,941
09	SUPERMAN	4	1,889,164,684
10	TEENAGE MUTANT NINJA TURTLES	5	1,517,034,755
		7	1,489,206,516
		5	418,505,332

Source: IMDB.com

X'TREME FACT: THOR

Inspired by the Norse god of the same name, Stan Lee, Jack Kirby, and Larry Lieber co-created Marvel's Thor in 1962 for the comic *Journey Into Mystery* #83.

10 QUICK FIRE FACTS

WOLVERINE

01	First appeared in *The Incredible Hulk* #180 (1974)
02	Hugh Jackman has played Logan in seven movies
03	Created by Roy Thomas, Len Wein, John Romita
04	Has featured in over 25 video games since 1989
05	*The Wolverine* (2013)'s box office: $414,828,246
06	Has highly developed super-senses
07	Wolverine comes from Alberta, Canada
08	Hugh Jackman first played him in 2000
09	Adamantium is fused to his entire skeleton
10	His healing abilities make his age unknown

CHECK IT OUT!

Captain America: before actor Chris Evans rocked the role of Steve Rogers/Captain America, he had already played another Marvel superhero... He was Johnny Storm/The Human Torch in *Fantastic Four* (2005) and *Fantastic Four: Rise Of The Silver Surfer* (2007)!

SUPERHERO & VILLAIN WEAPONS

TOP 10

THE T-10 UNOFFICIAL

XTREME FACT

WOLVERINE'S ADAMANTIUM-COATED CLAWS

It's not just Wolverine who has had an adamantium upgrade... *The Avengers: Age Of Ultron*'s titular villain upgraded his body with the virtually indestructible material.

		MOVIE(S)
01	WOLVERINE'S ADAMANTIUM-COATED CLAWS	*X-Men/Wolverine* movies
02	BATMAN'S EMP RIFLE	*The Dark Knight Rises*
03	IRON MAN MK 42 SUIT	*Iron Man 3*
04	DR. OCTOPUS'S METALLIC TENTACLES	*Spider-Man 2*
05	CAPTAIN AMERICA'S SHIELD	*Captain America/Avengers* movies
06	HAWKEYE'S BOW AND ARROWS/QUIVER	*The Avengers* movies
07	PETER PARKER'S WEBSLINGERS	*The Amazing Spider-Man* movies
08	LOKI'S STAFF	*The Avengers/Thor* movies
09	GREEN GOBLIN'S GLIDER	*Spider-Man*
10	THE JOKER'S SMILEX	*Batman*

CHECK IT OUT!

Green Goblin's Glider (top): the glider used by the Green Goblin can travel at a wild speed of 87 mph (140 kph).

CHECK IT OUT!

The Amazing Spider-Man : American by birth but raised in Britain, Andrew Garfield has played Peter "Spider-Man" Parker twice now, the latest being in *The Amazing Spider-Man 2* (2014). If you were to choose a director for Spidey movies, who better than the aptly named Marc WEBB!

BOX OFFICE 752 MILLION DOLLARS

TOP 10 COMIC BOOK SUPERHERO MOVIES

Team T-10 is very happy to see Batman and Iron Man movies doing so awesomely at the box office...

		YEAR	BOX OFFICE ($ WORLDWIDE)	RELATIVE SCALE:
01	THE AVENGERS	2012	1,518,594,910	100%
02	IRON MAN 3	2013	1,215,439,994	80%
03	THE DARK KNIGHT RISES	2012	1,084,439,099	71%
04	THE DARK KNIGHT	2008	1,004,558,444	66%
05	SPIDER-MAN 3	2007	890,871,626	59%
06	SPIDER-MAN	2002	821,708,551	54%
07	SPIDER-MAN 2	2004	783,766,341	52%
08	THE AMAZING SPIDER-MAN	2012	752,216,557	50%
09	MAN OF STEEL	2013	668,045,518	44%
10	THOR: THE DARK WORLD	2013	641,162,958	41%

Source: IMDB.com

XTREME FACT

MAN OF STEEL

When it was announced that the *Man Of Steel* (2013) sequel would be *Batman vs. Superman* (2015), the internet was ablaze with opinions about Ben Affleck's Bruce Wayne casting. But Heath Ledger's Joker casting received wild debate, too, and he won a posthumous Oscar.

MOST APPEARANCES AS THE SAME SUPERVILLAIN CHARACTER

TOP 10

Comic book movies these days attract the cream of the crop when it comes to acting talents, and these have happily played a key villain more than once...

		CHARACTER	NO. OF TIMES PLAYED
01	IAN McKELLEN	MAGNETO	5
02	REBECCA ROMIJN	MYSTIQUE	4
03	CILLIAN MURPHY	SCARECROW	3
=	TOM HIDDLESTON	LOKI	3
=	WILLEM DAFOE	GREEN GOBLIN	3
=	JAMES FRANCO	HARRY OSBORN	3
07	BENICIO DEL TORO	THE COLLECTOR	2
=	JULIAN McMAHON	DOCTOR DOOM	2
=	LIAM NEESON	RA'S AL GHUL	2
=	MICHAEL FASSBENDER	MAGNETO	2

CHECK IT OUT!

Michael Fassbender: acclaimed Irish-German actor Michael Fassbender (born April 2, 1977) first played the young Erik "Magneto" Lehnsherr in *X-Men: First Class* (2011), and then again in *X-Men: Days Of Future Past* (2014).

BEST POST-CREDITS SCENES

TOP 10 — THE T-10 UNOFFICIAL

		SCENE
01	IRON MAN 3	Tony Stark in thorapy with a bored Bruce Banner
02	THE AVENGERS	The Avengers, exhausted, silently eating shawarma
03	THE WOLVERINE	Wolverine approached by Magneto and Professor X (who he saw die)
04	IRON MAN 3	Agent Coulson reports finding a large hammer (Thor's)
05	CAPTAIN AMERICA: THE FIRST AVENGER	Nick Fury talks to Steve Rogers about his team idea
06	THOR: THE DARK WORLD	A frost monster continues to wreck London
07	THE AMAZING SPIDER-MAN	Curt Connors is asked about "the truth of Peter Parker's father"
08	X-MEN ORIGINS: WOLVERINE	Decapitated Deadpool's eyes open
09	IRON MAN	Nick Fury visits Tony Stark and mentions the Avengers Initiative
10	THE INCREDIBLE HULK	Tony Stark tells General Ross in a bar that a team is being formed

CHECK IT OUT!

Iron Man: in the movie's post-credits sequence, it was the first time that the Avengers Initiative had been mentioned, four years before *The Avengers* (2012) came to be.

TOP 10 COOLEST FEMALE HEROES

THE T-10 UNOFFICIAL

#		ACTOR
01	AGENT PEGGY CARTER	HAYLEY ATWELL
02	JEAN GREY	FAMKE JANSSEN
03	BLACK WIDOW	SCARLETT JOHANSSON
04	CATWOMAN	ANNE HATHAWAY
05	ELEKTRA	JENNIFER GARNER
06	SHADOWCAT	ELLEN PAGE
07	AGENT MARIA HILL	COBIE SMULDERS
08	INVISIBLE WOMAN	JESSICA ALBA
09	ROGUE	ANNA PAQUIN
10	STORM	HALLE BERRY

X-TREME FACT

ELEKTRA

A spin-off from *Daredevil* (2003), 2005's *Elektra* starred Jennifer Garner (from hit spy TV show *Alias*). Elektra Natchios first appeared in the Marvel comic *Daredevil* #168, published in January 1981.

TOP 10 BADDEST FEMME FATALES

THE T-10 UNOFFICIAL

#		ACTOR(S)
01	MYSTIQUE	JENNIFER LAWRENCE/REBECCA ROMIJN
02	FAORA-UL	ANTJE TRAUE
03	SCARLET WITCH	ELIZABETH OLSEN
04	VIPER	SVETLANA KHODCHENKOVA
05	YUKIO	RILA FUKUSHIMA
06	LADY DEATHSTRIKE	KELLY HU
07	ARCLIGHT	OMAHYRA
08	POISON IVY	UMA THURMAN
09	PSYLOCKE	MEI MELANÇON
10	EMMA FROST	JANUARY JONES

CHECK IT OUT!

Emma Frost: ranked 69th on Wizard's 200 Greatest Characters Of All Time list (published in 2008), Emma Frost was brought to life by January Jones in *X-Men: First Class* (2011).

TOP 10
MOST APPEARANCES AS THE SAME SUPERHERO CHARACTER

Comic book characters have never been more popular in movies, and these actors have played an iconic hero on more than one occasion...

	ACTOR	CHARACTER	NO. OF TIMES PLAYED
01	HUGH JACKMAN	WOLVERINE	7
=	SAMUEL L. JACKSON	NICK FURY	7
03	ROBERT DOWNEY, JR	IRON MAN	6
=	PATRICK STEWART	PROFESSOR X	6
05	FAMKE JANSSEN	JEAN GREY	4
=	HALLE BERRY	STORM	4
=	CHRISTOPHER REEVE	SUPERMAN	4
=	SCARLETT JOHANSSON	BLACK WIDOW	4
=	SHAWN ASHMORE	ICEMAN	4
10	CHRISTIAN BALE	BATMAN	3

XTREME FACT
HALLE BERRY

The star behind Storm has notched up loads of accolades outside of *X-Men* since her 1991 big screen debut, including five Best Actress awards and an Academy Award in 2001.

10 QUICK FIRE FACTS

STORM

01	Her real name is Ororo Munroe
02	Created by Len Wein and Dave Cockrum
03	Can manipulate the weather for battle/defence
04	First appeared in *Giant-Size X-Men* #1 (1975)
05	Part of the X-Men team
06	Actress Halle Berry has played Storm four times
07	Storm has featured in more than 26 video games
08	Is part of a Universal Studios theme park ride
09	Featured in *Marvel Universe: LIVE!* show (2014)
10	*The Wolverine* (2013) features a photo of Storm

OFF THE CHART

ACTOR	CHARACTER	NO. OF TIMES PLAYED
ANNA PAQUIN	ROGUE	3
CHRIS EVANS	CAPTAIN AMERICA	3
CHRIS HEMSWORTH	THOR	3
DANIEL CUDMORE	COLOSSUS	3
MARK RUFFALO	THE HULK	3

TIME TRAVEL

TOP 10 BIGGEST TIME-TRAVEL MOVIES

From flux capacitors to dimension-warping spaceships, these are the movies that have rocked time travel more than any others…

AUSTIN POWERS

		YEAR	BOX OFFICE ($ WORLDWIDE)
01	MEN IN BLACK 3	2012	624,026,776
02	STAR TREK	2009	385,680,446
03	BACK TO THE FUTURE	1985	381,109,762
04	BACK TO THE FUTURE PART II	1989	331,950,002
05	AUSTIN POWERS 2	1999	312,016,858
06	AUSTIN POWERS IN GOLDMEMBER	2002	296,655,431
07	BACK TO THE FUTURE PART III	1990	244,527,583
08	DÉJÀ VU	2006	180,557,550
09	MEET THE ROBINSONS	2007	169,333,034
10	SOURCE CODE	2011	147,332,697

Source: IMDB.com

XTREME FACT

AUSTIN POWERS 2

Before Austin was sent back to 1969 in a Volkswagen Beetle, Michael York (who plays Basil Exposition) improvised his line suggesting the audience not worry about how time travel works.

TOP 10 CRAZIEST TIME-TRAVEL DEVICES

THE T-10 UNOFFICIAL

		MOVIE(S)
01	DeLOREAN DMC-12	BACK TO THE FUTURE
02	MAILBOX	THE LAKE HOUSE
03	STEAM TRAIN	BACK TO THE FUTURE PART III
04	NEURAL SENSORY CHAMBER	SOURCE CODE
05	THE TARDIS	DOCTOR WHO
06	PHONE BOOTH	BILL & TED
07	TACHYON AMPLIFIER	LAND OF THE LOST
08	USS ENTERPRISE (NCC-1701)	STAR TREK
09	ALIEN SPACECRAFT	FLIGHT OF THE NAVIGATOR
10	HOMEMADE TIME MACHINE	THE TIME MACHINE

U.S.S. ENT
NCC-1

CHECK IT OUT!

USS Enterprise (NCC-1701): this spacecraft goes back in time via a slingshot effect around the sun in *Star Trek IV: The Voyage Home* (1986), and also via a time vortex in *Star Trek: First Contact* (1996).

X-PLORE
SOURCE CODE

Duncan Jones' *Source Code* (2011) deals with some very heady and complicated time-travel theories. The story involves Captain Colter Stevens (Jake Gyllenhaal) being transported into the last eight minutes of someone else's life before they are killed. Quantum physics and existential concepts fuel this thriller, and we love it for that!

XTREME FACT

MEN IN BLACK 3

The year 1969 strikes again! Agent J (Will Smith) travels back in time 43 years and sees a younger Agent K (Josh Brolin). However, Brolin is only 21-and-a-half years younger than actor Tommy Lee Jones, the present-day Agent K.

BOX OFFICE 624 MILLION DOLLARS

BOX OFFICE 147 MILLION DOLLARS

XTREME FACT

DeLOREAN DMC-12

It may be one of the coolest cars ever, but the DeLorean DMC-12 was the only product made by the DeLorean Motor Company (founded in 1975) before it went bankrupt in 1982. Shame it's not a real time machine!

TOP 10 BIGGEST FUTURE-SET MOVIES

Before we get to this list, remember that the *Star Wars* universe is set "a long time ago," so doesn't qualify. Here are the movies set in the future that do...

#		YEAR	BOX OFFICE ($ WORLDWIDE)
01	AVATAR	2009	2,782,275,172
02	THE HUNGER GAMES: CATCHING FIRE	2013	806,568,000
03	THE HUNGER GAMES	2012	691,247,768
04	I AM LEGEND	2007	585,349,010
05	WALL•E	2008	521,311,860
06	STAR TREK INTO DARKNESS	2013	467,365,246
07	X-MEN: THE LAST STAND	2006	459,359,555
08	PACIFIC RIM	2013	411,002,906
09	X2: X-MEN UNITED	2003	407,711,549
10	TRON LEGACY	2010	400,062,763

Source: IMDB.com

BOX OFFICE 691 MILLION DOLLARS

BOX OFFICE 411 MILLION DOLLARS

CHECK IT OUT!

The Hunger Games: Jennifer Lawrence (born August 15, 1990) has so far won an amazing 76 awards from 90 nominations since her acting career began in 2007.

XTREME FACT PACIFIC RIM

Pacific Rim director Guillermo del Toro brought in the big guns of visual effects to make the movie's monstrous battles truly epic. Shane Mahan (the genius behind the Iron Man suits), Industrial Light & Magic (*Star Wars'* effects and hundreds of other movies), and the likes of *Pirates Of The Caribbean*'s John Knoll and Hal T. Hickel were just a few of the other talents employed.

BIGGEST PREHISTORIC MOVIES

TOP 10

There have been plenty of dino-tastic movies made over the years. These are the Tyrannosaurus 10...

		YEAR	BOX OFFICE ($ WORLDWIDE)
01	JURASSIC PARK	1993	1,029,153,882
02	ICE AGE: DAWN OF THE DINOSAURS	2009	886,686,817
03	THE LOST WORLD: JURASSIC PARK	1997	618,638,999
04	JURASSIC PARK III	2001	368,780,809
05	DINOSAUR	2000	349,822,765
06	WALKING WITH DINOSAURS	2013	124,797,429
07	THE LAND BEFORE TIME	1988	84,460,846
08	LAND OF THE LOST	2009	68,777,554
09	BABY: SECRET OF THE LOST LEGEND	1985	14,972,297
10	BARNEY'S GREAT ADVENTURE	1998	12,218,638

Source: IMDB.com

BEEN & SEEN

When you've seen these futuristic movies, tick them off!

- [ ] REAL STEEL
- [ ] G.I. JOE: RETALIATION
- [ ] PACIFIC RIM
- [ ] THE HUNGER GAMES
- [ ] LOST IN SPACE
- [ ] STAR TREK INTO DARKNESS
- [ ] I, ROBOT
- [ ] X-MEN: DAYS OF FUTURE PAST
- [ ] A.I. ARTIFICIAL INTELLIGENCE
- [ ] ASTRO BOY

CHECK IT OUT!

Land Of The Lost: unlike the 1974-76 TV series of the same name, the 2009 movie version of *Land Of The Lost* features Sleestaks that can go out in daylight and have two sets of teeth.

TOP 10 BIGGEST ADVENTURE MOVIES

Pirates aside, here are the period movies which feature adventuring and questing that have claimed the most box office treasure...

#	Title	YEAR	BOX OFFICE ($ WORLDWIDE)
01	INDIANA JONES AND THE KINGDOM OF THE CRYSTAL SKULL	2008	786,636,033
02	RAIDERS OF THE LOST ARK	1981	389,925,971
03	KING KONG	2005	550,517,357
04	SHERLOCK HOLMES: A GAME OF SHADOWS	2011	545,448,418
05	SHERLOCK HOLMES	2009	524,028,679
06	INDIANA JONES AND THE LAST CRUSADE	1989	474,171,806
07	THE MUMMY RETURNS	2001	433,013,274
08	THE MUMMY	1999	415,933,406
09	THE MUMMY: TOMB OF THE DRAGON EMPEROR	2008	401,128,639
10	ROBIN HOOD: PRINCE OF THIEVES	1991	390,493,908

Source: IMDB.com

BOX OFFICE **786** MILLION DOLLARS

BOX OFFICE **433** MILLION DOLLARS

XTREME FACT
THE MUMMY RETURNS

Shooting his scenes as The Scorpion King for *The Mummy Returns* were quite a challenge for wrestling legend Dwayne "The Rock" Johnson. All of his lines were in Ancient Egyptian, and the actor also suffered sunstroke and food poisoning during production.

CHECK IT OUT!

Indiana Jones And The Kingdom Of The Crystal Skull: you can't have an Indy movie without that famous whip. However, studio executives originally wanted the whip work in this, the fourth Indy adventure, to be CGI, but actor Harrison Ford got to use a real one like in the previous movies.

MOVIE SHOWTIME

BOX OFFICE 123 MILLION DOLLARS

BIGGEST PIRATE MOVIES

Arrr, me hearties! Climb the riggin' and wash your linin', because it's time to present the 10 most successful swashbucklin' movies ever...

#	Title	Year	Box Office ($ Worldwide)	Relative Scale
01	PIRATES OF THE CARIBBEAN: DEAD MAN'S CHEST	2006	1,066,179,725	100%
02	PIRATES OF THE CARIBBEAN: ON STRANGER TIDES	2011	1,045,713,802	98%
03	PIRATES OF THE CARIBBEAN: AT WORLD'S END	2007	963,420,425	90%
04	PIRATES OF THE CARIBBEAN: THE CURSE OF THE BLACK PEARL	2003	654,264,015	61%
05	HOOK	1991	300,854,823	28%
06	CAPTAIN PHILLIPS	2013	217,657,113	20%
07	THE PIRATES! IN AN ADVENTURE WITH SCIENTISTS	2012	123,054,041	12%
08	RETURN TO NEVER LAND	2002	109,862,682	10%
09	TREASURE PLANET	2002	109,578,115	10%
10	SINBAD: LEGEND OF THE SEVEN SEAS	2003	80,767,884	8%

Source: IMDB.com

XTREME FACT
PIRATES OF THE CARIBBEAN: ON STRANGER TIDES

Johnny "Captain Jack Sparrow" Depp may play a loveable rogue in the *Pirates* movies, but in real life he shocked the *On Stranger Tides* crew members with his kindness when he bought waterproof coats for all 500 of them ($64,000) because of the bad weather.

CHECK IT OUT!

The Pirates! In An Adventure With Scientists (above): Aardman Animations, the team behind this swashbuckling comedy also made *Chicken Run* and the amazing *Wallace & Gromit* adventures. We love 'em!

255

YOUR SHOUT

Now your mind has been filled with loads of movie facts and figures, it's time to test your memory...

YOUR PICK OF THE... MOVIES

We've covered LOADS of awesome movies, but now it's over to you. What is YOUR Top 10?

01	
02	
03	
04	
05	
06	
07	
08	
09	
10	

ROUND 1: MULTIPLE CHOICE

01 Which of these movie actors is not in our Top 10 Most Bankable Stars list?

A JOHNNY DEPP
B EDDIE MURPHY
C CHRIS HEMSWORTH

02 Can you name the biggest stop-motion animated movie of all time?

A CORALINE
B THE CORPSE BRIDE
C CHICKEN RUN

03 *Batman* is the biggest superhero franchise ever, beating *Iron Man* and *Spider-Man* to the top spot. How much has the Caped Crusader taken worldwide at the box office?

A $4.728 BILLION
B $2.942 BILLION
C $1.259 BILLION

ROUND 2: QUESTION TIME

01 *Hook, Captain Phillips,* and *Return To Neverland* are all featured in the Biggest Pirate Movies, but can you name the franchise that occupies all four top spots on that list?

ANSWER:

ROUND 3:
PICTURE PUZZLES

Can you name the character that this piece of flying gear belongs to?

01

ANSWER:

Which character does this black costume and utility belt adorn?

02

ANSWER:

Clearly, this is Katniss Everdeen, but can you name the actress who plays her?

03

ANSWER:

ROUND 4:
WORDSEARCH

```
A C O R A L I N E C R E
T O L W V D O E S A V N
R I A O A V K E H K W O
A J D G V Q E S Y X O I
T Y W I A E A K H O E T
A O T J R E R Y I S V P
V J L I A V B F W I S E
A E O S V X R A I J F C
N O E B A A E L B E Z N
S H R E K A R L D V L I
C B O S G X E G B A C D
O D I N O S A U R O Z B
```

Take a look in the jumble of letters to the left and see how many of these movies you can find:

CLOVERFIELD

INCEPTION

AVATAR

CORALINE

GRAVITY

SKYFALL

DINOSAUR

SHREK

FIND THE ANSWERS ON PAGE 313

02 Samuel L. Jackson (right) has played this Marvel movie character seven times. Can you remember his name?

03 The entire Top 10 Biggest CGI Animated Movies list are sequels, except one. Can you name it?

ANSWER:

Find out which movie-related job is best suited to you on page 313

MOVIES
CAREER QUIZ

Which do you prefer to wear?
- **A** A DESIGNER JACKET
- **B** A BASEBALL CAP
- **C** A TRACKSUIT

Who would you rather hang out with for the day?
- **A** MORGAN FREEMAN
- **B** CHRISTOPHER NOLAN
- **C** TOM CRUISE

Which *The Dark Knight* character do you most relate to?
- **A** ALFRED
- **B** COMMISSIONER GORDON
- **C** BATMAN

If you were cornered by a blood-sucking vampire, what would you do?
- **A** PRETEND THAT YOU WERE A VAMPIRE AS WELL
- **B** TRY AND TALK HIM INTO A CHANGE OF DIRECTION
- **C** DROP TO THE FLOOR AND COMBAT-ROLL AWAY

If you were invited to a movie premiere, how would you arrive?
- **A** I'D WALK THE RED CARPET
- **B** I'D RATHER SNEAK IN THE BACK ENTRANCE
- **C** I'D BE TOO BUSY KEEPING FIT TO ATTEND

Which car would you like to own one day?
- **A** ASTON MARTIN
- **B** ROLLS ROYCE
- **C** DODGE VIPER

Which of the following statements best fits you?
- **A** I LOVE TO SHOW-OFF
- **B** I'M QUITE BOSSY
- **C** I'M NOT SCARED OF ANYTHING

ONLY HUMAN

63 158132-48781415213
154584337-4156456
56454456641-1545
514351-4564
213453434-4545433-4545435
5345435-4634354
2-45425 248-15455
57835-62798514
785456-45641
156684125-4848555451l
1456l5615-567897
63936 3-536398
45336l3-585
1253854-15862
8632863-556
1456l5615-567897
69756132-48781415213
154584337-4156456
56454456641-1545
514351-4564
213453434-4545433
45424-434354-45343541
15853-4552255862

CHECK IT OUT!

WEIGHT 10.8 OZ

Heart: beyond its biological functions, the heart is also associated with love and our emotions. Many ancient philosophers thought the heart (and not the brain) was where our thoughts and emotions were processed.

DANGER!

Looking after your heart is essential for keeping you healthy. Exercise, a low-fat diet, and minimizing emotional stress are key factors in helping to keep the heart healthy.

XTREME FACT

BRAIN

Based on the Human Genome Project, in 2013, the BRAIN Initiative (Brain Research through Advancing Innovative Neurotechnologies) was launched. Experts involved in the $300 million-a-year project are seeking to map each neuron in the human brain.

TOP 10 HEAVIEST HUMAN ORGANS

Before you read this list, have a guess at what the heaviest organ in your body is. You'll be very surprised at the ones that make the Top 10...

		AVERAGE WEIGHT IN ADULTS	
		(G)	(OZ)
01	SKIN	10,750	379.2
02	LIVER	1,500	53
03	BRAIN	1,350	47.6
04	LUNGS	830	29.3
05	HEART	308	10.8
06	KIDNEYS	270	9.5
07	SPLEEN	170	6
08	PANCREAS	68	2.4
09	THYROID	40	1.4
10	PROSTATE	25	0.9

WEIGHT 47.6 OZ

X-PLORE

ANATOMY OF THE HEART

Outer layer: **Epicardium**
Middle layer: **Myocardium**
Inner layer: **Endocardium**
Inner lining: **Endothelium**

The heart takes the de-oxygenated blood and pumps it into the lungs so carbon dioxide is left and oxygen is collected.

TOP 10

SMALLEST HUMAN BONES

THE T-10 UNOFFICIAL

#	Bone	LOCATION
01	STAPES	Middle ear
02	INCUS	Middle ear
03	MALLEUS	Middle ear
04	HYOID	Base of tongue
05	PHALANGES	Fingers & toes
06	TRIQUETRAL	Wrist
07	LUNATE	Wrist
08	SCAPHOID	Wrist
09	TRAPEZOID	Wrist
10	TRAPEZIUM	Wrist

CHECK IT OUT!

Stapes: among the 206 main bones that make up the structure of the human body, the stapes is the tiniest. It may be small, but this incredibly important bone transmits sound vibrations to the inner ear's membrane via the incus, and so is essential to hearing.

X-TREME FACT

INCUS

This tiny bone looks just like an anvil, which is why it is called the incus (latin for "anvil"). This bone transports sound from the malleus to the stapes.

CHECK IT OUT!

75-175 years old: this may look like a Mordor prop from *The Lord Of The Rings*, but it's actually an ornate artificial steel and brass hand and arm, dating from 1840-1940.

XTREME FACT
510 YEARS OLD

A section of the Mark I Iron Man suit? No, but this artificial arm is made of iron! It is believed to have been owned by a German knight called Götz von Berlichingen (1480-1562).

FIRST PROSTHETICS

Invented by smart thinkers, prosthetics (devices made to replace a missing body part) have helped people since way back in Ancient Egypt...

		PERSON/PLACE	YEARS AGO
01	ARTIFICIAL LEG	Vishpala (in ancient Indian text)	3,000+
02	WOODEN BIG TOE	Ancient Egypt	2,900
03	WOODEN FOOT	Hegesistratus, Greece	2,450
04	WOODEN & BRONZE LEG	Ancient Rome, Italy	2,300
05	IRON ARM	Gaius Plinius Secundus, Italy	1,960
06	IRON ARM WITH GRIPPING FINGERS	Götz von Berlichingen, Germany	510
07	ADJUSTABLE ARTIFICIAL LEGS AND FEET	Ambroise Paré, France	460+
08	IRON ARM	François de la Noue, France	444
09	IRON HOOK	Henri de Tonti, Italy	346
10	NON-LOCKING, BELOW-THE-KNEE LEG	Pieter Verduyn, The Netherlands	318

XTREME FACT
TODAY'S PROSTHETIC ARMS

From the makeshift limbs of old to the prosthetic limbs of the future. Dean Kamen (who also invented the Segway) invented this, the DEKA Arm, which is the most advanced of its kind. It is also called the Luke, named after Luke Skywalker (who has got a robotic hand). See www.dekaresearch.com.

SONGS ABOUT THE BODY

TOP 10

THE T-10 UNOFFICIAL

		BAND/ARTIST	YEAR
01	BONES	Radiohead	1995
02	FINGERPRINTS	Katy Perry	2008
03	STRUNG TO YOUR RIBCAGE	Biffy Clyro	2004
04	SKIN ON SKIN	The Unwinding Hours	2012
05	HEAD OVER FEET	Alanis Morissette	1995
06	PLACE YOUR HANDS	Reef	1996
07	SACRED HEART	The Civil Wars	2013
08	HEADLOCK	Imogen Heap	2005
09	HANDS HELD HIGH	Linkin Park	1997
10	EASY ON THE EYE	Gemma Hayes	2005

BIGGEST BRAINS: HUMANS VS. ANIMALS

TOP 10

Here is how our human brain stacks up against other animals in terms of brain-to-body weight ratio...

		RATIO
01	ANT	1:7
02	TREE SHREW	1:10
03	SMALL BIRD	1:12
04	HUMAN	1:40
05	MOUSE	1:40
06	DOLPHIN	1:50
07	CAT	1:100
08	CHIMPANZEE	1:113
09	DOG	1:125
10	SQUIRREL	1:150

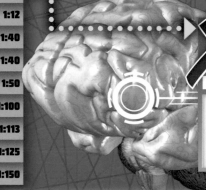

XTREME FACT

PREFRONTAL CORTEX

This is the region of the brain that you've probably heard of the most. This is because it is associated with a person's thought processes, decisions, and ideas.

CHECK IT OUT!

Daniel Kish, the real-life Batman: Blind from 13 months old, the American self-developed a form of echo-location, and can "see" by making a clicking noise and analyzing the sounds that come back, just like a bat. More than 500 blind children have learned his technique, thanks to Kish's organization: visit www.worldaccessfortheblind.org.

CHECK IT OUT!

Hand Transplant: Italian factory worker Stefano Silleoni, 42, lost both his forearms in a machinery accident. He was treated in Lyon, France, and had two new hands successfully transplanted.

X-PLORE
ISABELLE DINOIRE

Between 2005-06, Frenchwoman Isabelle Dinoire made medical history by being the first person to successfully receive a full face transplant. After takings pills, Isabelle fell so deeply asleep, and wouldn't wake up, that her dog accidentally mauled her while

desperately trying to wake her up. Dinoire will have to take anti-rejection drugs for the rest of her life so that her body doesn't reject and attack the new tissue grafted to her face.

MEDICAL MARVELS

TOP 10

THE T-10 UNOFFICIAL

		NAME	COUNTRY	YEAR
01	FEET FIXED INSIDE THE WOMB	Leah Bowlen	Australia	2008
02	FACE TRANSPLANT	Isabelle Dinoire	France	2005
03	SELF-APPENDECTOMY	Evan O'Neill Kane	USA	1921
04	WINDPIPE TRANSPLANT	Claudia Castillo	Colombia	2008
05	BOTH LUNGS TRANSPLANTED	Oli Lewington	UK	2007
06	FOUR EXTRA LIMBS REMOVED	Lakshmi Tatma	India	2007
07	EYELASH TRANSPLANT	Louise Thomas	UK	2009
08	HEART & LUNG TRANSPLANT	Lisa Williams	UK	2009
09	BOTH ARMS TRANSPLANTED	Karl Merk	Germany	2009
10	HAND TRANSPLANT	Stefano Silleoni	Italy	2012

OFF THE CHART

NOSE RECONSTRUCTION

In a scene straight out of a science fiction film, in 2013, doctors in Fuzhou, China, grew a new nose on a patient's forehead! This was to replace the patient's nose that had been irreparably damaged.

TOP 10 SHORTEST HUMANS ALIVE

In the previous T-10 book, we brought you the tallest people ever, so this time, we're looking at the littler people who have made the record books...

		COUNTRY	YEAR BORN	HEIGHT (CM)	HEIGHT (IN)
01	CHANDRA BAHADUR DANGI	Nepal	1939	54.6	21.5
02	JUNREY BALAWING	Philippines	1993	59.93	23.6
03	JYOTI AMGE	India	1993	62.7	24.7
04	MADGE BESTER	South Africa	1963	63	24.8
05	KHAGENDRA THAPA MAGAR	Nepal	1992	67	26.4
06	LIN YÜ-CHIH	Taiwan	1972	67.5	26.6
07	BRIDGETTE JORDAN	USA	1989	69	27.2
08	EDWARD NIÑO HERNÁNDEZ	Colombia	2010	70.2	27.6
09	HATICE KOCAMAN	Turkey	1989	71	28
10	AJAY KUMAR	India	1976	76	30

XTREME FACT — CHANDRA BAHADUR DANGI

At 75 years of age, Nepalese Chandra Bahadur Dangi is the shortest man in the world. Curiously, the rest of his family are of a more average height, and the medical condition which made Dangi this size is as yet unknown.

HEIGHT 24.7 IN

HEIGHT 21.5 IN

CHECK IT OUT!

Jyoti Amge: as the smallest woman in the world, 21-year-old Jyoti is from Nagpur in India. She was also a special guest housemate on *Big Boss*, India's own version of the reality TV show *Big Brother*.

TOP 10

NATIONS FIRST ASTRONAUTS

Here are the first 10 nations that managed to put a person successfully into space, and their superstar first astronauts...

#	NATION	ASTRONAUT	DATE
01	SOVIET UNION (NOW RUSSIA)	Yuri Gagarin	APR 12, 1961
02	USA	Alan Shepard	MAY 5, 1961
03	CZECHOSLOVAKIA	Vladimír Remek	MAR 2, 1978
04	POLAND	Mirosław Hermaszewski	JUN 27, 1978
05	EAST GERMANY (NOW GERMANY)	Sigmund Jähn	AUG 26, 1978
06	BULGARIA	Georgi Ivanov	APR 10, 1979
07	HUNGARY	Bertalan Farkas	MAY 26, 1980
08	VIETNAM	Pham Tuân	JUL 23, 1980
09	CUBA	Arnaldo Tamayo Méndez	SEP 18, 1980
10	MONGOLIA	Jügderdemidiin Gürragchaa	MAR 22, 1981

DATE
APR 12
1961

CHECK IT OUT!

USA: here's legendary American astronaut Alan Shepard on May 5, 1961, on his solo Mercury flight. A decade later, he went on to lead the Apollo 14 mission, and was responsible for the most accurate lunar landing in the history of moon missions.

XTREME FACT

SOVIET UNION

Here he is: the first-ever man in space. Russian Yuri Gagarin (March 9, 1934 to March 27, 1968) is in the Vostok 1 capsule, photographed on April 12, 1961. He was tragically killed piloting a MiG-15 jet in 1968.

CHECK IT OUT!

Robert Falcon Scott's camp, 1912: this stunning moonlit photo of Captain Scott's camp hut, by Mount Erebus, was taken on June 13, 1911.

Xtreme FACT

PRINCESS ELISABETH ANTARCTICA STATION

Although the Antarctic has always been a place of scientific research and exploration, the Princess Elisabeth Station is the first ever "zero emission" station. The structure was first built in Brussels, and it opened in February 2009. You can keep up to date with its activity at www.antarcticstation.org.

TOP 10
MOST RECENT ANTARCTIC EXPEDITIONS

Did you know that the South Pole wasn't actually reached by a human until 1911! Here are the most recent Antarctic daredevils...

#	Expedition	COUNTRY	PURPOSE	DATE
01	PARKER LIAUTAUD & DOUGLAS STOUP	USA	Scientific & speed record for unsupported skiing to the pole	DEC 2013
02	BEN SAUNDERS & TARKA L'HERPINIERE	UK	Recreate/complete R. F. Scott's 1912 Terra Nova Expedition	OCT 2013
03	TIM JARVIS & BARRY GRAY (+ 4 MORE)	UK/Australia	Shackleton re-enactment	FEB 2013
04	LIEUTENANT STUART FLETCHER (+23 MORE)	UK	Scientific research & centenary of R. F. Scott's 1912 expedition	2011–2012
05	SEBASTIAN COPELAND & ERIC McNAIR-LANDRY	USA	Opened a new route to the South pole	2011–2012
06	MOON REGAN TRANSANTARCTIC CROSSING	UK	First bio-fuel-based vehicle expedition	2010
07	CECILIE SKOG & RYAN WATERS	Norway	Unsupported skiing expedition	2009–10
08	FELICITY ASTON (+ 7 MORE)	Various	Celebrating the 60th anniversary of the Commonwealth	2009
09	HUSEYN BAHIROV & TARLAN RAMAZANON	Azerbaijan	Azerbaijan scientific expedition	2009
10	RAY ZAHAB, KEVIN VALLELY & RICHARD WEBER	Canada	Impossible 2 Possible (i2P) unsupported South Pole quest	2008–2009

OFF THE CHART
ANTARCTIC MARATHON

On November 18, 2014, the 10th Antarctic Ice Marathon took place at 80 Degrees South, near the South Pole. The race was in extreme temperatures, and you can learn more about it at www.icemarathon.com.

Xtreme Fact

JACQUES PICCARD AND DON WALSH

This amazing photo, taken on August 8, 1960, shows Jacques Piccard and Don Walsh emerging from their bathyscaphe. They had successfully explored the deepest point on the Earth (from surface to seabed) called the Challenger Deep, which is in the Mariana Trench in the Pacific Ocean.

TOP 10 FIRST MANNED DEEP-SEA EXPLORATIONS

We have been fascinated by the mysterious depths of our oceans for centuries. These were the first manned deep dives inside a mechanical device...

#		COUNTRY	EVENT	YEAR
01	WILLIAM BEEBE & OTIS BARTON	USA	First deep-sea divers inside the Bathysphere to 1,427 ft (435 m)	1930
02	WILLIAM BEEBE & OTIS BARTON	USA	Their Bathysphere gets to a depth of 3,028 ft (923 m)	1934
03	OTIS BARTON	USA	Bathysphere achieves a depth of 4,495 ft (1,370 m)	1948
=	AUGUSTE PICCARD	Switzerland	Inside his bathyscaphe vessel, reaches 4,600 ft (1,402 m)	1948
05	AUGUSTE PICCARD	Switzerland	Inside Trieste, he descends to 10,335 ft (3,150 m)	1953
06	AUGUSTE PICCARD	Switzerland	Piccard's bathyscaphe vessel gets to 13,125 ft (4,000 m)	1954
07	JACQUES PICCARD & DON WALSH	Switzerland/USA	Inside Trieste, they descend to 35,810 ft (10,915 m)	1960
08	BILL RAINNIE & MARAVIN McCAMIS	USA	DSV (Deep-sea Submergence Vehicle) Alvin reaches 5,905 ft (1,800)	1965
09	US NAVY	USA	Alvin recovers a lost hydrogen bomb at 2,985 ft (910 m)	1966
10	WOODS HOLE OCEANOGRAPHIC INSTITUTE	USA	Alvin is attacked by a swordfish at 2,001 ft (610 m)	1967

OFF THE CHART: SYLVIA EARLE, 1979

In 1979, US oceanographer Sylvia Earle set the ADS (Atmospheric Diving Suit) record of 1,250 ft (381 m). In 1998, Earle was named by *Time* magazine as its first Hero For The Planet.

MOST INFAMOUS PRISON BREAKOUTS

THE T-10 UNOFFICIAL

		PRISON	COUNTRY	YEAR
01	BILLY "THE KID" McCARTY, JR	Lincoln County, New Mexico	USA	1881
02	1,000 INMATES	Queyfiya	Libya	2013
03	JOHN DILLINGER	Indiana's Crown Point	USA	1934
04	CLARENCE ANGLIN, JOHN ANGLIN, FRANK MORRIS	Alcatraz	USA	1962
05	PASCAL PAYET	Luynes prison	France	2001
06	HUGO GROTIUS	Castle Loevestein	The Netherlands	1621
07	BILLY HAYES	İmralı prison	Turkey	1975
08	DANIEL RENWICK, TRACY PROVINCE, JOHN McCLUSKEY	Arizona State	USA	2010
09	APPROX 545 JAPANESE POWs	Number 12 POW Compound	Australia	1944
10	EDWARD SALAS & SEVEN OTHER INMATES	Curry County New Mexico	USA	2008

XTREME FACT
ALCATRAZ

Alcatraz, located in San Francisco Bay, California, USA, was a 312-capacity operational maximum security prison from August 11, 1934 to March 21, 1963. Now it is a museum that has 1.5 million visitors every year.

MOST EPIC ESCAPEES IN MOVIES

THE T-10 UNOFFICIAL

		MOVIE	YEAR RELEASED
01	EDMOND DANTÈS	The Count Of Monte Cristo	2002
02	TARA	Epic	2013
03	TONY STARK	Iron Man	2008
04	ANDY DUFRESNE	The Shawshank Redemption	1994
05	ROCKY & GINGER	Chicken Run	2000
06	HILTS	The Great Escape	1963
07	DIETER DENGLER	Rescue Dawn	2006
08	FRANK MORRIS	Escape From Alcatraz	1979
09	PHILIPPE	The Man In The Iron Mask	1998
10	LUKE	Cool Hand Luke	1967

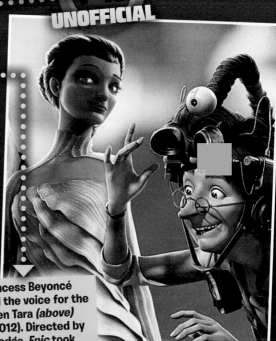

CHECK IT OUT! Tara: popstar princess Beyoncé Knowles provided the voice for the character of Queen Tara (above) in the film Epic (2012). Directed by Chris "Ice Age" Wedge, Epic took $268,426,634 at the box office.

OFF THE CHART

PTOLEMY'S WORLD MAP

Historic, and oh so artistic, too. This is the Ptolemaic World Map from Claudius Ptolemy's cartography tome, *Geographia Latin*. Ptolemy wrote AND illustrated this map and the whole book.

XTREME FACT

POSIDONIUS

Posidonius (135 BC–51 BC) certainly went out of his way to try and push scientific knowledge of our planet. He made a calculation of the size of the Moon and how far away it is, plus, he was correct in his theory that the Sun gave off an energy that affected all of the planets.

MOST ANCIENT CARTOGRAPHERS

TOP 10

When do you think cartographers (mapping experts) first attempted to log the planet's layout? It's a LOT longer ago than you'd ever imagine...

		COUNTRY/REGION	WORLD MAP NAME	YEARS AGO (APPROX)
01	(UNKNOWN)	Babylonia (present-day Iraq)	Imago Mundi	2,800+
02	ANAXIMANDER	Greece	Unnamed	2,500
03	HECATAEUS OF MILETUS	Greece	Ges Periodos	2,400
04	ERATOSTHENES	Greece	Unnamed	2,250
05	POSIDONIUS	Greece	Geographia (collected works)	2,120
06	STRABO	Greece	Geographia (collected works)	2,045
07	POMPONIUS MELA	Iulia Traducta (present-day Spain)	Unnamed	1,980
08	MARINUS OF TYRE	Greece	Unnamed	1,880
09	PTOLEMY	Egypt	Geographia (collected works)	1,860
10	(UNKNOWN)	Germany (discovered there)	Tabula Peutingeriana	1,800

CHECK IT OUT!

The planet as we know it: and here it is, a satellite view of our planet as we are familiar with it today. If you want to learn more scientific data about our world, check out: www.nationalgeographic.com.

TOP 10 MOST INFAMOUS PIRATES

THE T-10 UNOFFICIAL

		COUNTRY	KNOWN PIRATING YEARS
01	EDWARD "BLACKBEARD" TEACH	England	1716–1718
02	OLIVIER "THE BUZZARD" LEVASSEUR	France	1716–1730
03	BARTHOLOMEW "BLACK BART" ROBERTS	Wales	1719–1722
04	EDWARD "NED" LOW	England	1721–1724
05	RAHMAH IBN JABIR AL-JALAHIMAH	Kuwait	1780–1826
06	WILLIAM "CAPTAIN" KIDD	Scotland	1695–1699
07	CHARLES VANE	England	1716–1720
08	BLACK CAESAR	Africa	1700–1718
09	SAMUEL "BLACK SAM" BELLAMY	England	1716–1717
10	LARS & INGELA GATHENHIELM	Sweden	1710–1721

KNOWN PIRATING YEARS 1716–1718

BEEN & SEEN

When you've seen these pirate movies with your own eyes, tick them!

- [ ] PIRATES OF THE CARIBBEAN: ON STRANGER TIDES
- [ ] HOOK
- [ ] THE GOONIES
- [ ] PIRATES OF THE CARIBBEAN: AT WORLD'S END
- [ ] MUPPET TREASURE ISLAND
- [ ] PIRATES OF THE CARIBBEAN: THE CURSE OF THE BLACK PEARL
- [ ] TREASURE PLANET
- [ ] PIRATES OF THE CARIBBEAN: DEAD MAN'S CHEST
- [ ] PETER PAN
- [ ] CUTTHROAT ISLAND

XTREME FACT

BLACKBEARD

Born in Bristol, England, Edward Teach, better known as Blackbeard, was one of the most ruthless pirates to sail the seas. Although his pirating years were brief (approx. two years), stories of theft and murder around the West Indies and the eastern coast of the American colonies are legendary. This picture shows actor Ian McShane's potrayal of Blackbeard in *Pirates Of The Caribbean: On Stranger Tides*.

BIGGEST ANIMAL PHOBIAS

Many people have a psychological fear of certain animals. In order of the size of the feared creature, here are the 10 terms for those anxieties...

TOP 10

#		A FEAR OF...
01	SELACHOPHOBIA	SHARKS
02	EQUINOPHOBIA/HIPPOPHOBIA	HORSES
03	BOVINOPHOBIA	CATTLE
04	CYNOPHOBIA	DOGS
05	AILUROPHOBIA	CATS
06	ORNITHOPHOBIA	BIRDS
07	OPHIDIOPHOBIA	SNAKES
08	CHIROPTOPHOBIA	BATS
09	ICHTHYOPHOBIA	FISH
10	MUSOPHOBIA	RATS & MICE

DID YOU KNOW?

ZOOPHOBIA: As you can see, we've listed some animal phobias on the left, but did you know there is also a term for simply being afraid of animals? It's appropriately called "zoophobia."

MOST UNUSUAL PHOBIAS

TOP 10

THE T-10 UNOFFICIAL

#		A FEAR OF...
01	TETRAPHOBIA	THE NUMBER FOUR
02	POGONOPHOBIA	BEARDS
03	TUROPHOBIA	CHEESE
04	BAROPHOBIA	GRAVITY
05	ANTHOPHOBIA	FLOWERS
06	CHAETOPHOBIA	HAIR
07	SESQUIPEDALOPHOBIA	LONG WORDS
08	PAPAPHOBIA	THE POPE
09	KOUMPOUNOPHOBIA	BUTTONS
10	OMBROPHOBIA	RAIN

CHECK IT OUT!

Turophobia: Cheddar, Brie, Pepperjack—keep them all away from those who fear cheese!

XTREME FACT
CHIROPTOPHOBIA

One of the most famous fictional characters to have suffered from chiroptophobia is Bruce "Batman" Wayne. However, it was filmmaker Christopher Nolan and writer David S. Goyer who fleshed out that aspect of his past, not the comics.

TRY THE TEST

WRITE WHAT YOU SEE HERE:

X-PLORE
THE RORSCHACH TEST

Swiss psychiatrist and psychoanalyst Hermann Rorschach invented the Rorschach inkblot test in 1921. The tests are designed to unveil unconscious thoughts, depending on what the subject sees. What can you make out in this inkblot *(left)*?

XTREME FACT
SELACHOPHOBIA

One of mankind's most common phobias is a fear of sharks. We are pretty useless in the open ocean compared to these incredible, toothy, intelligent predators.

TOP 10 FAMOUS PSYCHIATRISTS
THE T-10 UNOFFICIAL

#	Name	COUNTRY	LIFETIME
01	SIGMUND FREUD	Austria	MAY 6 1856–SEP 23, 1939
02	ELISABETH KÜBLER-ROSS	Switzerland	JUL 8, 1926–AUG 24, 2004
03	MELANIE KLEIN	Austria	MAR 30, 1882–SEP 22, 1960
04	MICHAEL SHEPHERD	UK	JUL 30, 1923–AUG 21, 1995
05	ALFRED ADLER	Austria	FEB 7, 1870–MAY 28, 1937
06	SULA WOLFF	Germany	MAR 1, 1924–SEP 21, 2009
07	PHILIPPE PINEL	France	APRIL 20, 1745–OCT 25, 1826
08	ABRAHAM MASLOW	USA	APR 1, 1908–JUN 8, 1970
09	RD LAING	Scotland	OCT 7, 1927–AUG 23, 1989
10	KAREN HORNEY	Germany	SEP 16, 1885–DEC 4, 1952

CHECK IT OUT!

Sigmund Freud: he is considered the founder of what we call psychoanalysis (the study of the mind and its relationship to our thoughts and feelings). The term "Freudian" describes something as being psychoanalytical.

Xtreme Fact

SHERLOCK HOLMES

Created by Sir Arthur Conan Doyle in 1886, Sherlock Holmes (with help from Dr. Watson) is a fictional detective who solves seemingly uncrackable cases.

BOX OFFICE **959** MILLION DOLLARS

TOP 10

MOVIE MASTERMINDS

There have been plenty of super-smart geniuses to grace the movie screens over the years, but these are the ones with the biggest box office takings...

		NUMBER OF MOVIES	MOVIE(S)/YEAR(S)	BOX OFFICE ($ WORLDWIDE)	RELATIVE SCALE:
01	Q	22	*James Bond* movies (1962–present)	4,903,880,166	100%
02	TONY STARK	4	*Iron Man & Avengers* movies (2008–present)	3,935,753,517	80%
03	BRUCE WAYNE	8	*Batman* movies (1966–present)	3,712,725,948	76%
04	PROFESSOR X	5	*X-Men* movies (2000–present)	1,508,665,385	31%
05	MR. SPOCK	7	*Star Trek* movies (1979–present)	1,297,290,285	26%
06	BENJI DUNN	2	*M:I III* (2006) and *M:I Ghost Protocol* (2011)	1,092,563,392	22%
07	SHERLOCK HOLMES	37	*Sherlock Holmes* movies (1943–2011)	959,845,743	20%
08	DR. EMMETT BROWN	3	*Back To The Future* trilogy (1985–90)	957,587,347	20%
09	DOMINIC COBB	1	*Inception* (2011)	825,532,764	17%
10	FORREST GUMP	1	*Forrest Gump* (1994)	677,387,716	14%

Source: IMDB.com

CHECK IT OUT!

Bruce Wayne: Christian Bale has played Bruce Wayne/Batman on the big screen three times—more than any other actor in that role.

MOST ED EDUCATED COUNTRIES

TOP 10

Learning new information expands the mind. Here are the 10 countries with the highest percentage of residents who have studied beyond the age of 16...

		POPULATION WITH POST-SECONDARY SCHOOL EDUCATION
01	RUSSIA	53.5%
02	CANADA	51.3%
03	JAPAN	46.4%
=	ISRAEL	46.4%
05	USA	42.5%
06	KOREA	40.4%
07	UK	39.4%
08	NEW ZEALAND	39.3%
=	FINLAND	39.3%
10	AUSTRALIA	38.3%

46.4%
POST-SECONDARY SCHOOL EDUCATION

XTREME FACT

JAPAN

Japan is also third in the chart of countries with the highest average IQ (a measure of intelligence). In Japan, the average IQ is 105. The top two countries are Hong Kong (107) and South Korea (106).

GREATEST CODEBREAKERS

TOP 10

THE T-10 UNOFFICIAL

		COUNTRY	LIFETIME	FAMOUS FOR
01	GIOVANNI SORO	Italy	Unknown-1544	The father of modern cryptology, worked for first secret service in 1506
02	WILLIAM F. FRIEDMAN	Moldova	Sep 24, 1891-Nov 12, 1969	Dean of American cryptology
03	ELIZEBETH SMITH FRIEDMAN	USA	Aug 26, 1892-Oct 31, 1980	Being the first female cryptanalyst, cracked hugely complex codes
04	JOHN WALLIS	UK	Nov 23, 1616-Oct 28, 1703	Chief parliamentary cryptographer, invented the infinity symbol
05	HERBERT YARDLEY	USA	Apr 13, 1889-Aug 7, 1958	Founder/head of the Cipher Bureau, famed author on cryptology
06	MEREDITH GARDNER	USA	Oct 20, 1912-Aug 9, 2002	Decoding secret Soviet intelligence about spies in USA
07	CHARLES BABBAGE	UK	Dec 26, 1791-Oct 18, 1871	Father of the computer: developed first mechanical, programmable one
08	AGNES MEYER DRISCOLL	USA	Jul 24, 1889-Sep 16, 1971	Known as "Madame X," worked intelligence for WWI and WWII
09	MARIAN REJEWSKI	Poland	Aug 16, 1905-Feb 13, 1980	Solved the Enigma machine in 1932, which helped Britain crack it
10	WILLIAM "BILL" TUTTE	UK	May 14, 1917-May 2, 2002	Helped crack Germany's Lorenz cipher in World War II

DID YOU KNOW?

Cryptology: the scientific study of cryptography (the process of reading or writing secret codes or messages) and cryptanalysis (the solving of such secret codes).

WORLD CHAMPIONSHIP TITLES
15

X TREME FACT
GARRY KASPAROV

Not just a multiple-time world chess champion, Russian Garry Kasparov has many other talents. He's an author, human rights activist, business speaker, and pro-democracy leader. Find out more at www.kasparov.com.

TOP 10
GREATEST CHESS PLAYERS

Becoming a master of chess requires a ton of brainpower and the ability to predict the game's potential progress, several moves ahead. These are the all-time masters...

		COUNTRY	TOTAL WORLD CHAMPIONSHIP TITLES
01	EMANUEL LASKER	Germany	27
02	ALEXANDER ALEKHINE	Russia	17
03	ANATOLY KARPOV	Russia	16
04	GARRY KASPAROV	Russia	15
05	MIKHAIL BOTVINNIK	Russia	13
06	WILHELM STEINITZ	Austria	8
07	VISWANATHAN ANAND	India	7
=	VLADIMIR KRAMNIK	Russia	7
09	TIGRAN PETROSIAN	Russia	6
=	JOSÉ RAÚL CAPABLANCA	Cuba	6

WORLD CHAMPIONSHIP TITLES
27

CHECK IT OUT!

Emanuel Lasker: here's Dr. Lasker in 1910, halfway through his 1894-1921 chess championship reign. Aside from his love of the game, he wrote extensively about philosophy and mathematics.

PSYCHICS IN FICTION

TOP 10

THE T-10 UNOFFICIAL

		FROM
01	JEAN GREY	*X-Men* (1963-present comics/movie franchise)
02	RIVER TAM	*Firefly* (2002-03 TV series), *Serenity* (2005 movie) & comics (2007-present)
03	NIBBLER	*Futurama* (1999–2013 TV series)
04	ANDREW DETMER	*Chronicle* (2012 movie)
05	CHARLES XAVIER	*X-Men* (1963-present comics/movie franchise)
06	ELEANOR "NELL" LANCE	*The Haunting* (1963 movie)
07	CLYDE BRUCKMAN	*The X-Files* (1993-2002 TV series)
08	GEORGE LONEGAN	*Hereafter* (2010 movie)
09	ODA MAE BROWN	*Ghost* (1990 movie)
10	ALLISON DUBOIS	*Medium* (2005-2011 TV series)

X TREME FACT

ANDREW DETMER

American actor Dane DeHaan played Andrew Detmer in Josh Trank's 2012 directorial debut *Chronicle*. With a budget of $12 million, the psychic thriller went on to take a massive $126,636,097 worldwide.

BEST "POKER FACE"

TOP 10

The card game of Poker is all-out psychological warfare. Players must not show any reaction to their hand of cards, especially when the stakes are into the $ millions...

		COUNTRY	TOTAL TOURNAMENT EARNINGS ($)
01	PHIL HELLMUTH	USA	15,852,878
02	JAMIE GOLD	USA	12,238,161
03	JONATHAN DUHAMEL	Canada	11,928,281
04	JOE HACHEM	Australia	11,707,569
05	PETER EASTGATE	Denmark	11,535,337
06	CARLOS MORTENSEN	Spain	11,328,240
07	GREG MERSON	USA	10,756,287
08	JOE CADA	USA	9,388,619
09	PIUS HEINZ	Germany	8,899,080
10	JERRY YANG	Laos	8,408,530

CHECK IT OUT!

Peter Eastgate: when Peter won the 2008 World Series of Poker Main Event aged 23, he was the youngest-ever player to do so.

277

CHECK IT OUT!

Fahrenheit 9/11: Considering it's a documentary (and not an action blockbuster), taking nearly $223 million is crazy. *Fahrenheit 9/11* remains one of the most controversial docs ever, delving into the George W. Bush presidency and the terrorism around the 9/11 Twin Towers destruction.

TOP 10 MOST SUCCESSFUL DOCUMENTARIES

Documentaries can often get crucial information about our world to us. Here are the 10 most successful of all time, showing the documentary filmmakers who are making the biggest connections with us...

		DIRECTOR	YEAR RELEASED	BOX OFFICE (WORLDWIDE $ MILLIONS)
01	FAHRENHEIT 9/11	Michael Moore	2004	222,446,882
02	MARCH OF THE PENGUINS	Luc Jacquet	2005	127,392,693
03	EARTH	Alastair Fothergill & Mark Linfield	2007	108,975,160
04	JUSTIN BIEBER: NEVER SAY NEVER	Jon Chu	2011	99,036,827
05	OCEANS	Jacques Perrin & Jacques Cluzaud	2010	82,651,439
06	BOWLING FOR COLUMBINE	Michael Moore	2002	58,008,423
07	AN INCONVENIENT TRUTH	Davis Guggenheim	2006	49,756,507
08	SICKO	Michael Moore	2007	36,088,109
09	CHIMPANZEE	Alastair Fothergill & Mark Linfield	2012	34,823,764
10	2016: OBAMA'S AMERICA	Dinesh D'Souza & John Sullivan	2012	33,449,086

Source: IMDB.com

XTREME FACT

JUSTIN BIEBER: NEVER SAY NEVER

Justin Bieber's first big-screen documentary *Never Say Never* featured a star-studded string of A-listers including Usher, Miley Cyrus, LA Reid, and Jaden Smith.

MOST RECENT NOBEL PEACE PRIZE WINNERS

Presented every year since 1901, here are the 10 most recent individuals who have been awarded for their outstanding contributions to peace...

		OCCUPATION	COUNTRY	YEAR
01	TAWAKKOL KARMAN	Human rights activist, journalist, politician	Yemen	2011
=	LEYMAH GBOWEE	Peace activist	Liberia	2011
=	ELLEN JOHNSON SIRLEAF	24th president of Liberia	Liberia	2011
04	LIU XIAOBO	Human rights activist, writer, critic	China	2010
05	BARACK OBAMA	44th president of USA	USA	2009
06	MARTTI AHTISAARI	10th president of Finland	Finland	2008
07	AL GORE	45th vice president of USA, philanthropist	USA	2007
08	MUHAMMAD YUNUS	Economist	Bangladesh	2006
09	MOHAMED ELBARADEI	Director general International Atomic Energy Agency	Egypt	2005
10	WANGARI MAATHAI	Political activist	Kenya	2004

DID YOU KNOW?

In 1901, Alfred Nobel created the Nobel Prizes in Peace, Literature, Physics, Chemistry, Physiology or Medicine. The Nobel Peace Prize is awarded to those deemed to have "done the most or best work for fraternity between nations; for the abolition or reduction of standing armies and for the holding and promotion of peace congresses." Find out more at www.nobelprize.org.

MOST RECENT SAINTS

In order of the year they died, these are the 10 most modern sainted figures...

		COUNTRY	LIFETIME
01	SAINT JOSEMARÍA ESCRIVÁ	Spain	JAN 9, 1902–JUN 26, 1975
02	POPE CYRIL VI OF ALEXANDRIA	Egypt	AUG 2, 1902–MAR 9, 1971
03	SAINT AMPHILOCHIUS OF POCHAYIV	Ukraine	NOV 27, 1894–JAN 1, 1971
04	SAINT PIO OF PIETRELCINA	Italy	MAY 25, 1887–SEP 23, 1968
05	SAINT JOHN OF SHANGHAI AND SAN FRANCISCO	Ukraine	JUN 4, 1896–JUL 2, 1966
06	SAINT GEORGE PRECA	Malta	FEB 12, 1880–JUL 26, 1962
07	SAINT GIANNA BERETTA MOLLA	Italy	OCT 4, 1922–APR 28, 1962
08	SAINT NIKOLAI VELIMIROVIĆ	Serbia	JAN 4, 1881–MAR 18, 1956
09	SAINT KATHARINE DREXEL	USA	NOV 26, 1858–MAR 3, 1955
10	SAINT ALBERTO HURTADO CRUCHAGA	Chile	JAN 22, 1901–AUG 18, 1952

OFF THE CHART

THE BLESSED TERESA OF CALCUTTA

Here is Mother Teresa, photographed on February 3, 1986. She was born August 26, 1910, in Üsküp, Kosovo Vilayet (now Skopje, Republic of Macedonia) and died aged 87 in Calcutta, West Bengal, India, on September 5, 1997. She was awarded the Nobel Peace Prize in 1979.

CHECK IT OUT!

Inspector Jacques Clouseau: British comic genius Peter Sellers (*above*) (1925-1980) created and starred as Inspector Jacques Clouseau in six films. The first was the 1963 classic *The Pink Panther*.

XTREME FACT
LLOYD CHRISTMAS

The chipped tooth that Canadian-born actor Jim Carrey has as Lloyd Christmas is real. He had it capped for later roles, but exposed it again for the hilarious 2014 sequel, *Dumb And Dumber To*.

DUMBEST CHARACTERS

TOP 10

THE T-10 UNOFFICIAL

		FAMOUS FROM	EXAMPLE OF THEIR "WISDOM"
01	HOMER SIMPSON	*The Simpsons* TV series & movie	"Just because I don't care doesn't mean I don't understand."
02	INSPECTOR JACQUES CLOUSEAU	*The Pink Panther* movies	"I suspect everyone and I suspect no one."
03	LLOYD CHRISTMAS	*Dumb & Dumber* movies	"Austria? Well, then. G'day mate!"
04	HARRY DUNNE	*Dumb & Dumber* movies	"According to the map, we've only gone four inches."
05	GARTH MARENGHI	*Darkplace* TV series	"I'm one of the few people you'll meet who's written more books than they've read."
06	ALAN PARTRIDGE	*Alan Partridge* TV series & movie	"Can I just read you something from *Top Gear* magazine?"
07	PHILIP J. FRY	*Futurama*	"I can't wait until I'm old enough to feel ways about stuff."
08	DEREK ZOOLANDER	*Zoolander*	"Moisture is the essence of wetness, and wetness is the essence of beauty."
09	CHIEF WIGGUM	*The Simpsons* TV series & movie	"Hey, I'm the chief here. Bake him away, toys!"
10	WHITE GOODMAN	*Dodgeball: A True Underdog Story*	"Nobody makes me bleed my own blood!"

XTREME FACT
HOMER SIMPSON

American actor Dan Castellaneta has provided the iconic voice of Homer Simpson since 1989 for more than 550 episodes, plus, *The Simpsons Movie* (2007).

ONLY HUMAN

FIRST-EVER FBI "MOST WANTED" CRIMINALS

The FBI's "Top 10 Most Wanted" has been going for many, many years. Here are the first 10 ever to have gained such infamy...

#	Name	DATE ADDED TO THE "MOST WANTED" LIST
01	THOMAS JAMES HOLDEN	
02	MORLEY VERNON KING	MAR 14, 1950
03	WILLIAM RAYMOND NESBIT	MAR 15, 1950
04	HENRY RANDOLPH MITCHELL	MAR 16, 1950
05	OMAR AUGUST PINSON	MAR 17, 1950
06	LEE EMORY DOWNS	MAR 18, 1950
07	ORBA ELMER JACKSON	MAR 20, 1950
08	GLEN ROY WRIGHT	MAR 21, 1950
09	HENRY HARLAND SHELTON	MAR 22, 1950
10	MORRIS GURALNICK	MAR 23, 1950
		MAR 24, 1950

X-PLORE J. EDGAR HOOVER

Hoover was the first-ever director of the FBI (Federal Bureau of Investigation), founded in 1935. Prior to this, he was the director of its predecessor, the Bureau of Investigation. His history with the FBI is smothered in secrecy... More specifically, the controversial secret actions Hoover was involved in, like power-plays and going beyond the laws governing how the FBI should operate.

281

TOP 10 FIRST & FASTEST CIRCUMNAVIGATIONS

The late 16th and early 17th centuries saw brave explorers set sail around the globe. Many failed, many died, but these were the first captains to succeed in the quickest times...

#	Name	COUNTRY	VESSEL(S)/FLEET	YEARS TAKEN (EACH ATTEMPT)
01	THOMAS CAVENDISH	UK	Desire	2 (1586–1588)
02	WILLEM SCHOUTEN & JACOB LE MAIRE	Holland	Eendracht, Hoorn	2 (1615–1617)
03	JUAN SEBASTIÁN ELCANO	Spain	Nao Victoria	3 (1519–1522)
04	FRANCIS DRAKE	UK	The Golden Hind	3 (1577–1580)
05	JACQUES MAHU	Holland	Fleet of five ships	3 (1598–1601)
06	JORIS VAN SPILBERGEN	Holland	The Aeolus	3 (1614–1617)
07	JACQUES L'HERMITE & JOHN HUGO SCHAPENHAM	Holland	Fleet of 11 ships	3 (1623–1626)
08	OLIVIER VAN NOORT	Holland	The Mauritius	3 (1598–1601)
09	MARTÍN IGNACIO DE LOYOLA*	Spain	Nuestra Señora de Esperanza**	4 (1580–1584/1585–1589)
10	ANDRÉS DE URDANETA	Spain	Santa María de la Victoria	6 (1525–1536)

*First person to circumnavigate the world twice in both directions.
**One of his galleons
All other explorers listed only sailed westward.

YEARS TAKEN **3** (1577–1580)

CHECK IT OUT!

The Golden Hind: arguably England's most famous ship, this was captained by Sir Francis Drake from 1577 to 1580. Originally called *Pelican*, the galleon circumnavigated the globe and was renamed by Drake, mid-voyage, in 1578.

XTREME FACT — FRANCIS DRAKE

Knighted in 1581, Sir Francis Drake (1540-96) and his nautical adventure "firsts" are legendary. To the Spanish, whose armada he defeated in 1588, he was more of a pirate and called "El Draque"—the Dragon!

TOP 10 MASTERS & APPRENTICES

Behind every experienced legend there is always a naïve but enthusiastic rookie. Here we celebrate the most successful team-ups of teacher and student...

	MASTER	APPRENTICE(S)	MOVIE	BOX OFFICE ($ WORLDWIDE)
01	QUI-GONN JINN, EMPEROR PALPATINE	OBI-WAN KENOBI, DARTH MAUL	Stars Wars Episode I: The Phantom Menace	1,027,044,677
02	OBI-WAN KENOBI	ANAKIN SKYWALKER	Stars Wars Episode III: Revenge Of The Sith	848,754,768
03	DR. HENRY "INDIANA" JONES	HENRY "MUTT" WILLIAMS	Indiana Jones & The Kingdom Of The Crystal Skull	786,636,033
04	OBI-WAN KENOBI	LUKE SKYWALKER	Stars Wars Episode IV: A New Hope	775,398,007
05	HAYMITCH ABERNATHY	KATNISS EVERDEEN	The Hunger Games	691,247,768
06	OBI-WAN KENOBI	ANAKIN SKYWALKER	Stars Wars Episode II: Attack Of The Clones	649,398,328
07	MASTER SHIFU	PO	Kung Fu Panda	631,744,560
08	AGENT K	AGENT J	Men In Black	589,390,539
09	YODA	LUKE SKYWALKER	Stars Wars Episode V: The Empire Strikes Back	538,375,067
10	DR. EMMETT BROWN	MARTY McFLY	Back To The Future	381,109,762

Source: IMDB.com

10 QUICK FIRE FACTS

YODA

01	Originally voiced and puppeteered by Frank Oz
02	Tom Kane voices him for the *Clones Wars* TV series
03	First appeared in *Star Wars Episode V: The Empire Strikes Back*
04	A spin-off Yoda movie is being developed
05	First LEGO Minifigure to have shorter legs
06	Full name/title: Grand Jedi Master Yoda
07	Has a green lightsaber
08	Trained Obi-Wan Kenobi and Luke Skywalker
09	Died on Dagobah
10	Turntablist Duncan Beiny is better known as DJ Yoda

XTREME FACT
YODA

The man behind the voice (and puppet movement) of Yoda, Frank Oz, has had an incredible career. He also voices many Muppets (including Miss Piggy, Animal, and Fozzie Bear), has 116 acting credits, and has directed 15 movies including *The Dark Crystal* (1982) and Bill Murray classic *What About Bob?* (1991).

DID YOU KNOW?

In *Indiana Jones And The Last Crusade* (1989), Sean Connery played Jones' dad. However, Connery was only 12 years older than co-star Harrison "Indy" Ford.

283

YOUR SHOUT

This section of the book is dedicated to testing your knowledge on the crazy world of humans!

YOUR PICK OF THE... HUMANS

You've seen the lists and studied the facts, so now you can tell us your 10 greatest humans...

01
02
03
04
05
06
07
08
09
10

ROUND 1: MULTIPLE CHOICE

01 Which organ is the heaviest in the human body at 379.2 ounces (10,750 grams)?

A **HEART**
B **BRAIN**
C **SKIN**

02 In our Top 10 Unofficial Most Unusual Phobias, what is turophobia a fear of?

A **CHEESE**
B **BUTTONS**
C **RAIN**

03 In *Stars Wars Episode IV: A New Hope* who is Obi-Wan Kenobi's pupil, as seen in our Top 10 Masters & Apprentices movie list?

A **LUKE SKYWALKER**
B **DARTH MAUL**
C **YODA**

ROUND 2: QUESTION TIME

01 On April 12, 1961 Soviet Union (now Russia) sent the first man into space. He was tragically killed piloting a MiG-15 jet seven years later. Can you tell us his name?

ANSWER:

ROUND 3:
PICTURE PUZZLES

In which part of the body can the incus and stapes bones (seen here) be found?

01

ANSWER:

Emanuel Lasker is the greatest champion of which strategy game?

02

ANSWER:

Can you name the hapless character in this extreme close-up?

03

ANSWER:

ROUND 4:
WORDSEARCH

Take a look in the jumble of letters to the left and see how many of these human organs you can find:

```
E X V A K I D N E Y S R
H J N G B Z C B N O U W
E Y I H B N D E S A X O
P Z A T R K O W A B M H
A A R O W D S I E V N E
N V B I N W A K L U P A
C D S P L E E N I Y C R
R W E G I A G A V N F T
E A E S N Q E U E O D B
A C B M E U W V R M E X
S C H E N C L I N A W U
R N E O Y B N W R A E X
```

SKIN

LIVER

BRAIN

LUNGS

HEART

KIDNEYS

SPLEEN

PANCREAS

FIND THE ANSWERS ON PAGE 313

02 Five of the smallest bones in the human skeleton are in one specific area of the body. Can you name where?

03 What is the goal of the BRAIN (Brain Research through Advancing Innovative Neurotechnologies) Initiative?

ANSWER:

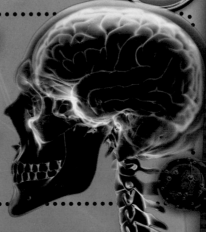

INFINITE SPACE

3-4534354
346425
39369-535398
4533653-565
248-15465
54935-62798514
786456-45641
158584125-484855554511
1456156I5-1567897
69756132-487814I5213
15458I337-4156456
5645445641-1545
514351-1564
I253854-15862
8632863-556
1456I56I5-1567897
69756I32-487814I5213
15458433I-4156456
5645445641-1545
514351-4564
2I3453434-4545433
454424-434354-45343541

TOP 10 MOST SPACEWALKS

		COUNTRY	TOTAL SPACEWALKS
01	ANATOLY SOLOVYEV	Russia (includes Soviet Union era)	16
02	ALEKSANDR SEREBROV	Russia (includes Soviet Union era)	10
=	SERGEI AVDEYEV	Russia	10
=	MICHAEL LÓPEZ-ALEGRIA	USA	10
05	JERRY L ROSS	USA	9
=	VLADIMIR DEZHUROV	USA	9
=	GENNADY PADALKA	Russia	9
=	MICHAEL FINCKE	Russia	9
09	LEONID KIZIM	USA	8
=	VLADIMIR SOLOVYOV	Russia (Soviet Union era)	8

Team T-10 were so blown away by the 2013 movie *Gravity* and its amazing astronaut action, it inspired us to do this list...

XTREME FACT

MICHAEL FINCKE

Pennsylvania-born US astronaut Michael Fincke holds the record for the longest amount of time an American has spent in space... Just under 382 days!

SPACEWALKS **9**

OFF THE CHART

MIKE FOSSUM

Since his first mission into space on July 4, 2006, American astronaut Mike Fossum has completed seven spacewalks, and so just misses out on a place in the Top 10. His most recent was on July 12, 2011, with Ronald J. Garan, Jr.

288

Xtreme Fact

GRAVITY

Mexican moviemaker Alfonso Cuarón directed the extraordinarily immersive, multi-award-winning *Gravity*. Some of the actors' zero-gravity appearance was achieved by the genius puppeteers from *War Horse* working them like, well, puppets!

BOX OFFICE 700.8 MILLION DOLLARS

TOP 10 BIGGEST ASTRONAUT MOVIES

We're not looking to the *Star Wars* saga or sci-fi space pilots—we're only concerned with movies that feature normal, human astronauts in classic spacesuits...

		RELEASED	BOX OFFICE ($ WORLDWIDE)
01	TRANSFORMERS: DARK OF THE MOON	2011	1,123,794,079
02	INDEPENDENCE DAY	1996	817,400,891
03	GRAVITY	2013	700,862,383
04	ARMAGEDDON	1998	553,709,788
05	PLANET OF THE APES	2001	362,211,740
06	APOLLO 13	1995	355,237,933
07	FANTASTIC FOUR	2005	330,579,719
08	MOONRAKER	1979	210,308,099
09	SPACE COWBOYS	2000	128,884,132
10	MISSION TO MARS	2000	110,983,407

Source: IMDB.com

CHECK IT OUT!

Fantastic Four: 10 years on from when the first *Fantastic Four* movie came out *(below)*, *The Fantastic Four* (released June 19, 2015) restarts the franchise's cinema life with *Chronicle* director Josh Trank at the helm.

TOP 10 FINAL SHUTTLE FLIGHTS

NASA's Space Shuttles have officially retired. These were the final 10 flights...

		LAST LAUNCH DATE
01	ATLANTIS (STS-135)	JUL 8, 2011
02	ENDEAVOUR (STS-134)	MAY 16, 2011
03	DISCOVERY (STS-133)	FEB 24, 2011
04	ATLANTIS (STS-132)	MAY 14, 2010
05	DISCOVERY (STS-131)	APR 5, 2010
06	ENDEAVOUR (STS-130)	FEB 8, 2010
07	ATLANTIS (STS-129)	NOV 16, 2009
08	DISCOVERY (STS-128)	AUG 28, 2009
09	ENDEAVOUR (STS-127)	JUL 15, 2009
10	ATLANTIS (STS-125)	MAY 11, 2009

XTREME FACT
ATLANTIS

Look closely at the photo, above... This shows where Atlantis now resides, inside the Kennedy Space Center Visitor Complex at Cape Canaveral, Florida, USA. Since its first flight in October 1985, Atlantis completed 33 missions.

TOP 10 MOST ASTRONAUTS LAUNCHED BY A NATION

A total of 533 human beings have been launched into space, and this is how it is split across the different countries...

		TOTAL PEOPLE SENT INTO SPACE
01	USA	333
02	RUSSIA	118
03	CHINA	10
=	GERMANY	10
05	CANADA	9
=	FRANCE	9
=	JAPAN	9
08	ITALY	6
09	BULGARIA	2
=	NETHERLANDS	2

OFF THE CHART

A total of 24 nations have only sent a single person into space, including the UK, Mexico, Malaysia, India, Vietnam, and Poland.

XTREME FACT
USA

This photo was taken on May 17, 2013. It shows NASA astronaut Karen Nyberg carrying out her preflight training at the Baikonur Cosmodrome, which is the world's largest (and first) launch site, based in Kazakhstan.

LAST FLIGHT JUL 8, 2011

Atlantis

X-PLORE

EUROPEAN SPACE AGENCY

The ESA (European Space Agency) is made up of 18 countries (Austria, Belgium, Czech Republic, Denmark, Finland, France, Germany, Greece, Ireland, Italy, Luxembourg, Netherlands, Norway, Portugal, Spain, Sweden, Switzerland, and United Kingdom). It has sent 34 people into space.

TOP 10 MOST INTERNATIONAL SPACE STATION VISITS BY A NATION

The amazing super-structure ISS (International Space Station) has had more humans visit it and work in it than you'd think...

		INDIVIDUAL(S)	ISS CREW MEMBER(S)
		139	42
01	USA	42	35
02	RUSSIA	7	2
03	CANADA	6	4
04	JAPAN	4	2
05	ITALY	3	1
06	FRANCE	2	1
07	GERMANY	1	1
08	BELGIUM	1	1
=	NETHERLANDS	1	0
10	SWEDEN		

XTREME FACT

RUSSIA

Here's a shot of the Soyuz-FG rocket (with the Soyuz TMA-10M spacecraft) taking off from Russia's Baikonur Cosmodrome in Kazakhstan.

TOP 10 FIRST LIVING THINGS SENT INTO SPACE/ORBIT

Before humans plucked up the courage to rocket themselves into space, a range of different, smaller organisms were launched toward the stars...

		SPACECRAFT	DATE
01	FRUIT FLIES	V2	FEB 20, 1947
02	MOSS	V2	VARIOUS, 1947
03	RHESUS MONKEY (ALBERT II)	V2	JUN 14, 1949
04	MOUSE	V2	AUG 31, 1950
05	DOG (LAIKA)	Sputnik 2	NOV 3, 1957
06	SQUIRREL MONKEY (GORDO)	Jupiter IRBM AM-13	DEC 13, 1958
07	RABBIT (MARFUSA)	R2	JUL 2, 1959
08	CHIMPANZEE (HAM)	Mercury-Redstone 2	JAN 31, 1961
09	GUINEA PIG, FROGS & MICE	Vostok-3A	MAR 9, 1961
10	TORTOISE	Zond 5	SEP 18, 1968

XTREME FACT

LAIKA

To celebrate Laika (which means "Barker") and her significant part of the history of space exploration, on April 11, 2008, an official monument (a dog standing on a rocket) was built next to the Moscow research lab where Laika lived.

TOP 10 LONGEST HUMAN SPACE FLIGHTS

If you had the chance, how long would you like to spend in space? Team T-10 isn't sure we'd be able to cope with the lengths these legends achieved...

		COUNTRY	DAYS IN SPACE
01	VALERI POLYAKOV	Russia	437.7
02	SERGEI AVDEYEV	Russia	379.6
03	VLADIMIR TITOV	Russia	364.9
	MUSA MANAROV	Russia (Soviet Union era)	364.9
05	YURI ROMANENKO	Russia (Soviet Union era)	326.5
=		Russia & Soviet Union era	311.8
06	SERGEI KRIKALEV	Russia (Soviet Union era)	240.9
07	VALERI POLYAKOV	Russia (Soviet Union era)	237
08	LEONID KIZIM	Russia (Soviet Union era)	237
=	VLADIMIR SOLOVYOV	Russia (Soviet Union era)	237
=	OLEG ATKOV		

XTREME FACT

LEONID KIZIM

This photo of Leonid Kizim was taken in 1984 by his fellow cosmonaut, Vladimir Solovyov. During his life, Kizim was given many awards, including Hero Of The Soviet Union, in 1980 and 1984.

TOP 10 NATIONS' FIRST SATELLITES

There are loads of satellite systems spinning around in orbit, but these were the "firsts" for the initial 10 nations to get them up there...

		SATELLITE	DATE
01	RUSSIA (SOVIET UNION ERA)	Sputnik 1	OCT 4, 1957
02	USA	Explorer 1	FEB 1, 1958
03	FRANCE	Astérix	NOV 26, 1965
04	JAPAN	Ōsumi	FEB 11, 1970
05	CHINA	Dong Fang Hong I	APR 24, 1970
06	UK	Prospero	OCT 28, 1971
07	ESA*	CAT-1	DEC 24, 1979
08	INDIA	Rohini D1	JUL 18, 1980
09	ISRAEL	Ofeq	SEP 19, 1988
10	UKRAINE	Strela-3	SEP 28, 1991

*Collaboration between many countries that comprise the European Space Agency.

TOP 10 SONGS ABOUT SPACE

THE T-10 UNOFFICIAL

		ARTIST/BAND	RELEASED
01	SUPERMASSIVE BLACK HOLE	Muse	2006
02	STARS 4-EVER	Robyn	2010
03	PLANET EARTH	Duran Duran	1981
04	STELLAR	Incubus	1999
05	STARMAN	David Bowie	1972
06	MOON	Sia	2004
07	PLANET SMASHER	Devin Townsend	2007
08	E.T.	Katy Perry	2011
09	SAIL TO THE MOON	Radiohead	2003
10	ACROSS THE UNIVERSE	The Beatles	1969

CHECK IT OUT!

Sergei Krikalev: here, the cosmonaut checks his headset is OK before launch on April 14, 2005.

CHECK IT OUT!

Starman: this very popular song almost never was... It was a very late addition to the 1972 album *The Rise And Fall Of Ziggy Stardust And The Spiders From Mars*, and replaced a cover of Chuck Berry's *Around And Around*.

TOP 10 BIGGEST MOUNTAINS ON THE MOON

Don't be fooled into thinking our moon is a dull, flat rock—or even made of cheese! Its landscape features many startling mountains...

#		DIAMETER KM	MI
01	MONS RÜMKER	70	43.5
02	MONS ARGAEUS	50	31.1
03	MONS HUYGENS	40	24.9
04	MONS WOLFF	35	21.7
05	MONS AMPÈRE	30	18.6
=	MONS BRADLEY	30	18.6
=	MONS DELISLE	30	18.6
=	MONS HANSTEEN	30	18.6
=	MONS PENCK	30	18.6
10	MONS HADLEY	25	15.5

XTREME FACT — MONS RÜMKER

This volcanic formation on the moon has a maximum height of 3,608.9 ft (1,100 m). It was named after German astronomer Karl Ludwig Christian Rümker (May 28, 1788-December 21, 1862).

DIAMETER 43.5 MILES

TOP 10 LONGEST MOUNTAIN RANGES ON THE MOON

It's not just the size of the individual mountains that's mind-blowing —check out the lengths of the rocky ranges on the moon...

#		LENGTH OF RANGE KM	MI
01	MONTES ROOK	791	491.5
02	MONTES CORDILLERA	574	356.7
03	MONTES HAEMUS	560	348
04	MONTES CAUCASUS	445	276.5
05	MONTES JURA	422	262.2
06	MONTES APENNINUS	401	249.2
07	MONTES CARPATUS	281	175
08	MONTES ALPES	189	117.4
09	MONTES RIPHAEUS	182	113.1
10	MONTES TENERIFFE		

MONS RÜMKER
---- MONTES APENNINUS

& ANOTHER THING!

Experts believe the Moon's craters were formed around 3.5-4.5 billion years ago by meteors hitting the surface.

RANGE LENGTH
249.2
MILES

XTREME FACT
MONTES APENNINUS

This arced mountain range is named after Italy's Apennine Mountains, which in turn takes its name from the Apennine Peninsula, the majority of which is in Italy. One of the range's valleys is where Apollo 15 famously landed in 1971.

BEEN & SEEN

When you've watched these moon-related movies, tick them off!

- [ ] **APOLLO 13**
- [ ] **CAPRICORN ONE**
- [ ] **IN THE SHADOW OF THE MOON**
- [ ] **DIAMONDS ARE FOREVER**
- [ ] **TRANSFORMERS:** DARK OF THE MOON
- [ ] **SPACECAMP**
- [ ] **A GRAND DAY OUT**
- [ ] **MAGNIFICENT DESOLATION:** WALKING ON THE MOON 3D
- [ ] **DESPICABLE ME**
- [ ] **A TRIP TO THE MOON**

DID YOU KNOW?

This amazing photo of the Himilayas mountain range shows (left to right): Changtse, 24,747 ft (7,543 m); Mount Everest, 29,029 ft (8,848 m); Nuptse, 25,791 ft (7,861 m); Ama Dablam, 22,349 ft (6,812 m); and Thamserku, 21,729 ft (6,623 m), which are not dissimilar to Montes Apenninus' maximum height of 3.1 mi (5 km).

FUTURE SOLAR & LUNAR ECLIPSES

TOP 10

Time to get your daily planners out, because we can tell you when the next total lunar and solar eclipses are going to be, and their maximum duration...

#	Date & Time	ECLIPSE TYPE
01	OCT 8, 2014: 10:55	
02	MAR 20, 2015: 09:46:47	LUNAR
03	APR 4, 2015: 12:00	SOLAR
04	SEP 28, 2015: 02:47	LUNAR
05	MAR 9, 2016: 01:26:40	LUNAR
06	AUG 21, 2017: 18:26:40	SOLAR
07	JAN 31, 2018: 13:30	SOLAR
08	JUN 27, 2018: 20:22	LUNAR
09	JUL 2, 2019: 19:24:08	LUNAR
10	DEC 14, 2020: 16:14:39	SOLAR
		SOLAR

OFF THE CHART

ANNULAR ECLIPSE

This sci-fi-esque annular eclipse (when the Moon doesn't quite block out the Sun) occurred in Tokyo, Japan, at 07:33 on May 21, 2012.

All the times shown *(left and above)* are UTC, which means *Temps Universel Coordonné* (French for "Coordinated Universal Time"), the primary time the world's clocks are regulated by.

BIGGEST MASSES IN OUR SOLAR SYSTEM

TOP 10

We know that the sun is the central mass of our solar system, but prepare yourself for a shock as to just how big it is compared to its adjacent planets...

#	Name	MASS
01	SUN	$1,989,100,000 \times 10^{30}$ KG
02	JUPITER	$1,898,600 \times 10^{27}$ KG
03	SATURN	$568,460 \times 10^{26}$ KG
04	NEPTUNE	$102,430 \times 10^{26}$ KG
05	URANUS	$86,832 \times 10^{25}$ KG
06	EARTH	$5,973.6 \times 10^{24}$ KG
07	VENUS	$4,868.5 \times 10^{24}$ KG
08	MARS	641.85×10^{23} KG
09	MERCURY	330.2×10^{23} KG
10	GANYMEDE (A JUPITER MOON)	148.2×10^{23} KG

Xtreme FACT

NEPTUNE

Neptune is the farthest planet from the Sun in our solar system. This beautiful image of Neptune was taken from Voyager 2, which launched August 20, 1977, and is STILL exploring outer space!

CHECK IT OUT!

Ganymede: on January 7, 1610, Italian astronomer and science genius Galileo Galilei discovered Ganymede. It was named by German astronomer Simon Marius in the 1600s, after Zeus's lover from Greek mythology.

X TREME FACT

JUPITER

As the biggest planet in our solar system, and the fifth planet away from the Sun, Jupiter is mainly made of hydrogen. Although its core contains more solid rock and hydrogen metals, it has no solid surface, unlike Earth.

EQUIVALENT EARTH TIME
9.8 HOURS

LONGEST DAYS OF PLANETS & DWARF PLANETS

We like this list a lot! How long would a day last on the other planets? Compared to our 24 hours, there are some wildly different time lengths...

TOP 10

X TREME FACT

VENUS

Before we knew that Venus was a planet, it was called the "Morning Star" and the "Evening Star." Our first exploration of Venus began with the Venera 1 probe on February 12, 1961.

#	Planet	EQUIVALENT EARTH TIME
01	VENUS	243 DAYS
02	MERCURY	58.65 DAYS
03	PLUTO	6.4 DAYS
04	ERIS	23.75 HOURS
05	NEPTUNE	19.1 HOURS
06	URANUS	17.9 HOURS
07	SATURN	10.2 HOURS
08	JUPITER	9.8 HOURS
09	CERES	9.1 HOURS
10	HAUMEA	3.9 HOURS

EQUIVALENT EARTH TIME
243 DAYS

& ANOTHER THING!

Venus is often described as being our "sister planet" because of its similar gravity and size.

TOP 10 BIGGEST ALIEN/HUMAN ENCOUNTER MOVIES

Of all the hundreds of movies made where we have come into contact with alien beings, these are the biggest box office invasions...

		ALIEN(S) ENCOUNTERED	RELEASED	BOX OFFICE ($ WORLDWIDE)
01	AVATAR	Pandorians	2009	2,782,275,172
02	THE AVENGERS	Chitauri	2012	1,518,594,910
03	TRANSFORMERS: DARK OF THE MOON	Autobots & Decepticons	2011	1,123,794,079
04	TRANSFORMERS: REVENGE OF THE FALLEN	Autobots & Decepticons	2009	836,303,693
05	INDEPENDENCE DAY	Unnamed aliens	1996	817,400,891
06	E.T. THE EXTRA-TERRESTRIAL	E.T.	1982	792,910,554
07	TRANSFORMERS	Autobots & Decepticons	2007	709,709,780
08	MAN OF STEEL	Kryptonians	2013	668,045,518
09	THOR: THE DARK WORLD	Asgardians	2013	639,317,634
10	MEN IN BLACK 3	Several	2012	624,026,776

Source: IMDB.com

XTREME FACT AVATAR

Avatar's writer-director James Cameron has held the top spot for "most successful movie ever" for a long time. Before Avatar took the prize, his 1997 epic *Titanic* held that multibillion-dollar accolade for 12 years.

10 QUICK FIRE FACTS — THE AVENGERS

01	Sixth movie in the Marvel Cinematic Universe
02	Released May 4, 2012
03	*The Avengers: Age Of Ultron* is released May 1, 2015
04	Fourth movie to feature Iron Man
05	Running time 2 hours 22 minutes
06	Shown in 4,349 cinemas
07	Cost $220 million to make
08	Second film to feature Black Widow
09	Nominated for an Academy Award: Visual Effects
10	Third most successful movie of all time

► CHECK IT OUT!

The Avengers: these superheroes really showed their box office superpowers... This is the fastest movie to break the billion-dollar mark. The Marvel blockbuster also holds the record for the biggest weekend opening across North America.

BOX OFFICE **2.78 MILLION DOLLARS**

TOP 10

SCARIEST MOVIE ALIENS

THE T-10 UNOFFICIAL

BOX OFFICE **1.52 MILLION DOLLARS**

		MOVIE
01	XENOMORPH	Alien vs Predator (2004)
02	THE GREYS	Dark Skies (2013)
03	LONG-CLAWED ALIEN	The X-Files: Fight The Future (1998)
04	TRIPODS	War Of The Worlds (2005)
05	THE THING	The Thing From Another World (1951)
06	INVADERS	Signs (2002)
07	ALIEN ABDUCTORS	Fire In The Sky (1993)
08	WHITE APE	John Carter (2012)
09	RANCOR	Star Wars Episode VI: Return Of The Jedi (1983)
10	FROST GIANTS	Thor (2011)

DID YOU KNOW?
Before writer-director Scott Stewart helmed the super-scary *Dark Skies*, he worked at visual-effects company The Orphanage, which worked on *Iron Man* and *Iron Man 2*.

COOLEST TV ALIENS

TOP 10

THE T-10 UNOFFICIAL

		TV SERIES
01	MORBO	Futurama (1999-2013)
02	IRISA NYRIRA	Defiance (2013-present)
03	ALF	ALF (1986-90)
04	TRIFFID	The Day Of The Triffids (1981)
05	DALEK	Doctor Who (1963*-present)
06	DIANA	V (1983-84, 2009-11)
07	KANG AND KODOS	The Simpsons (1990*-present)
08	MR. SPOCK	Star Trek (1966-1991**)
09	SEVEN OF NINE	Star Trek: Voyager (1997-2001)
10	ZELDA	Terrahawks (1983-86)

*Character's first appearance
**Last appearance in a Star Trek TV show

XTREME FACT

MR. SPOCK

Spock's first screen appearance was in the episode *The Man Trap* of the original *Star Trek* TV series in 1966.

OLDEST RECORDED UFO SIGHTINGS

TOP 10

There are many ancient descriptions of UFOs, in engravings, drawings, and journals, and these are 10 of the oldest we know of...

		LOCATION	YEAR(S)
01	CIRCLE OF FIRE/SAUCERS IN THE SKY	Egypt	1504–1450 BC
02	A SHIELD IN THE SKY	Rome	216 BC
03	SHIPS IN THE SKY	Rome	214 BC
04	SPHERE IN THE SKY	Tarquinia	99 BC
05	FLAMING VASE	Rome	74 BC
06	CHARIOTS THROUGH THE CLOUDS	Jerusalem	70 BC
07	CREATURE SHAPED LIKE A VASE	Rome	150
08	STRANGE LIGHTS IN THE SKY	Rome	393
09	FLAMING, CIGAR-SHAPED OBJECT	France	1034
10	FLYING VESSEL	Japan	1180

OFF THE CHART

EXTRATERRESTRIALS & SHIPS IN THE SKY

Photographed on April 28, 2005, here is Dr. Sun Shili proudly showing his sketches of UFO sightings that he experienced in Beijing, China. Shili is one of China's leading UFO researchers and authorities on the subject.

XTREME FACT
DALEK

With appearances in 99 episodes of *Doctor Who* (up to December 2013), the Daleks were created by writer Terry Nation and designer Raymond Cusick. The Dalek is actually an organic mutant that pilots the metallic, weaponized shell.

X-PLORE
UK UFO TRAIL

The reason this UFO Trail exists in Rendlesham Forest, Suffolk, UK, is because of the multiple UFO sightings that occurred there in 1980.

The Rendlesham Forest
UFO Trail

TOP 10 BIGGEST "ALIEN REALMS" VIDEO GAMES

So many video games, so many creative environments and worlds! Here are the 10 best-selling ones featuring out-of-this world alien-esque galactic worlds...

#	Title	Platform	Released	Unit Sales (Millions)
01	SUPER MARIO GALAXY	Wii	2007	11.03
02	FINAL FANTASY VII	PlayStation	1997	9.72
03	FINAL FANTASY X	PS2	2001	8.05
04	MYST	PC	1994	8.03
05	FINAL FANTASY VIII	PlayStation	1999	7.86
06	CRASH BANDICOOT 2: CORTEX STRIKES BACK	PlayStation	1997	7.58
07	SUPER MARIO GALAXY 2	Wii	2010	7.19
08	LEGO STARS WARS: THE COMPLETE SAGA	Wii	2007	5.27
09	ASTEROIDS	Atari 2600	1980	4.31
10	STAR FOX 64	N64	1997	4.03

OFF THE CHART

LEGO MARVEL SUPER HEROES

Released on October 22, 2013, the fantastic LEGO Marvel Super Heroes (Xbox 360) has sold in excess of one million units worldwide!

XTREME FACT

FINAL FANTASY

Created by Japanese video game legend Hironobu Sakaguchi, the Final Fantasy franchise began in 1987 and it has had more than 50 games released under its banner.

TOP 10 COOLEST ALIEN PLANETS IN MOVIES

THE T-10 UNOFFICIAL

		MOVIE(S)	RELEASED
01	ASGARD	Thor: The Dark World, Thor	2013, 2011
02	CYBERTRON	Transformers movies	1986–2014
03	PANDORA	Avatar	2009
04	CETI ALPHA V	Star Trek II: The Wrath Of Khan	1982
05	MARS	John Carter	2012
06	HOTH	Star Wars Episode V: The Empire Strikes Back	1980
07	ALTAIR IV	Forbidden Planet	1956
08	KRULL	Krull	1983
09	KRYPTON	Man Of Steel	2013
10	ABYDOS	Stargate	1994

BEEN & SEEN

When you've seen these fantastical movie worlds, tick them off!

- [ ] ASGARD
- [ ] CYBERTRON
- [ ] PANDORA
- [ ] CETI ALPHA V
- [ ] MARS
- [ ] HOTH
- [ ] ALTAIR IV
- [ ] KRULL
- [ ] KRYPTON
- [ ] ABYDOS

XTREME FACT KRYPTON

Superman's home planet was created by Jerry Siegel and Joe Shuster. Although it made its first appearance in *Superman* #1 (1939), it was mentioned the year before in *Action Comics* #1 (1938).

CHECK IT OUT!

▶ **Pandora:** home to the Na'vi, the fictional planet of Pandora in 2009's *Avatar* was also home to the rare (and somewhat dumbly named) material "unobtanium." Ahem...

COOLEST MOVIE ALIEN CRAFTS

THE T-10 UNOFFICIAL

		MOVIE
01	AQUATIC SHIP	The Abyss (1989)
02	UFO	The X-Files: Fight The Future (1998)
03	MOTHERSHIP UFO	Close Encounters Of The Third Kind (1977)
04	TRIMAXIAN DRONE SHIP	Flight Of The Navigator (1986)
05	ALIEN ATTACK SHIPS	Battleship (2012)
06	NARADA	Star Trek (2009)
07	MARTIANS' SAUCERS	Mars Attacks! (1996)
08	SLAVE I	Star Wars Episode V: The Empire Strikes Back (1980)
09	PREDATOR SHIP	Aliens vs Predator (2004)
10	CHITAURI SPEEDERS	The Avengers (2012)

XTREME FACT

TRIMAXIAN DRONE SHIP

The voice of the alien craft "Max" in *Flight Of The Navigator* was provided by American comedy actor and writer Paul Reubens, best known for his comedy character Pee-wee Herman.

BIGGEST STAR WARS LEGO SPACESHIPS

Star Wars fan? Lover of LEGO? This may be the best T-10 list ever! The spaceship sets with the most pieces ever are...

		RELEASED	NUMBER OF PIECES	RELATIVE SCALE:
01	MILLENNIUM FALCON	2007	5,195	100%
02	DEATH STAR	2008	3,803	73%
03	DEATH STAR II	2005	3,449	66%
04	SUPER STAR DESTROYER	2011	3,152	61%
05	IMPERIAL STAR DESTROYER	2002	3,104	60%
06	IMPERIAL SHUTTLE	2010	2,503	48%
07	R2-D2	2012	2,127	41%
08	EWOK VILLAGE	2013	1,990	38%
09	DARTH MAUL BUST	2001	1,860	36%
10	REPUBLIC DROPSHIP WITH AT-OT	2009	1,758	34%

XTREME FACT

DEATH STAR

This massive and highly detailed play set contains —among MANY other things—24 minifigures and droids, plus the trash compactor creature featured in *Star Wars Episode IV: A New Hope*. It's 16 in (41 cm) tall, and costs—brace yourself—$400!

CHECK IT OUT!

Alien Attack Ships: no one was more surprised than us that an alien invasion movie (starring Rihanna) based on strategy board game *Battleships* was made! American composer Steve Jablonsky (who had previously scored two monster invasion movies in 2007: *Transformers* and *Dragon Wars*) created the music, with Rage Against The Machine's Tom Morello providing guitars.

3,803 LEGO PIECES

OFF THE CHART

V-19 TORRENT

This is the awesome LEGO *Star Wars* V-19 Torrent! Team T-10 has got one, but it doesn't quite get into the Top 10 as it only has 471 pieces. The set features a new kind of Clone Trooper pilot minifigure.

CHECK IT OUT!

Optimus Prime: how well do you know the ever-heroic Autobot leader? Did you know that he was previously called Orion Pax and had a girlfriend called Ariel? Well, you do now! Check out the amazing *The Transformers* episode *War Dawn* to see Prime in original Pax mode.

APPEARED IN 5 MOVIES

TOP 10

MOST APPEARANCES BY A TRANSFORMER IN THE MOVIES

Many Transformers have made an appearance on the big screen, so we thought it was time to discover the ones that have been featured the most...

NUMBER OF MOVIES

01	OPTIMUS PRIME	5
=	BUMBLEBEE	4
03	IRONHIDE	4
=	MEGATRON	4
=	STARSCREAM	3
=	RATCHET	3
=	SOUNDWAVE	2
07	WHEELIE	2
=	JAZZ	
09	GRIMLOCK	
=		

XTREME FACT

BUMBLEBEE

He's one of the most popular Autobots, and rightly so. Bumblebee was the second character to be introduced in the first series of *The Transformers*. He even got renamed Goldbug (by Prime) after a major reconstruction.

&...ANOTHER THING!

Megatron is the founder of the Decepticon uprising. In the original animated movie, Megatron is rebuilt into Galvatron.

TOP 10 LONGEST-RUNNING TRANSFORMERS TV SERIES

For over 30 years, those awesome robots in disguise have waged war on Cybertron and Earth. Of all the TV series, these are the biggest hits...

#	Series	YEAR(S) ON AIR	TOTAL EPISODES
01	THE TRANSFORMERS	3 (1984–87)	98
02	TRANSFORMERS: PRIME	3 (2010–2013)	65
03	TRANSFORMERS: ARMADA	1 (2002–03)	52
=	TRANSFORMERS: CYBERTRON	1 (2005–06)	52
=	BEAST WARS: TRANSFORMERS	3 (1996–99)	52
=	TRANSFORMERS: ENERGON	1 (2004)	51
06	BEAST WARS II	1 (1998–99)	43
07	TRANSFORMERS: SUPER-GOD MASTERFORCE	1 (1988–89)	42
08	TRANSFORMERS ANIMATED	3 (2007–09)	42
=	TRANSFORMERS: ROBOTS IN DISGUISE	1 (2000–01)	39
10			

RELATIVE SCALE: 100% 66% 53% 53% 52% 44% 43% 43% 40%

154584337-4156456
5645445641-1545
514351-4564
213453434-4545433-4545435
5345435-4534354
42-45425
639363-535398
4533653-565
1253854-15862

YOUR SHOUT

This section of the book is dedicated to letting your mind free-fall into the giddy infinity of space...

YOUR PICK OF THE... SPACE

You've gone through all of the lists and studied the facts... Now tell us YOUR space top 10!

01	
02	
03	
04	
05	
06	
07	
08	
09	
10	

ROUND 1: MULTIPLE CHOICE

01 What year was the final Space Shuttle launched from the Kennedy Space Center in USA?

A 2013
B 2011
C 2008

02 Venus tops our Planets/Dwarfs With The Longest Day list, but which has the closest day length to Earth's?

A PLUTO
B ERIS
C NEPTUNE

03 What was the name of the first dog sent into space by the Soviet Union in their Sputnik 2 rocket?

A MARFUSA
B HAM
C LAIKA

ROUND 2: QUESTION TIME

01 The Top 10 Biggest Alien/Human Encounter Movies has *Avatar* placed in the number one spot with a worldwide box office gross of $2.782 million. Can you name the movie in second place with $1.511 million?

ANSWER:

ROUND 3:
PICTURE PUZZLES

Can you tell us the planet that this Man of Steel originates from?

01

ANSWER:

What is the name of this planet, the farthest from the Sun in our solar system?

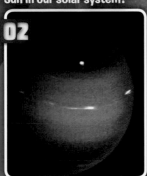

02

ANSWER:

Sergei Krikalev, pictured here, spent over 311 days in space. Which country is he from?

03

ANSWER:

ROUND 4:
WORDSEARCH

```
A S C B O S U N A R U F
D F B O W A V N E V N W
I L A C N L E R M A C G
E R M N E J C I A R T S
Y E N E P T U N E H H J
R W I A R D X P Y O A E
O P N R F C V U I A U G
F E R T G A U R Y T M S
O I U H E R O R T E E Z
U S T V A D G H Y O A R
T G A N Y M E D E Y E Y
A D S F G S J I T E U B
```

Take a look at the letters to the left, and see how many of these planets, dwarf planets, and moons you can find:

JUPITER

HAUMEA

NEPTUNE

URANUS

EARTH

GANYMEDE

SATURN

MERCURY

FIND THE ANSWERS ON PAGE 313

02 Can you name the sci-fi character on the right that first appeared on screen in *Star Trek* in 1966?

03 EAS is an organization made up of 18 countries, including France, Italy, and the UK. Can you tell us what the letters stand for?

ANSWER:

SPACE
CAREER
QUIZ

Which of these places would you most like to visit?

☐ **A A PLANE COCKPIT**
☐ **B AN AIRPORT CONTROL TOWER**
☐ **C A HANGAR FULL OF FIGHTER JETS**

Which of the following is your idea of fun?

☐ **A A ROLLER COASTER**
☐ **B STRATEGY COMPUTER GAMES**
☐ **C A SCIENCE MUSEUM**

Which of these movies do you like the most?

☐ **A GRAVITY**
☐ **B APOLLO 13**
☐ **C IRON MAN 3**

If your spacecraft entered a meteor shower, what would you do?

☐ **A TURN THE AUTOPILOT OFF AND TRY TO STEER HOME**
☐ **B RECONFIGURE THE NAVAGATION SYSTEM**
☐ **C DESIGN A HYPER-DRIVE FROM SPARE PARTS**

Which *Avengers* character are you most similar to?

☐ **A CAPTAIN AMERICA**
☐ **B NICK FURY**
☐ **C TONY STARK**

Which of these gifts would you rather receive?

☐ **A A CRASH HELMET**
☐ **B REMOTE-CONTROLLED CAR**
☐ **C A GIANT MODEL KIT**

Which of the following statements best fits you?

☐ **A I'M TOTALLY FEARLESS**
☐ **B I MAKE DECISIONS QUICKLY**
☐ **C I LOVE SCIENCE**

Find out which space-related job is best suited to you on page 313

THE ULTIMATE YOUR SHOUT ROUND-UP

TOP 10

Now push your brain cells to the max with this, the Ultimate Your Shout Challenge!

YOUR TOP 10 PICK OF THE... EVERYTHING!

You've seen ALL the lists and read ALL the facts...
Now tell us your ultimate TOP 10 OF EVERYTHING!

01
02
0
04
05
06
07
08
09
10

ROUND 1: MULTIPLE CHOICE

01 The biggest vehicle in the world is the AAR Standard S-4200 at 12,001 ft (3,658 m) long, but what type of vehicle is it?

A TRAIN
B SHIP
C AIRCRAFT CARRIER

02 What is the heaviest creature in the ocean?

A COLOSSAL SQUID
B WHALE SHARK
C BLUE WHALE

03 Which of the following tops our Biggest Selling Console Games Of 2013 list with over nine million sales?

A POKÉMON X/Y
B FIFA SOCCER 14
C MINECRAFT

ROUND 2: QUESTION TIME

01 Tan Boon Heong of Malaysia generated the fastest recorded swing in sport in 2010. But in which sport was the eye-popping 261.6 mph (421 kph) racket head speed achieved?

ANSWER:

ROUND 3:
PICTURE PUZZLES

01 What is the name of this structure that was used in 2007 as a huge cinema screen?

ANSWER:

02 Name the only movie from the *Batman* franchise to make it into the Top 10 Biggest Movies...

ANSWER:

03 The biggest planet in our solar system has a day that lasts only 9.8 hours. What is its name?

ANSWER:

ROUND 4:
WORDSEARCH

```
A W H A I T I R I E R V
S E S P A R T A C U S N
D B G J E H A T K C D P
A A K I T E U L J G I A
C T S N B M U S V N N V
X M T I A E E B O B O T
V A S N T P O W V S R B
R N G T A N R G M O A T
M R I E A F A G E D U M
E C A N K N A L T M R A
L O R D E X E O T R U V
A E O O N B C A V A S E
```

Take a look in the jumble of letters to the left and see how many of these Top 10 number ones you can find:

SPINOSAURUS
ROBOBEE
ATLANTIS
NINTENDO
SPARTACUS
LORDE
BATMAN
WHAITIRI

FIND THE ANSWERS ON PAGE 312

02 Where did the world's largest earthquake take place on May 22, 1960? It measured a staggering 9.5 on the Richter scale...

03 Name the seventh most downloaded song ever by the star pictured on the right? It's worth a gamble...

ANSWER:

NAME THAT...
ZONE!

Can you name which zone these obscure words come from? Tick the box next to your choice...

01 Word: **ULURU**
- A **ANIMAL KINGDOM**
- B **EPIC STRUCTURES**
- C **FORCES OF NATURE**

02 Word: **TYRANNOTITAN**
- A **MUSIC MASH-UP**
- B **ANIMAL KINGDOM**
- C **INFINITE SPACE**

03 Word: **ELEKTRA**
- A **MECHANICAL MARVELS**
- B **SPORT ZONE**
- C **MOVIE SHOWTIME**

04 Word: **HAUMEA**
- A **INFINITE SPACE**
- B **GAMING GALAXY**
- C **FORCES OF NATURE**

05 Word: **PÉTANQUE**
- A **ONLY HUMAN**
- B **SPORT ZONE**
- C **EPIC STRUCTURES**

06 Word: **BJORK**
- A **MUSIC MASH-UP**
- B **ANIMAL KINGDOM**
- C **FORCES OF NATURE**

07 Word: **TETRIS**
- A **EPIC STRUCTURES**
- B **MOVIE SHOWTIME**
- C **GAMING GALAXY**

MECHANICAL MARVELS
PAGES: 34-35

MULTIPLE CHOICE
01: C. HOVERCRAFT
02: A. 1.97 SEC
03: A. ROBOBEE

QUESTION TIME
01: USA
02: JAY Z
03: THE INTERNATIONAL SPACE STATION

PICTURE PUZZLES
01: QUADRICYCLE
02: IRON MAN SUIT
03: APOLLO 10

WORDSEARCH

CAREER QUIZ
MOSTLY As: TEST PILOT
You're more comfortable in the air than a Peregrine Falcon, and adrenaline-based activities, like flying, give you a real buzz.

MOSTLY Bs: RACING CAR DRIVER
You can burn more rubber than Sebastian Vettel and Jeff Gordon put together. Plus, you take tactical risks, which make you hard to beat.

MOSTLY Cs: MILITARY ENGINEER
At home in a workshop or a lab, you prefer to have your feet firmly rooted on the ground. Being highly intelligent and strategic makes you a great engineer.

ANIMAL KINGDOM
PAGES: 72-73

MULTIPLE CHOICE
01: A. PRONGHORN ANTELOPE
02: B. 133.5 IN (339 CM)
03: A. AMPHIBIANS, FISH, & SNAKES

QUESTION TIME
01: GREAT BARRIER REEF
02: JAGUAR
03: BALD EAGLE

PICTURE PUZZLES
01: SCORPION
02: NAKED MOLE-RAT
03: FLYING FROG

WORDSEARCH

CAREER QUIZ
MOSTLY As: MARINE BIOLOGIST
You love the water and everything in it. When you're not in the sea, you are constantly thinking about it.

MOSTLY Bs: VETERINARIAN
You care about animals, especially pets, and are happy for them to come to you. Clever and nurturing are two of your strongest traits.

MOSTLY Cs: SAFARI GUIDE
You can't get enough of the wild. You like the adrenaline rush and unpredictability of adventure and discovery.

GAMING GALAXY
PAGES: 100-101

MULTIPLE CHOICE
01: B. SPORT
02: A. 157.68 MILLION
03: A. MISSISSIPPI, USA

QUESTION TIME
01: 2012
02: PLAYSTATION 4
03: CANDY CRUSH SAGA

PICTURE PUZZLES
01: LUIGI
02: GAMECUBE
03: KINECT ADVENTURES!

WORDSEARCH

CAREER QUIZ
MOSTLY As: DEVELOPER
You're imagination is too big to stay in your brain! Creating gaming worlds and the characters in them would suit you best. Get thinking!

MOSTLY Bs: COMPOSER
You're life is set to music! You'd make a great composer, bringing the whole gaming universe to life with your magical sounds.

MOSTLY Cs: JOURNALIST
You can't stop reading and writing, especially about gaming! Telling everyone which games and consoles you love, and why, would come easily to you.

SPORT ZONE
PAGES: 136-137

MULTIPLE CHOICE
01: B. 9.58 SECONDS
02: A. TOUR DE FRANCE
03: A. SNAEFELL MOUNTAIN COURSE

QUESTION TIME
01: ACROBATICS
02: HANDBALL
03: BASEBALL

PICTURE PUZZLES
01: ABDOMINALS
02: YUKON QUEST
03: MICHAEL JORDAN

WORDSEARCH

CAREER QUIZ
MOSTLY As: SOLO ATHLETE
Self-motivated, you excel as an individual, based on your sharp, competitive edge. You prefer to get the job done alone.

MOSTLY Bs: TEAM ATHLETE
You thrive on a group structure and feed off your teammates' energy. Winning feels so much better for you when it's shared.

MOSTLY Cs: COACH
Your sporting brain is so strong that you can tell the best how it's done. Strategic, tactical, and smart, you make winning possible.

FORCES OF NATURE
PAGES: 162-163

MULTIPLE CHOICE
01: B. 2012
02: B. 379.66 FT (115.72 M)
03: C. 40%

QUESTION TIME
01: 5
02: THUNDER AND LIGHTNING
03: MAMMOTH CAVE (OR) FISHER RIDGE CAVES

PICTURE PUZZLES
01: SRI LANKA
02: JADEITE
03: AUSTRALIA

WORDSEARCH

CAREER QUIZ
MOSTLY As: METEOROLOGIST
The skies fascinate you. The study of weather and predicting its next move would be a job suited perfectly to you.

MOSTLY Bs: BOTANIST
If it grows out of the ground, you find it interesting. Investigating the science of plant biology could be your ultimate career.

MOSTLY Cs: SEISMOLOGIST
To you, the Earth and its instability is exciting. The scientific study of predicting earthquakes and volcanic movement is for you.

ULTIMATE ROUND-UP
PAGES: 310-311

MULTIPLE CHOICE
01: A. TRAIN
02: C. BLUE WHALE
03: A. POKÉMON X/Y

QUESTION TIME
01: BADMINTON
02: VALDIVIA, CHILE
03: POKER FACE

PICTURE PUZZLES
01: LOVELL RADIO TELESCOPE
02: THE DARK KNIGHT RISES
03: JUPITER

WORDSEARCH

MUSIC MASH-UP

MULTIPLE CHOICE

01: B. 8,438,000
02: A. HO HEY
03: C. RIHANNA

QUESTION TIME

01: MADONNA
02: P!NK
03: THE 20/20 EXPERIENCE

PICTURE PUZZLES

01: ALICA KEYS
02: METALLICA
03: BAAUER

WORDSEARCH

```
A S D A C I L L A T E M
H O I D B H S E F Z J A
C N R I H A N N A G E R
B U M E A D V B E W N I
I X K C E W E G I N A S
G U O T A L A D V N I E
I A Z E T A S E M U M P
C D E L T Y U O E A D F
A D H E R T B M A F H O
```

CAREER QUIZ

MOSTLY As:
POP STAR
You have confidence and a larger-than-life personality. This makes you the perfect music megastar! You should be hangin' with JT and Rihanna.

MOSTLY Bs:
PRODUCER
Your brain is always two steps ahead, and because music is your entire world, you know every trick in the book when it comes to making a hit single.

MOSTLY Cs:
PROMOTER
Your list of contacts is bigger than Shakira's hair. You're friends with almost everybody and using social media comes as easily as breathing.

EPIC STRUCTURES

MULTIPLE CHOICE

01: A. 149 MPH (240 KPH)
02: C. CHINA
03: B. RUNGNADO MAY DAY STADIUM

QUESTION TIME

01: X-WING FIGHTER
02: ONE WORLD TRADE CENTER
03: JAPAN

PICTURE PUZZLES

01: LONDON
02: LOUVRE
03: 6TH

WORDSEARCH

```
S A Q U A R I U M R E G
O R F A V M E G D I R B
O N E D W V K E J N S X
I S B A D R I U X M U Q
X C E D N U J O S K D A
C B N U Y T E W E I R J
S B E M F T N P W U P
H E O W C U H S E O
B U Q E C E O S V R
```

CAREER QUIZ

MOSTLY As:
ARCHITECT
You love to design structures that make everyone's jaw drop. With a great eye for style you'd make an awesome architect.

MOSTLY Bs:
RIDE DESIGNER
Not content with designing buildings, your creations twist and contort, giving passengers a taste of the adrenaline rush you love.

MOSTLY Cs:
BUILDING HISTORIAN
You love books and research, looking back through history to see how buildings have developed.

MOVIE SHOWTIME

MULTIPLE CHOICE

01: C. CHRIS HEMSWORTH
02: C. CHICKEN RUN
03: A. $4.728 BILLION

QUESTION TIME

01: PIRATES OF THE CARIBBEAN
02: NICK FURY
03: FINDING NEMO

PICTURE PUZZLES

01: GREEN GOBLIN
02: CAT WOMAN
03: JENNIFER LAWRENCE

WORDSEARCH

```
A C O R A L I N E C R E
T O L W V D O E S A V M
R A I A O A V K E H K W
A J D C Y W I A E A K H O
V A O T J R E R V F W I
A J E O S V X R A I S F C
N O E B A A E L B E A I
S H R E K A R L D V L L
C B O S G X E G B A C D
O D I N O S A U R O Z B
```

CAREER QUIZ

MOSTLY As:
ACTOR
You love performing and bask in the attention of your adoring fans. All in all, this makes you a fantastic global movie star.

MOSTLY Bs:
DIRECTOR
You have a great imagination and a strong vision of what you want. Others can take the credit, but your determination means nobody can stand in your way.

MOSTLY Cs:
STUNTMAN
Happiest away from the paparazzi. Anonymity gives you the power to focus on your craft of being the craziest person on set!

ONLY HUMAN

MULTIPLE CHOICE

01: C. SKIN
02: A. CHEESE
03: A. LUKE SKYWALKER

QUESTION TIME

01: YURI GAGARIN
02: THE WRIST
03: TO MAP EACH NEURON IN THE BRAIN

PICTURE PUZZLES

01: THE EAR
02: CHESS
03: HOMER SIMPSON

WORDSEARCH

```
E X V A K I D N E Y S R
H J Y Z A V R O D N O U
A I T R K Q W A B M X O
P A R B I N W A K J U P
N C O S P L E E N Y F T
R E A S N Q E U E O D B
A S C H E N C L I N A W U
R N E O V B N W R A E X
```

CAREER QUIZ

MOSTLY As:
SURGEON
The human body fascinates you. That, coupled with your intelligence and dedication, means you'd make an amazing surgeon.

MOSTLY Bs:
EXPLORER
You love surprises. Your thirst for discovery is huge. This job could take you anywhere—the desert, the ocean, even outer space!

MOSTLY Cs:
TEACHER
You are great at sharing your encyclopedic knowledge and wisdom, making you a fantastic and inspiring teacher.

INFINITE SPACE

MULTIPLE CHOICE

01: B. 2011
02: B. ERIS
03: C. LAIKA

QUESTION TIME

01: THE AVENGERS
02: MR. SPOCK
03: EUROPEAN SPACE AGENCY

PICTURE PUZZLES

01: KRYPTON
02: NEPTUNE
03: RUSSIA

WORDSEARCH

```
A S C B O S U N A R U F
D F B O W A V N E V N W
I L A C N L E R M A C G
E R M E N J C I A R T S
V E N E P T U N E H A U
R W I A R D X P Y O A U
O P F R U V C V U I A G
F U I N R T G A U R Y T M
O U S T V A D G H Y E Z
T G A N Y M E D E Y E V
O A D S F G S J I T E U B
```

CAREER QUIZ

MOSTLY As:
ASTRONAUT
No desk job for you—you need the adrenaline rush of being at the heart of the action: behind the controls of a 1.2 million pounds-of-thrust engine.

MOSTLY Bs:
HEAD OF MISSION CONTROL
You can keep cool in high pressure situations. You could be in charge of the first manned mission to Mars!

MOSTLY Cs:
ROCKET DESIGNER
It all starts with you! Your vision and imagination have the ability to push the human race to the edges of the universe. Hopefully you can bring them back, too!

NAME THAT ZONE!

01: C. FORCES OF NATURE
02: B. ANIMAL KINGDOM
03: C. MOVIE SHOWTIME
04: A. INFINITE SPACE
05: B. SPORT ZONE
06: A. MUSIC MASH-UP
07: C. GAMING GALAXY

INDEX BY CATEGORY

INDEX BY A-Z

PICTURE CREDITS

T: top **B**: bottom **L**: left **C**: center **R**: right **BG**: background

All images supplied by © **Getty Images**

Except:

The Kobal Collection

P25: (BG) The Kobal Collection / Warner Bros., (BL) Dark Side Productions / The Kobal Collection, P25: (BG) Marvel/Paramount / The Kobal Collection, P28: (BG) The Kobal Collection / Paramount Pictures, P29: (BG) The Kobal Collection / Warner Bros./DC Comics, P32: (BG) Legendary Pictures / The Kobal Collection, (BR) The Kobal Collection / Halcyon Company, The, P41: (T) Marvel Enterprises / The Kobal Collection, (BR) Columbia Tristar / The Kobal Collection, P44: (BG) The Kobal Collection / Dreamworks SKG, P45: (BG) Walt Disney Pictures / The Kobal Collection, P53 (T) The Kobal Collection / Paramount Pictures, P95: (B) The Kobal Collection / Lawrence Gordon/Mutual Film/Paramount, P99: Dimension/Miramax / The Kobal Collection, (BG) The Kobal Collection / Walt Disney Productions, P128: (T) Dreamworks Animation / The Kobal Collection, P129 (BG) Canal + / The Kobal Collection / Aeder, Erik, P141: (BG) Warner Bros. / The Kobal Collection, P145: (TR) Marvel Studios / The Kobal Collection, P147: (BC) The Kobal Collection / Walt Disney Pictures, P192: (BL) Universal / The Kobal Collection, (BG) Fox 2000/20th Century Fox / The Kobal Collection / Tenner, Suzanne, P213: (BG) The Kobal Collection / Tohokushinsha Film Corp/Ntv/Tokuma Shoten, P226: (T) Universal Pictures / The Kobal Collection, (B) Universal Pictures / The Kobal Collection, P228: (BG) The Kobal Collection / Warner Bros., (TL) Amblin/Universal / The Kobal Collection, P234: (BG) Warner Bros. Pictures / The Kobal Collection, (B) Danjaq / EON Productions / The Kobal Collection, P235: (BG) erry Bruckheimer Films / The Kobal Collection, (BC) Marvel Enterprises / The Kobal Collection, P236: (BG) Twentieth Century Fox Film / The Kobal Collection, (R) The Kobal Collection / Lucasfilm/20th Century Fox, P238: (BG) Columbia Pictures / The Kobal Collection, (BR) Illumination Entertainment / The Kobal Collection, P239: (T) Warner Bros. Pictures / The Kobal Collection, (R) Marvel Enterprises / The Kobal Collection, (BR) Marvel Enterprises / The Kobal Collection, P240: (BG) The Kobal Collection, (TR) Dreamworks Animation / The Kobal Collection, (BR) Illumination Entertainment / The Kobal Collection, P241: (BR) Dreamworks Animation / The Kobal Collection, P242: (BG) Laika Entrtainment / The Kobal Collection, P243: (BR) The Kobal Collection / Studio Ghibli, P244: (BG) Marvel Enterprises / The Kobal Collection, (BL) Marvel/Paramount / The Kobal Collection, P245: (BG) The Kobal Collection / Marvel/20th Century Fox, (TR) The Kobal Collection / Columbia/Marvel, P246: (BG) Warner Bros / The Kobal Collection, (TC) Columbia Pictures / The Kobal Collection, P247: (BL) Marvel/Paramount / The Kobal Collection, P248: (R) The Kobal Collection / 20th Century Fox/Marvel Ent./Regency Ent., (BR) Bad Hat Productions / The Kobal Collection, P249: (BG) 20th Century Fox / The Kobal Collection, P251: (BG) Amblin Entertainment / The Kobal Collection, (BL) The Kobal Collection / Amblin/Universal, (BR) Kpg Digital For Film / The Kobal Collection, P252: (BG) Legendary Pictures / The Kobal Collection, (BL) ionsgate / The Kobal Collection, P253: (T) Animal Logic/BBC Earth/BBC Worldwide/Evergreen Films/Reliance Big Entertainment / The Kobal Collection, (BR) The Kobal Collection / Mosaic Media Group, P254: (BG) The Kobal Collection / Lucasfilm/Paramount Pictures, (BL) Alphaville/Imohotep Prod / The Kobal Collection / Hamshere, Keith, P255: (L) Walt Disney Pictures / The Kobal Collection, (R) Sony Pictures Animation / The Kobal Collection, P269: (BR) Twentieth Century Fox / The Kobal Collection, P271: (BG) Walt Disney Pictures / The Kobal Collection, P274: (BG) The Kobal Collection / Silver Pictures, (BC) Warner Bros. Pictures / The Kobal Collection, P277: (T) Film Afrika Worldwilde / The Kobal Collection, P278: (BG) The Kobal Collection / Dog Eat Dog/Miramax, P280: (TR) New Line / The Kobal Collection, P283: (B) Lucasfilm/20th Century Fox / The Kobal Collection, P289: (BG) Warner Bros / The Kobal Collection, (BR) The Kobal Collection / 20th Century Fox/Marvel, P298: (B) Marvel Enterprises / The Kobal Collection, P299: (T) The Kobal Collection / Twentieth Century-Fox Film Corporation, (TR) The Kobal Collection / 20th Century Fox, P303: (R) Warner Bros / The Kobal Collection, (BR) The Kobal Collection / Twentieth Century-Fox Film Corporation, P304: (TR) Disney / The Kobal Collection, P305: (T) Battleship Delta Productions / The Kobal Collection, P306: (BG) Paramount Pictures / The Kobal Collection, (BR) The Kobal Collection / Dreamworks, P307: (BG) The Kobal Collection / Paramount Pictures

ACKNOWLEDGMENTS

Top 10 Of Everything 2015 Produced by SHUBROOK BROS. CREATIVE
Writer & Researcher: Paul Terry

Editorial Director: Trevor Davies
Chief Sub-editor: Amanda Alcindor

Special thanks to...

Ian Turp & Marc Glanville at Getty Images

Paul Palmer, Mick Lozen, Jim Duggan and Ryan Curtis at Headly Brothers

Helena Kosinski at Nielsen Music

Amy Trombetta and Nick Iademarco at Wright's Media

Billboard

David Martill

Car Consultant: Suzy Wallace

All lists credited to Billboard:
Copyrighted 2014. Prometheus Global Media. 107713:114AT

Box office information courtesy of The Internet Movie Database (http://www.imdb.com). Used with permission.

OF EVERYTHING
EXPERT
PANEL

Benjamin Baker
Dylan Enskat
Alex Jackson
Elliott Jackson
Ollie Jackson
Freddie Kamasa
Frank McCormick
Jack McCormick
Henry Shubrook
Marley Whitington